Property Rights and Property Wrongs

Secure property rights are central to economic development and stable government, yet difficult to create. Relying on surveys in Russia from 2000–2012, Timothy Frye examines how political power, institutions, and norms shape property rights for firms. Through a series of innovative survey experiments, *Property Rights and Property Wrongs* explores how political power, personal connections, elections, concerns for reputation, legal facts, and social norms influence property rights disputes from hostile corporate takeovers to debt collection to renationalization. This work looks beyond high-profile cases of economic conflict and departs from the common view that property rights in Russia are uniformly weak by probing Russia's "legal dualism." The result is a nuanced view of the political economy of Russia that contributes to central debates in economic development, comparative politics, and legal studies.

TIMOTHY FRYE is the Marshall D. Shulman Professor of Post-Soviet Foreign Policy at Columbia University and the former Director of the Harriman Institute. Professor Frye received a BA in Russian language and literature from Middlebury College in 1986, an MIA from Columbia's School of International and Public Affairs in 1992, and a PhD from Columbia in 1997. He is the author of *Brokers and Bureaucrats: Building Markets in Russia*, which won the 2001 Hewett Prize from the American Association for the Advancement of Slavic Studies, and *Building States and Markets after Communism: The Perils of Polarized Democracy*. He has worked as a consultant for the World Bank, the European Bank for Reconstruction and Development, and the US Agency for International Development. He is also Director of the International Center for the Study of Institutions and Development at the Higher School of Economics in Moscow.

D0145510

Property Rights and Property Wrongs

How Power, Institutions, and Norms Shape Economic Conflict in Russia

TIMOTHY FRYE

Columbia University, New York

CAMBRIDGE
UNIVERSITY PRESS

University Printing House, Cambridge CB2 8BS, United Kingdom

One Liberty Plaza, 20th Floor, New York, NY 10006, USA

477 Williamstown Road, Port Melbourne, VIC 3207, Australia

4843/24, 2nd Floor, Ansari Road, Daryaganj, Delhi – 110002, India

79 Anson Road, #06-04/06, Singapore 079906

Cambridge University Press is part of the University of Cambridge.

It furthers the University's mission by disseminating knowledge in the pursuit of education, learning, and research at the highest international levels of excellence.

www.cambridge.org
Information on this title: www.cambridge.org/9781107156999
DOI: 10.1017/9781316661727

First published 2017

Printed in the United States of America by Sheridan Books, Inc

A catalog record for this publication is available from the British Library.

ISBN 978-1-107-15699-9 Hardback
ISBN 978-1-316-61010-7 Paperback

Cambridge University Press has no responsibility for the persistence or accuracy of URLs for external or third-party Internet websites referred to in this publication and does not guarantee that any content on such websites is, or will remain, accurate or appropriate.

Contents

List of figures		*page* vi
List of tables		vii
Acknowledgments		ix
Note on the text		xii
1	Introduction	1
2	Power and Property	38
3	Autocratic Elections and Property Rights	82
4	Courts and Connections	101
5	Reputation and the Rule of Law	138
6	Social Norms and the Banker's Gold Watch	163
7	Conclusion	197
Data Appendix		206
References		215
Index		240

Figures

2.1 Power and Property Rights   *page* 72
3.1 Elections and Property Rights   97
4.1 Disputes Before States Arbitration Courts   114
4.2 Strategies for Resolving Disputes   118
4.3 Effectiveness in Resolving Disputes   122
5.1 Reputation, Courts, and Property Rights to Trade   161

Tables

2.1 Perceived Threats of Hostile Takeover, 2011 Survey   *page* 63
2.2 Power and Perceptions of Property Rights, 2011 Survey   66
2.3 Perceived Threats of Hostile Takeover, 2008 Survey   74
2.4 Power and Perceptions of Property Rights, 2008 Survey   75
A2.1 Unpacking Property Rights: Different Threats   78
A2.2 Perceptions of the Security of Property Rights
       from Takeover   80
A2.3 Missing Observations   81
3.1 Balance Statistics   92
3.2 Elections and Perceptions of Property Rights, 2011
       Survey   96
A3.1 Balance by Region   100
4.1 Perceived Effectiveness of Courts   108
4.2 Rough Return Rates for Disputes with Private Firms   119
4.3 Rough Return Rates for Disputes with the Regional
       Government   120
4.4 Better to be Right or Connected: Using Only
       Negotiations   124
4.5 Better to be Right or Connected: Using Courts   126
4.6 Better to be Big or Connected: Using Only Negotiations   129
4.7 Better to be Big or Connected: Using Courts   130
4.8 The Value of Connections Before a Dispute   133
4.9 The Value of Connections During a Dispute   134
5.1 The Value of Reputation   146
5.2 The Sources of Reputation   148
5.3 The Benefits of Membership   149
5.4 The Propensity to Trade   152
5.5 Reputation and Courts   153
5.6 Reputation and Courts, 2008   155
5.7 No Reputation Versus a Good Reputation   156
5.8 Measuring Reputation   158

5.9 Reputation and Giving Credit   160
6.1 The Necessity of Privatization   174
6.2 The Frequency of Major Violations of Privatization   175
6.3 Turning to the Courts: Major Violations   176
6.4 Turning to the Courts: Minor Violations   177
6.5 Testing the Original Sin Argument   179
6.6 What Should the Courts Do? Major Violations   181
6.7 What Should the Courts Do? Minor Violations   182
6.8 Who Supports Revising Privatization and Why?   184
6.9 The Results in Comparative Perspective   191
DA1 Descriptive Statistics: Firm Survey 2000   207
DA2 Descriptive Statistics: Firm Survey 2005   208
DA3 Descriptive Statistics: Firm Survey 2008   209
DA4 Descriptive Statistics: Firm Survey 2011   210
DA5 Fieldwork Report: Mass Survey 2006   212
DA6 Description of Variables: Mass Survey 2006   213
DA7 Descriptive Statistics: Mass Survey 2006   214

Acknowledgments

When I told my brother Eric that I was writing a book on the security of property rights in Russia, he said: "It sounds like a short book." And it would be if I only focused on instances of secure property rights. But studying the insecurity of property rights is in many ways more interesting. Why has it been so difficult to build property rights in Russia over the last 25 years? Why are property rights secure for some right-holders, but not for others? Why does the security of property rights vary so dramatically across types of rights in Russia? How do power, institutions, and norms shape property rights? To try to answer these questions, I cast a wide net. Among other topics, I explore how political connections determine the likelihood of a violent corporate takeover, how gossip shapes property rights in trade, how autocratic elections influence perceptions of property rights, and whether right-holders can make an illegal privatization more legitimate in the eyes of the public by providing public goods. While it was great fun to research each of these individual questions, the hope is that taken together these chapters yield broader lessons for economic development, comparative politics, and the study of Russia.

The main sources of evidence for the book are five surveys conducted in Russia between November 2000 and December 2011. I am especially grateful to the Levada Center and to Alexei Grazhdankin in particular who oversaw five of these surveys cited in the manuscript. I have worked with Alexei on about 20 surveys over the years and his insights, professionalism, and deep knowledge have immeasurably improved my work.

I am immensely grateful to my survey respondents, all 4188 of them who were willing to answer my questions. Special thanks go to the 2586 businesspeople who sat for interviews that often took an hour or more to complete. Thank you for taking time from your busy schedule.

I am also thankful to the following organizations that provided funds to conduct the surveys, including the National Council on

East European and Eurasian Research, the Olin Foundation, the Mershon Center of The Ohio State University, the Harriman Institute at Columbia University, the Social Science Research Council, and the William Davidson Institute at the University of Michigan. Parts of Chapters 2 and 3 were prepared within the framework of the Basic Research Program at the National Research University Higher School of Economics (HSE) and supported within the framework of a subsidy granted to the HSE by the Government of the Russian Federation for the implementation of the Global Competitiveness Program. (Note that I received funding from both the Russian and the US governments and from the University of Michigan and The Ohio State University).

For comments on earlier versions of papers that became these chapters, I thank Quintin Beazer, Gregory Caldeira, Randy Calvert, Jim Fearon, Ray Fisman, Venelin Ganev, Jordan Gans-Morse, Scott Gehlbach, Rick Herrmann, John Huber, Ichiro Iwasaki, Pauline Jones-Luong, Kathleen McGraw, Tom Nelson, Will Pyle, Aleksander Radigin, Thomas Remington, David Samuels, Alberto Simpser, Daniel Treisman, Joshua Tucker, Andrei Yakovlev, and Ekaterina Zhuravskaya. I also thank seminar participants at CEFIR in Moscow, the Mershon Center, the William Davidson Institute, the Harriman Institute, the University of Wisconsin-Madison, the Davis Center, and New York University. I much appreciate two anonymous reviewers at Cambridge University Press whose thoughtful remarks sparked a re-organization of the manuscript. I also thank my colleagues at The Ohio State University and Columbia University. I've learned so much from my interactions with all of you. Special thanks go to my colleagues at the International Center for the Study of Institutions and Development at the Higher School of Economics in Moscow.

I thank Ichiro Iwasaki for inviting me to Hitotsubashi University to present what became Chapter 5. His hospitality and insights were much appreciated. I also thank the graduate students at Columbia who read earlier versions of this chapter in the seminar "Comparing Institutions." Chapter 6 benefitted from related research conducted with Irina Denisova, Markus Eller, and Ekaterina Zhuravskaya. I thank Dave Weimer, who along with William Riker, first stoked my interest in property rights as a pre-doctoral fellow at the University of Rochester in 1992–1993. I also thank Suzanne Freeman, Matthew Van Meter, and, especially, Deborah Renshaw for assistance in editing the final version of the manuscript.

I also give thanks to my sherpas at Cambridge University Press, Lew Bateman, Robert Dreesen, and John Haslam who guided the project through to publication.

My greatest thanks go to my wife Kira whose encouragement and love made this book possible and to my son Vanya whose smile and enthusiasm make it all worthwhile.

Chapter 6 borrows the theoretical discussion from "Original Sin, Good Works and Privatization in Russia" published in *World Politics*, 58:4, July 2006, but is significantly reworked with data from a different source and an analysis of the perceptions of citizens rather than firm managers. Chapter 3 borrows the research design and some data from "Elections and Property Rights: A Natural Experiment in Russia," *Comparative Political Studies*, (2016), but makes new theoretical arguments and uses different empirical tests.

This book is dedicated to Sergei and Katia and Andrei and Larisa.

Note on the text

I use the modified Library of Congress system of transliteration from English into Russian. I bow to convention for words and names that have a standard English usage, such as Yeltsin or Magnitsky. I also follow the transliteration used by Russian authors when citing their own works.

1 | *Introduction*

We know how to do a lot of things, but deep down we don't really know what we are doing.

A long-time rule-of-law practitioner (Carothers 2006: 15)

The importance of secure property rights for economic development and stable government is readily acknowledged. In the now orthodox account of economic development, secure property rights can account for *The Rise of The Western World* and *Why Nations Fail*, to quote two influential works (North and Thomas 1973; Acemoglu and Robinson 2012). But if secure property rights are so beneficial, then why are they so rare? Throughout history most owners and citizens have faced great obstacles to exercising the rights to their property. The costs of guarding property, bribing state officials, identifying honest trading partners, measuring the quality of goods, and enforcing contracts prevent businesses and citizens from making investments and trades that would benefit them and society as well. Most citizens and countries miss out on the substantial gains that can accrue from the investment and trade that flow from secure property rights.

Scholars and policy advisors have pointed to a number of sources for insecure property rights. Some argue that influential politicians and their supporters who benefit from weak property rights are the problem. Others blame incapable formal institutions, such as courts and the police that fail to protect the property of right-holders in ways both big and small. Others focus on weak informal institutions, such as social trust and concerns for reputation that make it hard for businesses to rely on social sanctions to protect property. Still others cite social norms, including religions, ideologies, or cultures that promote attitudes and values inimical to secure property rights as the major culprit.[1]

---

[1] Demonstrating empirically the impact of property rights on economic outcomes is a challenge due to measurement issues, endogeneity, unobserved

Each of these broad approaches to property rights has a long social science pedigree. Moreover, each of these approaches is familiar to observers of Russia. Rapacious elites? Check. Weak courts, low social trust, and anti-market norms? Check, check, and check. But within each of these broad approaches many puzzles remain. Of all the dimensions of political power, which are most important for protecting property? If political power both shapes and is shaped by property rights, then how can we know whether the former influences the latter or vice versa? Can social norms about property change? If so, under what conditions? When using courts to protect property is it better to have a strong legal case or friends in high places? Why is privatization so unpopular? Are informal and formal institutions that protect property substitutes or complements? I explore these and others puzzles by mining a range of evidence from Russia, including a survey of the mass public, four surveys of businesspeople, statistical data on court use and economic crimes, as well as background interviews with policymakers, academics, and businesspeople between 2000 and 2012.[2]

Postcommunist Russia offers an excellent opportunity to study these issues. The sheer scale of property rights change over the last quarter-century invites investigation. The 1990s saw perhaps the greatest transfer of property in world history as state assets moved to private hands via privatization, theft, and in many cases a mix of both. The 2000s saw the state claw back large sections of the economy through legal subterfuge and coercion. Attempts to seize and protect property in Russia over the last 25 years have been accompanied by efforts to build institutions and change norms on a massive scale – efforts that have produced very mixed results.

Beyond the scope of change in property rights, however, it is the very unevenness of Russian institutions and norms that make an exploration of this particular case so valuable. Developed economies are marked by supportive social norms, strong public institutions, and robust private institutions, which make it difficult to identify precisely why rights are respected. We see a businessperson who abides by a contract, but are they responding to high levels of social trust, strong

heterogeneity, and a host of other problems. See among others Besley and Ghatak (2009), Fenske (2011), DFID (2014) and Frye (2015).

[2] See Data Appendix for survey details. There is also a rich case study literature on property rights in Russia (cf. Barnes 2006; Hendley 1998; Spence 2006; Alina-Pisano 2008; Ledeneva 2013: Ch. 4).

social networks, or efficient courts? That all of these good institutions and norms coexist makes it difficult to identify the relative importance of each of these factors on property rights. In contrast, Russia is marked by a state that is too capacious to be irrelevant but too disorganized to be a reliable backstop for disputes, by social norms that both underpin and undermine property, and by a rich range of informal institutions from political connections to concerns for reputation that many argue are central to property rights protection. The great heterogeneity of power relations, institutions, and norms in Russia better positions us to identify their impact on property rights.

An exploration of how power, institutions, and norms shape economic conflict over property can tell us a great deal about property rights and politics, but it can also shed light on important debates in comparative politics, such as the role of institutions in competitive autocracies.[3] Scholars of autocracy have increasingly examined whether formal institutions, such as elections and courts, are consequential or merely well-scripted theater (c.f. Magaloni 2006; Gandhi 2008; Lust-Okar 2006a). They have also begun to identify the conditions under which autocrats have incentives to strengthen or weaken property rights and to explore the roots of legal dualism, in which property rights institutions may benefit some right-holders, but not others (Haber et al. 2003; Moustafa 2008; Besley and Kudamatsu 2009; Hendley 2011).

In addition, this exploration can also help us understand contemporary Russia and its prospects for economic development. Russia watchers have long debated whether formal institutions are facades or constraints, whether connections (*blat*) promote or undercut markets, and whether the mass public supports or opposes private property. They have debated why reforms to support market institutions have been so difficult to implement and asked whether Russia's weak

---

[3] During the period under study, Russia is a good example of a competitive autocracy in which there is open competition for power but the political playing field is tipped significantly in favor of the incumbent. Russia's political regime has become much less competitive and more repressive following Vladimir Putin's return to the presidency in May 2012. More research is needed to understand precisely how these most recent changes in political regime affect property rights. However, many of the findings presented here continue to inform our understanding of property rights in Russia. Indeed, that changes in political power between rulers and right-holders shape property rights is a recurring theme in this work.

property rights are best seen as a halfway house between communism and capitalism, the result of a weak state, or a reflection of deep-rooted cultural factors.

The chapters that follow provide a host of evidence that speak to these important debates.

Bargaining Power

Consider explanations of property rights rooted in bargaining power. Scholars often analyze property rights as a bargain between rulers and right-holders. Rulers who control the state seek to retain office, while also obtaining as much revenue as possible. Right-holders seek to maximize revenue from the property under their control. Rulers exchange secure property rights for revenue and political support from right-holders. The terms of this exchange depend on the resources that each side can muster. As Levi (1988: 1) famously paraphrased: "Rulers maximize revenue, but not as they please." They must constantly bargain with constituents who have varying degrees of bargaining power vis-a-vis the ruler. Where rulers (and by extension their agents) do not depend on assets controlled by right-holders for revenue, they offer right-holders far less generous terms for property rights. For example, rulers with easy access to oil revenue may offer weaker property rights to those outside this sector because the ruler depends far less on their revenue to retain office (Haber et al. 2003). Rulers with great personal popularity, large majorities in parliament, or other valuable political resources are able to design property rights regimes that are more favorable to their interests. Similarly, when rulers experience shocks that weaken their bargaining power, such as ill health, political defeats, or fiscal shortages, they grant more favorable property rights to groups on whom they depend for support (North 1981; Fisman 2001).

Rulers are not alone in bargaining as right-holders also seek more favorable terms for their property rights using all tools at their disposal. The owners of mobile firms who can threaten to move to another jurisdiction or to less easily taxed lines of production may be able to strike more favorable terms than their less mobile counterparts (Bates 1981; Bates and Lien 1985). Large firms that are able to mobilize workers/voters during elections, politically connected firms on whom the government depends for support, and firms in economically important sectors receive better treatment than smaller, less mobile, and less connected firms (Umbeck 1981; Bates 1989; Haber et al. 2003; Frye 2004; Markus 2015; Wang 2015). Holmes (2003: 21) sums up the bargaining power view succinctly in his discussion of the development of property rights in England, the "rights of big landowners were secured long before the rights of orphans." In this view, property rights largely benefit powerful rulers and right-holders typically at the expense of the weak and, especially, at the expense of future right-holders.

There is much to this view, but it also raises three sets of questions. First, to say that the property rights of the politically powerful are better protected is helpful, but rather blunt, in part because political power has many dimensions. Is political power reducible to personal connections with high officials? The size of the firm? Membership in business organizations? Wealth? To gain a more nuanced picture of the relationship between power and property, it is important to explore the different means by which political power is exercised to protect assets. Second, a more refined view would give a rough estimate of the relative magnitude of the importance of particular types of power, such as political connections versus economic size versus asset mobility. Which aspects of political power are more important than others? Is political power more important than other factors?

Third, political power may be more salient for some types of property rights disputes than for others, which begs the question: Under what conditions is political power especially important? Are political connections more important for long-term investments than for daily business transactions between firms? Are they more important when businesses use informal or formal means to resolve disputes? The extent to which political power is fungible in its capacity to protect property should be established rather than asserted.

In Chapter 2, I examine how bargaining power shapes right-holders' perceptions of the likelihood of a hostile corporate takeover in Russia. These are hostile takeovers in the most literal sense and frequently come with threats of violence and incarceration. I explore how asset mobility, firm size, and various forms of political connections shape perceptions of property rights. Using a survey of more than 900 firms in 2011, I find that firms with immobile assets, state ownership, and fewer workers viewed themselves as particularly likely to be the target of a hostile corporate takeover.

In addition, I unpack the concept of political connections into four elements: property-based connections that measure the extent of state ownership in a firm; institutional connections that measure a manager's prior work experience in the local or regional government; personal connections that capture whether a firm's manager knows the governor personally; and partisan connections that measure the political affiliations of top managers.

The results indicate that while state ownership and prior work experience in the government are associated with perceptions of less secure property rights, personal connections with the governor are associated with more secure property rights. Thus, different types of political connections have different effects. More generally, this chapter enriches the literature on business–state relations by examining the independent impact of political relationships that are often lumped together under the umbrella terms of "political power" and "political connections."

Explanations for property rights that invoke bargaining power also face a more general problem: causal identification. Bargaining power both influences and is influenced by property rights, which makes it difficult to identify how a change in one affects a change in the other. This potential endogeneity runs deeper than a simple problem of reverse causation because rulers may use expansions of power to gain greater control over property, and greater control over property may increase a ruler's bargaining power. Because bargaining power and property rights are so closely tied to each other, it is difficult to untangle their relationship and make strong claims about how bargaining power affects property rights.

In Chapter 3, I explore a plausibly exogenous shift in bargaining power induced by the surprisingly poor showing of the ruling United Russia party in parliamentary elections of December 2011. I take advantage of the timing at which businesspeople were interviewed in a large national survey conducted in the weeks before and after the election of December 4th. Because the pre-election and post-election groups of firms are identical in almost all factors, we can attribute any differences in the perceptions of property rights between the "control" group of respondents interviewed before the election and the "treatment" group of respondents interviewed after the election to the shift in bargaining power induced by the election.

I find that a negative shock to the bargaining power of the ruling party helped to level the playing field. Firms with immobile assets, fewer workers, and state ownership viewed their property rights as more secure after the elections than before. This suggests that exogenous changes in bargaining power can influence perceptions of property rights; it also reveals that even Russia's highly imperfect elections shape expectations about property rights.

Formal Institutions: Courts and Connections

Rulers and right-holders bargain over claims to property not in a vacuum, but in particular institutional and normative settings that may influence their strategies. In accounting for broad patterns of property rights, many argue that rulers and right-holders may be constrained by a range of formal and informal institutions. Formal institutions, such as courts, police forces, and bureaucracies, have the advantage of economies of scope and scale in organizing the coercion necessary to sanction violators of property rights and thereby persuade businesses that their investments and innovations will be protected. These formal institutions may limit rulers by increasing the costs of arbitrarily raising tax rates, manipulating regulatory institutions, or simply seizing property. Formal institutions also may constrain right-holders by raising the costs of reneging on contracts, engaging in theft, and bribing state officials. Those countries with the most capable institutions and most effective bureaucracies are often thought to have the strongest property rights (North 1990; Knack and Keefer 1995; Rauch and Evans 2000).

However, expanding the capacity of the state to protect property raises a well-known problem: states that have the capacity to protect property rights are also well placed to usurp those rights (Weingast 1997). Because the state is sovereign and claims a monopoly on the use of force over a given territory, its actors are uniquely positioned to both threaten and to protect property rights. Examples of state officials using their power to expropriate the assets of private right-holders or gaining compliance by threatening to do so are commonplace in low- and middle-income countries (Bates 1981; Volkov 2002). Yet, some countries at some times have been able to create relatively secure property rights by raising the costs to state officials of engaging in predation.

In the canonical case, North and Weingast (1989) argue that decades of political struggle in seventeenth-century England yielded a balance of power between the king and parliament that helped to usher in a period of relatively stable property rights. Key to this arrangement was a mutual dependence of the Crown on parliament for taxes and the parliament on the Crown for repayment.[4] Stasavage (2003) refines the argument to suggest that partisan factions in parliament with an interest in repayment of loans were central to increasing confidence that loans would be repaid to private lenders. Others point to different mechanisms that allow powerful elites to constrain each other in ways that generate stronger property rights. Deirmeier et al. (1997) argue that credible commitments to property rights can emerge through the strategic action of investors and the state in some circumstances. They develop an "overlapping generations" model in which ambitious politicians in the lower party ranks who hope to be in power in the future constrain current rulers from preying on property and thereby reassure right-holders that their property will be respected. Similarly, Haber et al. (2003) argue that despite great political instability, successive governments in Mexico around the turn of the twentieth century made credible commitments to investments in the oil sector via strategic alliances with foreign investors. Because the government of Mexico was dependent on foreign investors for tax revenue and lacked the technical expertise to extract the oil, the government was better off taxing the privately produced oil than expropriating the investment and running the company on its own. In this case foreign investors were better off investing in Mexico and paying taxes in Mexico given the opportunities for profit and the reduced risk of expropriation.[5]

Even among those who emphasize the importance of public institutions for secure property rights there is much debate.[6] Which public

---

[4] For alternative views, see Pincus and Robinson (2014) and Jha (2015).
[5] Credible commitment is achieved only with the loss of discretion, and some argue that such discretion is especially important in a highly uncertain transition environment (Holmes 1995: 75; Stiglitz 1999).
[6] Commitment may emerge from far-sighted rulers who create institutions that constrain themselves and their subordinates (Campos and Root 1994; Gehlbach and Keefer 2012), but the conditions under which this occurs are far from clear and examples of autocratic officials usurping property rights seem to outnumber those protecting them. Albertus and Menaldo (2012) argue that by expropriating the pre-existing elite, rulers can demonstrate their loyalty to their core supporters and enjoy longer tenures.

institutions are most relevant? Are businesses more concerned about institutions that protect property rights in disputes with state officials or with private sector competitors (Frye 2004; Acemoglu and Johnson 2005)? The theoretical and policy implications of these two interpretations differ. If private businesses primarily fear disputes with state officials, as John Locke would suggest, then policies to insulate judges from political pressure are in order. If however, private businesses primarily fear the corruption of judges by private competitors, as Thomas Hobbes would suggest, policies should be designed to weaken ties between judges and economic actors. This might mean increasing the number of judges hearing cases or rotating judges to other districts more frequently.

Acemoglu and Johnson (2005) find that "property rights" institutions that protect citizens against expropriation by the state are critical for economic growth, investment, and financial development, but that "contracting" institutions that enable contracts between citizens are only correlated with financial development. Research from Russia suggests that investment decisions depend on firms' perceptions that they can use courts in disputes with regional and local officials (Frye 2004). However, we do not know whether these firms' confidence in their ability to use courts in disputes with state officials is because they believe the courts work well or because these firms have unidentified sources of power that give them leverage over state officials and judges too.

In addition, the problem of measuring political power is apparent in court cases as well. Is it better to have the facts on one's side or good political connections? Is it better to be economically powerful or a friend of the governor? Because political power comes in a variety of forms ranging from personal connections to economic size to prior experience in government, it is helpful to understand the relative importance of these different types of power for everyday disputes.

I explore these issues in Chapter 4 by examining perceptions of the performance of state courts of arbitration in resolving everyday disputes. I find that businesspeople perceive political connections to be an important resource in run-of-the-mill economic disputes heard by state arbitration courts. Indeed, in one vignette having good political connections increases a respondent's perceived chances of winning a dispute by as much as increasing the size of the firm by almost 3000

workers. More surprising, however, is that respondents also believe
that it is important to have the facts of the case on one's side. That
success in court is perceived to depend not only on political connections and economic power but also on the facts of the case suggests a
much more nuanced interpretation of the effectiveness of state courts
of arbitration than is found in much of the literature.

Informal Institutions: Reputation and Rights

For other scholars, the key to generating secure property rights lies
in the quality of informal institutions, such as social networks, concerns for reputation, ethnic ties, and other forms of social sanctions.[7]
Because even the best-governed state lacks the resources to resolve
every potential dispute, informal solutions that encourage investment and innovation are critical in even highly developed economies
(Macauley 1963; Granovetter 1985; Bernstein 1992). Scholars point
to social networks, business organizations, professional associations,
and identity groups as informal institutions that provide a means to
sanction cheating and promote cooperation without relying on the
state for enforcement (Milgrom et al. 1990; Ellickson, 1991; Bernstein
1992; McMillan and Woodruff 1999; 2000; Frye 2000). Ostrom
(1990) notes how farming communities are able to create self-govern-
ing organizations that monitor property and deliver sanctions against
violators while Frye (2000) finds similar informal institutions at work
in brokers associations in Moscow in the 1990s. Observers of Russia
have contributed to this debate by studying how trading networks
based on long-standing social ties, "*blat*," and a concern for reputation
can promote production and trade (Ledeneva 1998, 2006; Hendley et
al. 2000; 2001; Gaddy and Ickes 2002; Pyle 2005).

Informal institutions can heighten the costs to the state of engaging
in expropriation (North 1990; Putnam 1993; Weingast 1997; Greif

---

[7] The terminology of informal/formal institutions is often unclear. Some view
institutions as informal because they are unreported and untaxed. Others treat
institutions as informal because they are unwritten. I view formal institutions
as ultimately backed by state coercion and informal institutions as ultimately
imposed by social actors. This creates an anomalous situation that business
organizations and professional associations who enforce property rights are
seen as informal institutions, when in practice they may be recognized by the
state. Thus, this wrinkle should be borne in mind.

2006; Tilly 2005.)[8] Civic institutions, such as business organizations, industrial groups, and labor unions can check state power and
enhance the impact of a rightholder's good reputation (Campos and
Root 1994; Haber et al. 2003). Frye (2004) finds that, controlling for
a range of factors, members of business organizations are more likely
to invest than non-members and attributes this outcome primarily
to the greater costs of expropriation. Similarly, Markus (2012) finds
that firms in Russia and Ukraine raised the costs of private or public
expropriation by creating strategic alliances with other firms, community associations, and foreign investors and thereby generated stronger
property rights. Most generally, Putnam (1993) and Weingast (1997)
find that civic associations promote good governance and more secure
property by improving the monitoring of state officials.

Yet, we have little empirical research on how a concern for a business reputation is generated and replicated over space and time, particularly in Russia. How valuable is a good reputation relative to other
factors? What sources do individuals and businesses use to evaluate
the trustworthiness of potential trading partners? Under what conditions can business organizations serve as a check on cheating by firms?
Identifying the relative impact of formal and informal institutions and
understanding better how these institutions work are central tasks for
scholars of economic development.

Moreover, while much work tends to focus on either the impact
of informal and formal institutions on economic behavior, it is also
essential to explore the interaction of these institutions. Some argue
that informal institutions, such as trust-based social networks, reduce
incentives to develop strong public institutions, such as independent courts and powerful bureaucracies (Migdal 1988; Frey 1997).
According to this substitution view, individuals and firms would tend
to use either formal or informal institutions to guide their decisions
to invest and innovate. This would suggest that informal and formal
institutions undermine each other.

Others argue that strong social networks that rely on concerns
for reputation are critical to building capable state institutions
(North 1990; Putnam 1993). When state courts work relatively well,

[8] I draw a distinction between social norms and general levels of trust in that the
former emphasizes the normative content of the attitudes and values of citizens
within a society, while the latter does not.

trust-based social networks can be even more effective at reducing cheating because information about misbehavior can be transmitted more cheaply. According to this complements view, strong formal institutions and strong informal institutions go hand in hand.[9]

Chapter 5 uses surveys of business elites in Russia in 2005, 2008, and 2011 to address these issues and finds that reputation is a potent stimulus to trade, that a bad reputation has a far more powerful effect than a good reputation, that businesspeople rely in equal measure on newspapers and gossip to verify reputations, and that courts play a non-trivial role in protecting property rights to trade. I also find little evidence that courts and reputation are substitutes for one another, but some weak evidence that they serve as complements. This suggests that at least in this case informal institutions do not undermine formal institutions as argued by Migdal (1988) and Frey (1997).

Social Norms

Finally, some scholars have pointed to the role that social norms play in underpinning economic institutions such as property rights. Whether generated by ideology, religion, tradition, or culture, social norms that identify appropriate and inappropriate behavior and help citizens make sense of the economic world around them are important elements of property rights (Kreps 1990). This literature has a long tradition, but a few recent works give the flavor of the argument.[10] Kuran (2005) argues that social values derived from the Koran inhibited the expansion of markets and property rights in the Middle East by discouraging the development of complex financial institutions among Muslims. He notes that Islam treats certain economic behaviors as normatively bad (e.g., lending with interest), although this practice may provide gains for society. In this way, the power of social norms about appropriate and inappropriate behavior shapes property rights and economic development.

---

[9] The evidence on this point is equivocal and likely depends on the specific formal and informal institutions in question (Bernstein 1992; Banerjee and Duflo 2010).

[10] For a good review of the law and society approach, see Abel (2010). For a long-run view of the impact of culture on economic outcomes see Richerson and Boyd (2005).

In attributing the growth of the industrial revolution in England to the ideas and values of the Enlightenment, Mokyr (2009: 1) argues that "economic change in all periods depends, more than most economists think, on what people believe." Mokyr puts ideas and values in the forefront of the argument, but avoids claims that they are the whole story. Drawing on the ideas of Weber, Landes (2000: 12) argues that culture makes "almost all the difference" in accounting for economic progress across countries and over time. Emphasizing the religious roots of the spectacular economic development of Northern Europe in the sixteenth to eighteenth centuries, he argues:

According to Calvinism, goodness was a plausible sign of selection. Anyone could be chosen, but it was only reasonable to suppose that most of the chosen would show by their character and ways the quality of their souls and the nature of their destiny. This implicit reassurance was a powerful incentive to proper thoughts and behavior. And while hard belief in pre-destination did not last more than a generation or two (it is not the kind of dogma that has lasting appeal), it was eventually converted into a secular code of behavior: hard work, honesty, seriousness, the thrifty use of money and time. All of these values help business and capital accumulation.

In Landes' view, it is the normative content of the social norms of Calvinism that encourage certain behaviors that generate economic development. To make the case in other settings, Landes (2000: 12) points to social norms carried by immigrant groups that are more economically successful than the ethnic groups of the host nation, such as "the Chinese in East and Southeast Asia, Indians in East Africa, Lebanese in West Africa, Jews and Calvinists throughout much of Europe, and on and on." Of course, not all immigrants prosper in their new setting and bad habits may die hard. Guiso, Sapienza, and Zingales (2004) find that emigrants from low-trust regions in southern Italy bring their mistrust with them to their new host countries.[11]

Demonstrating the impact of social norms and culture on property rights and economic development is a challenge. Social norms and cultural attitudes are as likely to be a by-product of secure property rights as a cause, and, of course, the two may reinforce each other, which makes it difficult to identify the causal impact of either (Guiso et al. 2006: 39;

---

[11] See Haley (1978) for a critique of cultural arguments that the Japanese avoid litigation.

Grosjean and Senik 2011; Simpser 2016). Even while recognizing that social norms and culture may be important, some argue that they are notoriously difficult to measure with any precision. Still others explore whether those features of culture that move slowly can account for variation in institutions and economic performance that change over time (Becker 1996; Roland 2000; 2004; 2012). This debate is easy to caricature, but the best participants recognize the potential impact of social norms and culture on behavior and the inherent difficulty of studying the topic.

One point of contention that is especially relevant is the malleability of social norms. Whether social norms can be changed by new information or are largely impervious to outside influences in the short run is an important topic (Denzau and North 1994; Roland 2012; Di Tella et al. 2012; Grosjean and Senik 2011). Some conceptions of how social norms influence economic practice suggest that these norms are remarkably robust to external influence and change slowly over time, while others suggest that new information can alter social norms and that culture is actually quite fluid.[12] This debate has important implications for understanding large-scale social change. To motivate their study of the impact of the Argentine government's anti-privatization campaign on beliefs about the renationalization of water services, Di Tella et al. (2012: 553) observe: "Indeed, if these beliefs were fixed, perhaps because they were historically determined, then the possibility of changing economic systems or of implementing long lasting market reforms might be limited." Examining the mutability of attitudes toward property relations is an important research agenda.

These debates have been prominent in the postcommunist world as many observers, particularly in the early 1990s, fretted over whether generations of citizens raised under communist rule could adopt social norms to support private property rights and the expansion of markets (Shiller et al. 1991; Hellman 1993).[13] With the case of Russia in

---

[12] Guiso et al. (2006: 23) define culture as "those customary beliefs and values that ethnic, religious, and social groups transmit fairly unchanged from generation to generation." This is a useful and clear definition, but also one that focuses on the static parts of culture. See also Banfield (1958).

[13] Landes (2000: 3-4) references the case of contemporary Russia: "Seventy-five years of anti-market, anti-profit schooling and insider privilege have planted and frozen anti-entrepreneurial attitudes. Even after the regime has fallen, people fear the uncertainties of the market and yearn for the safe tedium of state employment. Or they yearn for equality in poverty, a common feature of

mind, Shiller et al. (1991) note that "one view is that major obstacles (to the success of free markets) are the attitudes, morals and understandings of the people themselves, not just the institutions or politics they live with." Early studies from post-Soviet Russia find mixed evidence of support for private property (Finifter and Mickiewicz 1992; Duch 1993; Miller et al. 1994; Evans and Whitefield 1995; Gibson 1996).[14] These works capture initial responses to the collapse of the command economy and the introduction of political and economic reform, but it is difficult to draw lessons from these early studies given that many citizens had been exposed to privatized property for only a short time.[15]

In Chapter 6, I look at a critical issue for understanding the sources of social norms toward property: the legitimacy of privatized property rights. Several generations of Russians were nurtured on slogans linking private property with the great ills in the world, but in the first 15 years of the transition Russia experienced a vast expansion in private property rights in a historically short period of time. Using a survey of the mass public conducted in 2006, I find that the process by which property was obtained influences subsequent perceptions of the legitimacy of privatized property. That is, property rights privatized with more severe violations of the law are still seen as less legitimate ten years after the fact. However, right-holders who benefitted from illegal privatization can take steps to improve public perceptions of the legitimacy of their property rights by providing public goods and by investing in their firm.

Moreover, evidence from 27 postcommunist countries indicates that Russians oppose privatized property at rates quite similar to their counterparts in other postcommunist countries. In addition, Russians

---

peasant cultures around the world. As the Russian joke has it, peasant Ivan is jealous of neighbor Boris because Boris has a goat. A fairy comes along and offers Ivan a single wish. What does he wish for? That Boris's goat should drop dead. Fortunately, not all Russians think that way."

[14] Shiller et al. (1991) surveyed around 400 New Yorkers and 400 Muscovites in 1990 and found far greater similarities than differences in their normative assessment of markets, but also noted that Muscovites were much more likely to express negative associations with businesspeople.

[15] There is a long literature about the negative impact of Russian and orthodox culture on property relations predating Communist rule (Gerschenkron 1960: 60; Pipes, 1974), but more recent scholarship has been less critical of legal developments toward property in Russia (Burbank 2004; 2012; Antonov 2011).

are about as likely to oppose privatized property as counterparts in many Latin American countries. In a word, everyone hates privatization. Indeed, the evidence suggests a subtle form of reasoning about the legitimacy of private property rights obtained through privatization. The vast majority of Russians oppose privatization, but they also prefer that factories be held in private rather than state hands. The same result largely holds for citizens in other postcommunist countries as well. Despite the complexity of the issue of privatization, many Russians appear to hold rather sophisticated views on the topic.

While each empirical chapter aims to enrich long-standing debates on how power, institutions, and norms influence property rights, in Chapter 7 I tie together some of the threads that weave their way through the work to address broader issues in comparative politics, Russian studies, and economic development.

The Russia Angle

In addition to exploring general themes of interest to scholars of economic development and comparative politics, I make several broader points on economic conflict in Russia. Rather than making blanket statements about the state of property rights in Russia, I try to identify the conditions in which property rights are stronger and weaker in Russia. The conventional wisdom suggests that property rights in Russia are exceedingly weak; that formal legal institutions are inconsequential, and that political connections decide all. There is of course much to this view. Examples of spectacular and occasionally grotesque violations in property rights in Russia are easy to find. Take the case of Sergei Magnitsky, a 37-year-old Russian accountant who, while working for a large foreign investor, uncovered a tax fraud of more than $230 million by government officials, which he reported to the authorities. Rather than investigating, the authorities brought tax evasion charges against Magnitsky, placed him in pre-trial detention, and denied him basic medical attention which led to his death in custody in 2009. Not satisfied with the result, the authorities then put Magnitsky on trial and found him guilty even though he had been dead for more than three years.[16]

---

[16] The most spectacular abuses of justice occur in cases of human rights rather than property rights. By 2011 the European Court of Human Rights had received more than 50,000 complaints from Russia. Indeed, of the 47 countries

Neither is it difficult to find examples of Russian authorities bringing dubious charges of violations of property rights or tax laws to harass and imprison political opponents. Anti-corruption activist Alexei Navalny in 2013 received a five-year prison sentence in a case widely seen as political rather than legal.[17] In 2005, prominent businessman and Putin critic Mikhail Khodorkovsky was sentenced to eight years in prison for tax evasion and other economic crimes. Half way through his sentence, the state brought new charges against Khodorkovsky that even those unsympathetic to his plight saw as a mockery. His release from prison in early 2014 was largely due to the good graces of President Putin (and a desire for a public relations victory on the eve of the Olympic Games in Sochi) rather than to any admission of legal improprieties. In addition to these high-profile cases, more than 50 mayors were removed from office in 2011 in the wake of charges of economic illegalities.

And yet others argue that the story of property rights in Russia is more nuanced than the conventional wisdom suggests (Hendley et al. 2000; 2007; Gans-Morse 2012; Shvets 2013; Trochev 2012).[18] Alongside these abominations of justice, this revisionist view argues that businesses in Russia continue to turn to courts to resolve run-of-the-mill economic disputes. Despite considerable public distrust and cynicism toward courts, filings in the state courts of arbitration – the main forum for resolving business disputes – increased by more than more than 90 percent between 2000 and 2012. This growth in court use is perhaps not surprising as the Russian economy grew by more than 60 percent during this period, suggesting that many more transactions were taking place. Whether this increase in the use of courts means that property rights are being violated more frequently or that businesspeople are more comfortable using courts is difficult to know from the raw data, but it does suggest the value of examining the role of formal legal institutions in Russian economic life.

belonging to the EHCR, complaints from Russia make up of 25 percent of cases. See Riley (2011).

[17] Russian billionaire Mikhail Prokhorov noted after hearing the sentence: "Judge Blinov is apparently the only person in our country, who did not see a political dimension in the case of Navalny and Ofitserov." Interfax, July 18, 2013.

[18] This approach has been championed most forcefully by Hendley. See Hendley et al. (1999; 2000), Hendley 2002; 2004; 2009; 2011; 2012a).

The revisionists also point to considerable diversity in the likelihood of a private entity receiving an acquittal in different legal settings in Russia. Pity the entrepreneurs who face criminal charges in the courts of general jurisdiction where conviction rates are 97–99 percent (Volkov et al. 2011; Paneyakh 2014).[19] Win rates for private citizens in administrative law cases involving wrongdoing by state officials in these same courts routinely run above 50 percent (Trochev 2012). In state courts of arbitration private businesses win about half their cases (Satarov et al. 2010: 72). And courts are far from the only means of protecting property as right-holders rely on reputation, social ties, political coalitions, and a host of other means to make their rights to property more secure.

I contribute to this debate in three ways. Like the revisionists, I find a considerable degree of "legal dualism" in Russia.[20] Some parts of the Russian legal system work much better than others. State courts of arbitration, which hear most business disputes, far outperform courts of general jurisdiction that handle criminal cases. State arbitration courts work better in cases where political issues are less prominent. For example, businesspeople have more confidence in courts in cases of non-payment than in hostile corporate takeovers. I attribute this legal dualism not so much to Russia's transitional economy, cultural factors, or a weak state, but to a political logic common in autocracies that seeks to balance economic efficiency with retaining the ability to reward supporters and punish political opponents. This suggests the value of viewing secure property rights not as a state that marks the endpoint of a transition from communist rule or as a culturally defined constant that changes little over time, but as a fluid and dynamic

---

[19] However, this figure does not include cases where judges find that a crime has not been committed or where the judge turns the case back to the Prosecutor (Dzis'-Voinarskii 2012). Taking these cases into account the rate is about 76 percent. Conviction rates in the USA are often over 90 percent (Gordon and Huber 2002).

[20] "Legal dualism" has deep roots in Russian and Soviet history and scholars in recent years have consistently pushed back against the view that legal norms have been largely irrelevant (Burbank 2004; 2012; Antonov 2011; Hendley 2013). The term "legal dualism" is used in a variety of overlapping ways (Sharlet 1977). It can describe a tension between formal and customary/oral law (Burbank 2004; Antonov 2011); a recognition that legal institutions work differently in politically charged and routine cases; the gap between formal legal norms and the law as practiced in everyday life (Ross 2004); or the clash between traditional ideas and new laws (Medushevsky 2006).

relationship that depends on the bargaining power of right-holders and rulers and existing institutions.

In addition, I try to offer some richness to discussions about the role of political connections for protecting property rights in Russia. With the conventional wisdom, I find that political connections are important for protecting property rights, but I also find that larger firms, firms with more mobile assets, firms with better reputations, and members of business organizations also tend to have more secure property rights, even controlling for their political connections. Because these attributes of firms often go together, it is important not to reduce these firms' more secure property rights to their political connections alone without taking into account other factors that might be at work. Political connections matter, but so do other factors.

Moreover, it is important to unpack political connections as the term has many dimensions, some of which are much more important than others. The chapters that follow show that businesspeople perceive that personal relations with state officials, work experience in the government, and partisan political affiliations have different impacts on the security of property; it is imprecise to speak of the power of political connections *per se*. Different types of political connections have different impacts on property rights.

Institutions under Autocracy

The findings speak to a large body of recent work on the role of institutions under autocratic rule. The traditional view suggests that formal institutions under autocratic rule are little more than window dressing and have no real influence on policy outcomes or regime durability (Gasiorowski 1995: 883). In the last decade, however, scholars have explored how elections, parties, legislatures, and constitutions shape policy outcomes and the longevity of autocratic regimes (Lust-Okar 2006a; 2006b; Magaloni 2006; Greene 2007; Gandhi 2008; Boix and Svolik 2013; Reuter and Remington 2009; Blaydes 2011; Svolik 2012; Simpser 2013; Ginsburg and Simpser 2014). This impressive body of work offers an important corrective, but is subject to concerns about endogeneity: because autocrats shape these institutions to serve their own ends, it is often difficult to know whether these institutions have an independent effect on outcomes or are merely reflections of the underlying power of the autocrat (Pepinsky 2014). By exploring how an exogenous shift in bargaining power induced by an election shaped perceptions about the security of property rights, this work provides a sterner test of the exogenous impact of institutions on outcomes than is often the case. This result lends credence to the view that institutions matter even under autocratic rule.[21]

In addition, I contribute to the growing literature on legal institutions under autocracy. While research suggests that more democratic governments tend to have stronger property rights, scholars have also identified conditions under which autocrats may introduce stronger legal norms, including, in some cases, in the economic sphere (Leblang 1996). Moustafa (2007) argues that economic decline and a heightened need for foreign direct investment in Egypt compelled the Mubarak government to create separate courts for foreign investors in hopes of solving a severe budget crisis. Magaloni (2008) finds that in the face of increased political competition autocrats in Mexico created stronger legal institutions with the goal of enforcing political order on subnational politicians. Borrowing from McCubbins and Schwartz (1984), Ginsburg (2008) observes that autocrats can use administrative law to monitor lower-level bureaucrats. In other work, Ginsburg (2003) argues that autocrats who are concerned about the security of their rights after leaving office may strengthen legal institutions as "political insurance." On this view, autocrats with short time horizons anticipate losing office and empower stronger legal institutions in hopes of assuring a soft landing once they are out of power.[22] On the other hand, Olson (1993) suggests that only autocrats with long-time horizons who expect to stay in power will strengthen property rights. Only when the long-term benefits of the increased tax returns generated by stronger legal institutions exceed the short-term costs of empowering legal institutions will rulers introduce legal constraints on their power. Haber et al. (2003) find that vertical political integration can under strict circumstances increase the security of property rights for foreign investors. A simple statement that property rights are weak

---

[21] Several works in this camp analyze legal institutions, but these tend to examine the influence of high courts on political liberalization or the protection of human rights (Helmke 2005; Hilbink 2007). In contrast, this work focuses on the narrower issue of how legal institutions and elections influence perceptions of property rights under autocratic rule.

[22] Polischuk and Sunyaev (2013) provide a formal treatment and empirical test of this argument across regions in Russia.

under autocratic regimes hides as much as it reveals. By exploring the role of courts and elections in Russia, this work aims to provide further evidence about the conditions under which formal institutions influence outcomes under autocratic rule.

Methodological Contribution

Finally, the book hopes to make a methodological contribution to the study of property rights by relying on survey-based experiments and a natural experiment.[23] Most research on property rights has been observational in that it seeks to account for potential confounding influences by including control variables that may also be influencing the dependent variable of interest. Many case studies, survey-based analyses, and cross-national studies of property rights fall into this category, but these types of observational analysis are less suited to making causal claims due to endogeneity problems (Acemoglu et al. 2001). Endogeneity problems can arise if "good" institutions and "good" norms go together – a coincidence that makes it difficult to determine the individual impact of institutions and norms on property rights. For example, in settings with a dominant middle class, high levels of social trust, strong courts, and robust norms in support of private property, it is difficult to identify precisely which of these factors is influencing behavior and attitudes. In addition, observational studies may suffer from reverse causation. This possibility is especially relevant for survey analyses of property rights because perceptions of property rights may color perceptions of institutions rather than the other way around. These possibilities should be borne in mind in the observational analyses that follow.

In most analyses, however, I use survey-based "experiments" or a natural experiment that rely on randomization rather than the inclusion of control variables to help mitigate this problem.[24] For example, instead of asking a single question to all respondents and reporting the average response, I create very slightly different versions of the question and randomly assign which respondents receive which version of the question. When the number of respondents who receive each version

---

[23] Di Tella et al. (2012).
[24] Baird and Javeline (2007) use survey experiments to study Russia's Supreme and Constitutional Courts.

of the question is sufficiently large, the differences in the responses between the groups should only be attributable to the small changes in the question wording that each group received. Random assignment of the different versions of the question should ensure that all variables that may potentially influence the responses are distributed roughly equally across each version of the question. On average, the groups that receive each version of the question should be statistically indistinguishable from each other. There should be similar numbers of old and young, employed and unemployed, bright and not-so bright, and so on in each group. Even difficult to measure variables such as ideology, personality, and risk tolerance should be equally distributed across groups. Thus, these factors cannot account for differences in the responses between groups. Survey-based experiments can alleviate the endogeneity problem by ensuring that, at least in principle, independent variables of interest are not co-determined with the outcome.

Survey experiments can also provide greater confidence in making causal claims, in part because they require less stringent assumptions about the data than do standard multivariate analyses. Multivariate regression using observational data is a powerful tool that gives researchers leverage by controlling for other factors that may be influencing the results, but it also generates debates about how models should be specified (Gerber and Green 2012), and to the extent that results depend on the inclusion/exclusion of certain control variables, it becomes more difficult to identify which factors are shaping outcomes. In contrast, the analysis here relies on the principle of randomization to control for potential confounding relationships and allows us to draw more powerful conclusions based on simple comparisons of mean responses across groups. In other words, survey experiments instill greater discipline on the researcher and provide more transparency in the analysis than do traditional multivariate regression techniques.

Experimental questions are far less powerful in making general statements about the "average" respondent in the sample because the number of responses to the same question in a standard four-condition experiment is four times smaller than in observational analyses, but they do offer a valuable means of identifying relationships between independent and dependent variables. In other words, while we can rarely speak with great confidence that we have identified the precise "level" of the factor that we are trying to measure in a survey experiment, we can often be quite confident that we have captured the "change" in response across groups.

There is no free lunch in choosing research methods and survey-based experiments have their own shortcomings.[25] Most prominently, they raise issues of internal and external validity. Concerns about internal validity arise "when the treatment does not exactly correspond to the construct that is envisioned as the independent variable" (Green and Gerber 2002: 811). Internally valid experiments capture the true causal process claimed by the researcher. This is often a problem because there may be several possible paths by which independent variables are associated with dependent variables.

External validity generates concerns about whether the results produced in an experiment travel outside the setting in which the experiment is conducted. The latter is especially worrisome in this work because many of the survey experiments present respondents with different hypothetical scenarios and it is difficult to know whether respondents will actually behave in the real world as they say they will in the survey. The hypothetical scenarios have the advantage of reducing incentives for the respondent to dissemble because the responses do not require the revelation of sensitive information. When possible, I try to complement the responses to the hypothetical scenarios with analyses that focus on the respondent's behavior.

This approach occupies a useful middle ground between laboratory experiments and field experiments. While survey experiments lose some control relative to laboratory experiments, they raise fewer questions of external validity as the surveys are conducted at the workplace of the respondent as part of the normal course of business.[26] Ideally one would like to conduct a field experiment, but randomly violating property rights as proposed in these questions and examining the responses raises serious ethical and administrative concerns – let alone worries for the safety of the researcher.[27] The survey experiments here get around this problem by randomly assigning respondents to slightly different versions of questions that involve violations of property

---

[25] Gaines et al. (2007) discuss the potential drawbacks of survey-based experiments. For examples of natural experiments involving property rights, see Di Tella et al. (2007) and Field (2007).

[26] On "lab in the field" experiments, see Morton and Williams (2010: 296–300) and Grossman (2011).

[27] But see Blair et al. (2014).

rights. The hope is that by using both observational analyses and survey experiments, by employing measures of perception and behaviors, and by using administrative data where appropriate, we can gain a richer picture of how different factors shape property rights.

What are Property Rights?

Property rights typically invoke the image of words on paper, but in modern economic and political science, they are much more (Demsetz 1967; North 1990). To put some flesh on the concept, think of the owners of three identical construction firms in Mumbai, Moscow, and Minneapolis.[28] By dint of formal rights of ownership, they can claim rights to consume, sell, and earn income from the assets of their firm (Barzel 1989). Yet their ability to do so varies dramatically. Based only on the law on the books, the World Bank estimates that a typical business owner in Mumbai pays more than 7 percent of the value of the firm to register the title to the business and more than 18 times the average per capita income in India to obtain all necessary construction permits, and almost 40 percent of the value of the claim to enforce a contract in court. The same owner in Moscow pays less than 1 percent of the value of the firm to register title, about 2 times the average per capita income to obtain construction permits, and about 13 percent of the value of a claim to enforce a contract (World Bank 2012). The same rightholder in Minneapolis spends less than 1 percent of the value of the firm to register title, 13 percent of the average per capita income to obtain construction permits, and around 5 percent of the value of the claim to enforce a contract. Yet, these crude comparisons tell only part of the story as they capture the law on the books, which may differ sharply from the facts on the ground (Ellickson 1991).

Right-holders often face a range of constraints that are captured poorly by looking at the formal law. If our Moscow businessperson expects to be the target of a raid by tax police paid for by a business rival tomorrow, one can hardly expect him to view his property rights as secure today. Anticipating that his rights will be violated, he will invest his profits abroad or sell the assets of the firm cheaply. These

[28] For an insightful account of buying and selling apartments in Moscow and Chicago, see Derlugian (2000).

concerns are not likely at the top of the list of our businessperson in Minneapolis.

More technically, property rights are a bundle of rights that include the power to consume, obtain income from, and alienate assets, such as land, labor, or capital (Barzel 1989: 2; Riker and Weimer 1993). Individuals, groups, or the state may exercise rights over these assets as is typically the case with private, common, and state property, respectively. Property rights vary along many dimensions, but three have received special attention: the clarity of allocation, the ease of transfer, and the security from trespass.[29] Because the state plays a critical role in each of these dimensions of property rights, property rights are often conditional on political relationships – a theme that will become apparent in the empirical chapters that follow.

These features of property rights influence economic performance by determining the extent to which right-holders are rewarded for their efforts. If right-holders view their assets as subject to competing claims by others, difficult to sell, vulnerable to theft, or lacking in credibility, then the cost of exercising these rights increases. Where these costs exceed the expected return, right-holders will have little incentive to engage in productive economic behavior, and economic performance will suffer. In this way, the structure of property rights is widely believed to shape economic performance over time.

Property rights have not always been at the center of scholarly attention. The core results of neoclassical economics rely on the assumption that property rights are perfectly defined and enforced without cost. This seemingly innocuous assumption led many economists to take property rights for granted. The current resurgence of interest in property rights can be traced to Coase (1960), who challenged these assumptions. In "The Problem of Social Cost," Coase observes that if property rights were perfectly defined and costless to enforce, (as many economic models assumed) then the initial distribution of

---

[29] Consider Goldstein and Udry's (2008: 5) discussion of land tenure in Southern Ghana. They note "land is 'owned' by a paramount chief and is allocated [to individual farmers] locally through the matrilineage leadership ... but land rights are multifaceted. The act of cultivating a given plot may – or may not – also be associated with the right to produce trees on the land, the right to lend the plot to a family member, the right to rent out the land, the right to make improvements, or the right to pass cultivation to one's heirs ... and these many dimensions of land tenure are ambiguous and negotiable." Not surprisingly, conflicts over land are common.

property rights was of little consequence for social welfare because owners would simply exchange property rights until they reached an equilibrium outcome that left everyone satisfied. Those able to obtain greater economic gain from exercising a property right could compensate parties injured by the owners' exercise of that property right. If bargaining were costless, then steel producers could compensate those harmed by the pollution the steel plant produces while still exercising their right to produce steel. This arrangement would leave both parties better off than if the steel plant could not produce or if the victims could not protect themselves from pollution. Coase's argument marked a departure from prevailing thought which argued that government action was needed to assign penalties to polluters to make injured parties whole. Coase argued that in the absence of transaction costs market participants have many means to organize their transactions efficiently without state regulation.

Coase went on to argue, however that because in reality the cost of exercising property rights is never zero, the allocation of property rights is critical. The costs to the steel producers of identifying all those harmed by its pollution, measuring their losses, and paying compensation could easily exceed the gains from exercising the right to produce steel, thereby leading to social welfare losses. Indeed, many mutually beneficial exchanges of property rights go unmade precisely because the costs of transacting outweigh the gains from exercising the right.[30] Coase argued that when the transaction costs of exercising property rights were low, market-based solutions involving negotiations between parties were likely most efficient. But when these costs were high, government regulation was likely the best response. This insight laid the conceptual foundations for scholars to examine how a broad range of institutions from legal and political systems to social ties and ethnicity shape the security and distribution of property rights.

For political scientists a seminal work on property rights is Riker and Sened (1991), who trace the emergence of property rights not only to demands made by right-holders and those affected by the exercise of property rights, but also to political incentives to withhold or supply property rights. Whereas Demsetz (1967) argues in the neoclassical tradition that scarcity drives the emergence of property rights, Riker and Sened (1991) observe that this view is insufficient. Using the

[30] See Glaeser et al. (2001) for a discussion and application of Coase.

example of landing rights for airplanes, they argue that secure property rights will not emerge absent incentives for politicians to recognize these rights. This argument can help account for why rights to potentially valuable property may not emerge.

Right-holders have a rich menu of options to protect their property rights, but in complex economies the state can generally protect property rights more efficiently than any other organization due to its economies of scope and scale (North and Thomas 1973; Tilly 1992). Among their tasks, state agencies, such as the police, regulators, and prosecutors enable the state to make property rights free from trespass. Courts can increase the security of property rights by resolving disputes among private agents, but also by placing constraints on state officials. Yet, it is widely argued that because even the best functioning state cannot resolve every potential dispute, right-holders also turn to a rich array of private institutions, organizations, and relationships to help make their property rights secure (Macauley 1963).

The Importance of Property Rights

At the micro-level, property rights influence economic development through at least four channels (Besley and Ghatak 2009). First, secure property rights allow individuals to reap the fruits of their investment and efforts. Because much economic activity requires up-front investments of time, capital, and effort for benefits that accrue in the future, right-holders are vulnerable to arbitrary or unexpected changes in policy or laws. Where right-holders expect the government to change the tax rates or rivals to steal their output after they incur the sunk cost of investment, they will be reluctant to invest in the first place. This "commitment problem" robs the investor of a potentially lucrative investment, but it also robs the state of potential tax revenue.

Second, weak property rights compel economic agents to devote significant resources to defending their property rather than putting those assets to more productive uses. Each worker hired to protect property – be it a lawyer or a security guard – is a worker not hired to produce.

Third, secure property rights promote development by making it easier to trade. Economic development is more rapid when rights are assigned to those who can use the asset most efficiently, but weak property rights may prevent this beneficial outcome by deterring right-holders from selling or renting their assets to more productive agents. Landowners who have surplus land to sell may be reluctant to do so absent confidence in the enforcement of contracts with buyers. Fourth, where property rights are weak right-holders cannot use their property as collateral, which can hinder the development of markets for credit.[31]

One potential challenge to the importance of property rights for economic development comes from China, a country that has experienced spectacular growth amidst generally weak protections for property rights (Perenboom 2003; Huang 2008: 32). But scholars have shown how China has developed a rich array of informal, and to a lesser degree, formal institutions that allow right-holders to have reasonable confidence that they will be rewarded for their efforts under some circumstances. Qian (2003) argues that institutions such as anonymous banking, which makes it difficult for the state to expropriate specific depositors, have constrained state agents from seizing bank accounts and thereby spurred private savings and innovation in China. Others point to social networks, patronage ties, promotion patterns for regional officials, and other informal mechanisms as keys to investment in China (Tsai 2002; Landry 2008). In addition, Lu et al. (2013) use survey evidence to find that stronger formal institutions to protect property rights produced large gains for manufacturing firms in China. Mattingly (2016) shows that village councils that do not have clan leaders among their members experience lower levels of land seizure. Although the two are often used interchangeably, property rights are not synonymous with the rule of law. The latter implies stronger notions of equality before the law whereas property rights may be secure for some, but not for others (North 1981; Haber et al. 2003). Moreover, observers typically use the term the "rule of law" as a much broader concept that includes aspects of legality that do not concern property relations. Nor are property rights synonymous with private property as mixed and state property can also enhance efficiency depending on the local context.

Nor should property rights be equated with individual ownership. A main theme in the economics of transition from communism was the

---

[31] Some argue that strong private property rights also promote democracy (Lindblom 1977). Boone (2014) also analyzes the interaction of politics and the economics of property rights.

problem of competing claims of ownership. Boycko et al. (1995) justify voucher privatization in Russia as an attempt to limit the sponta-
neous privatization of firms by local governments, managers, workers,
and ministerial officials, each of whom claimed property rights and
were stripping the assets of firms for themselves before other claim-
ants did. In his study of the transformation of Hungarian corporations
in 1993–94, Stark (1996) sees a similar process, but with the opposite result. He describes how multiple actors with claims to revenue
from firms created "recombinant" property that put the pieces of the
socialist economy back together in a way that made economic sense.
In her study of the transformation of rights to land in a Romanian village, Verdery (1996: 54–55) refers to property rights as "fuzzy" in that
villagers often created "overlapping" rights that gave multiple actors
access to the benefits of property, while avoiding routinized rules about
the exercise of property rights.

And of course, property rights should not be restricted to formal
property rights. That the law on the books differs from the law in practice has been a theme of research for decades (Coase 1960; Macauley
1963; Ellickson 1991; DeSoto 1989).[32] It is the interplay of *de jure* and
de facto property relations that raises the most interesting questions
for research.

Property rights also emanate from power relations (Goldstein and
Udry 2008; Lawson-Remer 2012). Secure property rights entail the
capacity to exclude and right-holders ultimately rely on the use of
force to back up claims of exclusion. To this end, right-holders have
used both informal and formal agents of coercion to protect their
property (Polanyi 1957). In many cases in postcommunist Russia it is
not easy to tell if enforcers of property rights are working as private or
state agents (Volkov 2002; Firestone 2009). The importance of coercion in the exercise of property rights inevitably brings state agents
into the analysis and suggests the value of a wider angle of focus for
research than simply examining atomized right-holders. Indeed, this
work follows Verdery (1996: 54) in favoring a "property analysis that
invokes the total system of social, cultural and political relations and
inquires into, rather than assumes, the nature of property relations."
In the empirical chapters that follow, I ask more narrowly focused

---

[32] Alina-Pisano (2008) makes this case most forcefully in her study of land
privatization in the Black Earth region of the Russia and Ukraine.

questions that explore how bargaining power, social norms, reputation, courts and other factors influence the exercise of property rights
in specific settings.

It is also important not to idealize property rights. In contrast to
studies that try to reverse engineer the norms and institutions that support property rights in advanced economies, this work adopts an ends-
based notion of property which begins with how right-holders resolve
specific problems in their daily business in Russia. Rather than beginning with an idealized version of norms and institutions in a market
economy, it starts with the much messier proposition of exploring how
right-holders resolve disputes, protect property, and interact with the
state on a daily basis in a far from perfect institutional setting.

Empirical Difficulties of Studying Property Rights

Identifying the security of property rights is a challenge due to problems with sources, data, and methods. Collecting data requires great
effort so many observers rely on secondary sources that typically bring
strong biases to the issues. Brokers selling stocks generally express an
optimistic view on the legal environment to encourage investment.
Journalists may focus on spectacular cases that capture the reader's
attention rather than general trends that do not. Lawyers have often
invested heavily in understanding formal institutions, but may have
less feel for nuances of how social norms and informal institutions
shape business relations. Foreign investors likely face different sets
of legal issues than do domestic investors, but foreign investors are
much better at swaying media coverage of their disputes in their home
country media. Politicians in all countries tend to use the courts as
subjects of derision when judges rule against them and businesspeople
often complain about courts even in settings where they function well.
Political scientists have biases as well. We tend to favor things that are
easily counted, which may limit our search for answers. These biases
often make it difficult to establish baselines for evaluation. It is easy
to find tales of gross violations of property rights, but it is difficult to
know whether these are exceptions without also looking at cases where
property rights were not violated. Few headlines declare: "Business
Deal Completed Without Incident."

Moreover, sources themselves may have unrealistic benchmarks. In
the 1990s brokers on equity markets in Russia often complained to me

that the state courts of arbitration were a problem because even simple cases could take several months to be decided – a speed that would be envied in most parts of the world (Frye 2000).[33] In a word, we should recognize these biases and try to understand whether they inflate or deflate our estimates.

Evidence and Methods

So how best to obtain evidence on the security of property? One could look at the formal institutions and laws, but these often bear little resemblance to the state of affairs on the ground. One could look at changes in the rates at which businesspeople use courts. However, many disputes may be resolved before reaching courts. Only a small percentage of cases that could end up in court actually come before a tribunal. This "tip of the iceberg problem" is well known. Without knowing the "true" denominator – the number of actual violations that could have ended up in court – it is difficult to estimate the rate of change over time and determine whether right-holders believe that the quality of courts is improving. Ramseyer (1996: 5) pithily notes: "Reported (court) decisions are not a random sample of all litigated cases and litigated cases are not a random sample of disputes."

Relying on the use of courts as a proxy for the security of property rights may yield competing interpretations. If businesses use courts more frequently it could mean that the courts are working better and are a more attractive tool for victims of property rights violations. Or it could mean that their rights are violated more frequently. If businesses never use courts, it could mean that businesses view going to courts as a waste of time or that courts work extremely well and deter violations of property rights in the first place. Establishing the deterrent effect of courts – the threat of punishment by courts that deters cheating – is very difficult.

One can also examine the "win rates" of defendants in cases against state or private officials. However, making generalizations about the quality of legal institutions based on win rates in court cases is problematic because the cases that actually end up in court are unrepresentative of all disputes. If right-holders only bring very strong cases to court, win rates may be high, even if legal institutions are relatively

---

[33] Given the double digit inflation at the time, this was a reasonable concern.

weak. We can learn a great deal about the workings of the court system by examining win rates and court cases, but this approach is less useful in making statements about the broader legal environment (Trochev 2012; Shvets 2013).

Alternatively, one could examine cross-national measures of the security of property rights. Scales of governance and the security of property rights have become a cottage industry (Kurtz and Schrenk 2007; Kaufmann and Mastruzzi 2007), but rating a country's security of property rights by a single index or indicator reinforces the notion that property rights within a country are a public good available to all. But we know that some businesses can have strong property rights even as others do not within a single country.

One prominent approach to studying property rights is to conduct case studies of particular property rights regimes, disputes, or institutions (Bates 1981; 1989; Libecap 1992; Verdery 1996; Alina-Pisano 2008). Case studies have the great advantage of providing rich accounts of the context in which property rights are obtained and exercised. By tracing events and decisions over time, they may provide greater temporal depth than field experiments or surveys. They lend themselves to more elaborate conceptualizations of property and property rights than is typically possible with standard surveys. We have many excellent analyses of specific legal reforms, practices, and institutions in Russia and other low- and middle-income countries.[34] As against these advantages, case studies typically do not provide a sense of the magnitude of the importance of different factors that support property rights and are less powerful in controlling for potential confounding factors. This is a concern due to the problem of the endogeneity of institutions (Acemoglu et al. 2001), but also due to concerns for omitted variable bias. Informal practices may be correlated with other features of a relationship that may influence behavior. A firm with longstanding personal ties to a state official may be more likely to win in court, but it also may be more likely to win due to its experience with the legal system, size, the facts of the case, or the nature of the opponent. Without taking into account these factors, it is difficult to identify

---

[34] Field experiments are an important means of studying some forms of property rights (Olken 2007), but it is often difficult to randomly assign property rights given the implications for political and economic power.

the independent impact of personal ties on the likelihood of protecting property rights in court.

Surveys and Property Rights

To try to understand the security of property rights, I rely primarily on surveys of holders of property rights and surveys of the mass public. Surveys often lack the rich detail that case studies of specific disputes can provide and capture only snapshots of specific moments in time, but have several advantages. They collect information about the first-hand experience of respondents. Given the stakes, it is likely that respondents are highly motivated to understand the extent of threats to their property. Moreover, surveys gather information on a broader range of factors that may be contributing to the security of property rights than can be amassed in a single index or indicator.

Surveys of firms present at least three potential disadvantages. First, surveys can be affected by "survivor bias." Because we only survey firms that remain open, we do not capture the view of firms that have closed for whatever reason. Say that burdensome regulation leads firms to close their doors. If only firms that have managed to evade these heavy regulatory burdens end up in the sample, this could lead one to the erroneous conclusion that regulation is not a problem. This is likely to be a greater threat in surveys that include large numbers of small firms and may be less of a problem here. This bias can be assessed somewhat by exploring whether new and old firms have similar characteristics. As Russia has more than a million registered firms, it would take a very large and sustained period of corporate raiding to dramatically influence the population of firms. Moreover, firms may be raided repeatedly. This form of "permanent" redistribution suggests that in principle all existing firms are vulnerable to a corporate raid. While it is difficult to detect the impact of survivor bias, it is unlikely to have a large impact on the remaining population of firms in this survey. This problem is not unique to surveys as qualitative studies of firms also must deal with this "censored" sample.

The four firm surveys that I rely on contain a core set of questions that have been asked in each round in at least eight regions and have a common sampling frame, but each survey included different respondents.[35] Because these are not surveys of the same respondents, I make

---

[35] The 2008 and 2011 survey include firms from 11 and 15 regions respectively,

few claims from the surveys about changes in property rights over time.[36] I am much more confident in identifying relations between variables of interest at one point in time than in identifying trends through time.

Second, surveys are often an indirect way to study behavior. Rather than observing the behavior of respondents directly, survey researchers rely on reported behavior, which may differ from actual behavior for several reasons. Respondents suffer from all the same psychological biases that make it difficult for us to recall our behavior accurately (Gilbert 2007; Roese and Vohs 2012). In addition, surveys often measure the perceptions rather than the behavior of respondents. Some questions require respondents to give their subjective perceptions about the business environment and these responses may be less reliable than questions that ask respondents to recount their behavior. Others argue that perceptions of institutions and behavior nonetheless can offer important clues as to the security of property rights (McMillan and Woodruff 2000). It is important to bear in mind that some questions rely on subjective evaluations whereas others report behavior more directly.

Third, respondents in surveys and interviews on property rights also have incentives to lie if the questions probe economically sensitive topics, such as tax evasion, bribe payments, volumes of sales, and illegal activities. In addition, respondents may be unwilling to criticize public institutions in more autocratic settings for fear of reprisal. This is a serious worry, especially in recent years as the government in Russia has become more autocratic, but it should not be overstated. For example, Frye et al. (2016) find little dissembling in responses to the politically sensitive question of popular approval of Vladimir Putin, which suggests that respondents should be willing to give honest answers to the less sensitive questions posed in the surveys used here.

Nonetheless, with the Levada Center, one of the most respected polling agencies in Russia, we used several strategies to address this concern. We developed the questionnaires through extensive piloting with respondents who were known and unknown to the researchers. In addition, we often asked respondents in debriefings about

but even these surveys includes firms in the 8 core regions from the 2000 and 2004 surveys.
[36] For an insightful work that traces the shift from private threats to property to state threats to property in Russia see Volkov (2002; 2004) and Gans-Morse (2012; 2014).

which questions they thought would be unlikely to obtain accurate responses.

We also designed the survey instrument to avoid questions that were likely to heighten incentives to dissemble. We avoided questions about the "size of informal payments" to various state officials as requiring excessive demands on the recall and good will of the respondent. The questions used here are phrased so that respondents do not need to reveal sensitive economic information. In the rare cases where we raised potentially sensitive questions, we asked respondents to rely on their general perception of "firms like theirs" rather than their experience. For other types of sensitive question, we asked respondents to react to hypothetical situations, such as conflicts with other firms or state officials. These responses are not measuring past behavior directly, but are rooted in the experience of the respondents and give them a cloak for responding more truthfully than they otherwise might. The wager here is that the gains from added veracity of the responses by raising hypothetical questions outweigh the loss from measuring behavior directly.

We are fortunate that our group of respondents in the firm surveys – the business, financial, or legal heads of the firm – are typically well educated and often are powerful actors in their own right. This may allow them greater ability to comprehend more complex questions and greater authority to answer truthfully about the condition of property rights.

It is also important to keep in perspective the consequences of less than truthful responses. We can often identify the direction of bias in responses to sensitive questions. Respondents are likely to understate the extent to which they engage in corruption to avoid incriminating themselves and to overstate the efficacy of state institutions should they fear retribution for being critical. Recognizing these potential biases allows us to identify upper and lower bounds of responses.

The problems of survivor bias, misperceptions, and respondent veracity plague all studies based on interactions with subjects whether in structured surveys or informal interviews. For this project, I have also conducted numerous interviews of businesspeople, state officials, and academics working on the topic, and I make use of illustrative case studies, but their insights are not asked to carry the burden of proof.

What the Book does not Address

This book does not address more sophisticated forms of property rights, such as intellectual property, patent protection, or the legal implications of new technologies that are often topics of discussion in advanced economies. As in many postcommunist and developing countries, what need to be protected in Russia are basic rights to "truck and trade" rather than what might be seen as second-order property rights, such as patent protection.

Nor does it speak to the possibility for the spillover of the rule of law and secure property rights into issues of human or political rights. These are obviously important topics, but are simply too broad for the project at hand. Nor do the chapters here address all sectors of the Russian economy. They say little directly about property rights in agriculture, natural resources, or microbusiness. Instead, they focus on wholesale and retail trade, heavy and light industry, construction, finance, and a number of other sectors.

This book does not directly address how different distributions of property rights influence behavior. An alternative strategy would have been to examine how different distributions of property at the time of the transformation generated different political or economic outcomes across countries, regions, or sectors. This is an important topic, but is not addressed here.

This work focuses primarily on nonstrategic firms, and the results should not necessarily be generalized to the large politically important firms in the natural resource sector of the economy. Nor should they be extended to multinational foreign firms whose relations with the state likely differ from those of more typical Russian firms in the surveys. The firms under study are less likely to grab headlines than are Russia's natural resource giants or well-known foreign companies, but merit attention as they employ most Russians, are critical for efforts to diversify the economy from oil and gas, and are understudied. Moreover, these firms would most benefit from a reduction in corruption and improvements in the quality of property rights. If this work accomplishes anything, it hopes to draw a more nuanced picture of how bargaining power, formal institutions, informal institutions, and social norms shape different types of property relations in Russia.

The goal is not to develop a "unified theory of property rights" or to measure the extent to which property rights in Russia are secure on a scale of 1–100. It would be wonderful to report that on a scale of 1 to 100, Russia's property rights rating is 58.32 with a confidence interval of 52.0–64.3, but the concept is too complex for such precision.[37] This work takes a different tack. By analyzing the way in which ordinary Russian firms and citizens view how power, institutions, and social norms shape property rights, the chapters aim to provide a more theoretically nuanced and empirically rooted understanding of the determinants of secure property rights in Russia.

---

[37] This is a paraphrase from West (2005: 7).

2 | *Power and Property*

Police Officer: "Would you like to buy a cell phone?"
Our Hero: "Are you checking documents or selling cell phones?"
Police Officer: "Both."
From the movie *Boomer: Film Number Two* (2006)

It was a familiar, but frightening scene. On September 7, 2005, dozens of men in camouflage outfits and automatic weapons stormed into Togliattiazot, a large chemical factory in Togliatti about 600 miles east of Moscow. The deputy director of the firm noted: "We thought it was a terrorist attack" (Bush 2008). Far from being terrorists in the strict sense, these were members of the local OMON, a paramilitary branch of the police force accompanied by detectives from Moscow. They seized thousands of financial documents and soon the CEO and General Director of Togliattiazot faced charges of tax evasion and fraud. The two top managers fled the country, but did not sell their shares. Soon the company faced 270 court cases across Russia's regions aimed at paralyzing financial operations, depressing the value of the firm, and compelling the owners to sell at a knockdown price (*Rossisskaia Gazeta*, November 29, 2007). Investigations by the Ministry of Internal Affairs and the Tax Police followed, but the owners refused to sell (Tishchenko 2009).[1] Operating from outside Russia, the General Director rallied the workforce to take to the streets of Togliatti in protest at the hostile takeover attempt, helped publish a book, *Togliattiazot Against Raiders*, and turned to the powerful Union of Russian Industrialists and Entrepreneurs for defense. In addition, the owners managed to get the governor of the Samara Region, Konstantin Titov, to take their side (at least in public) in the dispute, and opened merger

---

[1] For a detailed treatment see Tishchenko (2009).

negotiations with several "White Knights," including energy sector giants, *Gazprom* and *Sibur*, in hopes of keeping a modicum of independence. They countersued state agencies who, in their view, had overstepped their authority. They also sued the firms thought to be organizing the raids. They even transferred ownership of the firm to the son of the Chairman of the Board, who was not under investigation.[2]

After five years of court cases, bureaucratic lobbying, and intense political maneuvering, the case was dropped, but only briefly. In 2012, the Investigative Committee brought new charges against Togliattiazot at the request of minority shareholders who accused the majority owners of engaging in transfer pricing to avoid taxes and cheat minority shareholders out of profits.[3] In 2013, the Investigative Committee brought new charges of asset-stripping against the firm, and in 2014, the majority owners of the firm were arrested in absentia and lost control of the firm.[4]

This example highlights a line of argument in the literature on property rights: the importance of power. In their essence, property rights entail the power to exclude others from enjoying the rights of one's property. Whether it is the power to call on the state to fend off a hostile (literally) corporate takeover in Russia, to employ a private security agency to guard one's factory from theft, to hire the Mafia to enforce contracts, or simply to use a handgun to protect one's claim to land during the California gold rush, the power to exclude lies at the heart of property rights (Firestone 2008; Gambetta 1994; Umbeck 1981). Certainly this close link between power and the security of property rights is familiar to observers of Russia who often point to

---

[2] Appealing to politicians, rallying the public, courting friendlier outsider investors, and filing countersuits are common in corporate battles in market economies, but threats of violence and forced flight abroad are not.

[3] Transfer pricing occurs when a company sell its products at below market price to a related company that then re-sells the goods at much higher prices, thereby cheating minority shareholders in the original company out of profits.

[4] As the book went to press the identities of the majority owners of the firm were unclear. In September 2015, former governor of Khalmykia Kirsan Ilyumzhinov announced that he held a majority of shares in the firm, but in November 2015, he renounced his claim two days after being put on the US sanctions list.

the politically contingent nature of property rights. The outcomes of high-profile struggles over property are frequently depicted as battles that reflect the relative political power of the combatants.

But to say that the powerful have stronger property rights raises a host of questions. What aspects of the power to protect property rights are most important? Personal connections? Wealth? Experience? Size? Asset mobility? Property type? How fungible is the power to protect property rights? Are the same dimensions of power relevant for everyday business disputes and for existential threats such as a hostile corporate takeover? Decomposing power into different dimensions is important because if we observe that managers of larger firms have better political connections and perceive their property rights as stronger than other firms, we cannot determine whether firm size or political connections are driving perceptions of stronger property rights. The link between power and property is more nuanced than simple statements that the powerful have stronger property rights.

This chapter uses data from two surveys of businesspeople in 2008 and 2011 to identify the impact of three factors: asset mobility, firm size, and various forms of political connections on the perceived likelihood of a hostile corporate raid. It finds that managers of firms whose assets are largely immobile, such as firms in the natural resources, industrial, and energy sectors, perceive their property rights as significantly more vulnerable to corporate raiding than do managers of firms with more mobile assets. In addition, size matters. Managers of smaller firms too view themselves as more likely to be the target of a corporate raid.

It also finds that political connections matter for the security of property rights, but not always as expected. It is perhaps not surprising that personal connections to the governor are generally positively correlated with perceptions of more secure property rights. But managers with prior work experience in local or regional government and managers of state-owned firms view their property rights as less secure from a hostile takeover. In these cases, closer ties with the state are associated with weaker perceived property rights. Once controls for other factors are introduced, being a member of the United Russia party is not associated with more secure property rights, but it is difficult to have great confidence in this result because it relies on relatively few observations. Thus, the direct effects of political connections on perceptions of the security of property rights depend on the type of political connection under study. Some help, but some do not.

Political connections also have important conditional effects on perceptions of property rights. Political connections are especially useful for firms with immobile assets. Managers of firms with immobile assets who know the governor or who have prior work experience in the government perceive their property rights as much stronger than managers of immobile assets who do not have these connections. Indeed, among the holders of immobile assets having personal connections or institutional connections decreases the perceived likelihood of a hostile corporate raid in the next two to three years by about 10 percentage points.

This chapter is not the first to identify state-backed corporate raiding as a significant source of weak property rights in Russia, but it differs from much existing literature in several ways. First, along with Gans-Morse (2012; 2017), Markus (2012), and Kapeliushnikov et al. (2013), it uses survey data to address the role of corporate raiding and state-backed violence on property rights in Russia. This approach helps to give some sense of the relative magnitude of the impact of fears of bureaucratic coercion and raiding on property rights.

Second, it unpacks political power into different components to offer a more nuanced interpretation of the relationship between power and property. Rather than simply stating that the powerful have stronger property rights, it probes how asset mobility, firm size, and political connections shape perceptions of property rights. Similarly, it unpacks political connections into ties generated through state ownership, personal connections (a right-holder knows the governor personally), institutional connections (a right-holder has previous work experience within the state), and partisan connections (a right-holder is a member of United Russia). Many studies point to the importance of political connections, but few decompose political connections into finer categories. This is important because these measures have different impacts on perceptions of property rights.

For example, it is particularly interesting that managers of state-owned firms view their property rights as more vulnerable to a hostile takeover than do managers of private firms, which suggests that state ownership is no panacea against corporate raiding. This finding points to the great fragmentation of the Russian state, as being owned by one part of the state provides little protection from being raided by another part of the state (Easter 2012).

Third, this work more explicitly integrates politics into the study of the property rights of firms by treating businesspeople not just as economic agents but also as political players. Many surveys of firms explore how different economic factors, such as size, type of property, strategy, and evaluations of state institutions shape economic behavior, but few such surveys include explicitly political variables, such as personal relationships with public officials, partisan affiliations, or prior work experience in the government. Viewing businesspeople as economic and political actors seems appropriate for settings such as Russia where there is an especially close relation between business and politics.

The results in this chapter rely on standard regression techniques so the usual concerns about causal identification arise (Gerber and Green 2012). Because the variables of interest, political connections, firm size, and asset immobility are not randomly assigned, we cannot be certain that unobserved factors beyond the control variables included in the analysis are influencing the results. And, in some cases, reverse causality may be a cause for concern. The next chapter takes advantage of an exogenous shift in the bargaining power of the ruler to achieve stronger causal identification, but here we must be content with traditional regression techniques to identify relationships.

In this chapter, I focus on the factors that provide a defense against corporate raiding rather than on the types of firm that initiate corporate takeovers. This decision is motivated by pragmatism. Firm managers are much more likely to express views about their potential to be a victim of a corporate raid than to discuss their roles as initiators in corporate raids. It is not against the law to be the victim of a corporate raid, but in many cases the tactics used in corporate raids clearly skirt the law, which makes them far more difficult to research.

This chapter begins with a discussion of corporate raiding Russian style with a special emphasis on the role played by state officials with access to coercion. This section illustrates the great variety of forms that hostile takeovers may take, while also recognizing commonalities in corporate raiding. It then turns to survey evidence to explore the determinants of perceptions about the likelihood of corporate raiding, before discussing the implications of the findings for our understanding of property rights and the case of Russia.

Raiding Russian Style: Economic Use of Coercion

In textbook treatments of exchange between economic agents, coercion plays no role. Relying on the notion of comparative advantage, economic agents trade items that they can produce more cheaply for items that they produce at greater expense. Rational traders make themselves better off by engaging in these trades thus nullifying the value of the costly act of coercion. Yet, in recent years, scholars have recognized the importance of understanding how coercion shapes economic development (North et al. 2009). To cite just a few examples, scholars have examined how civil wars shape economic growth (e.g., Murdoch and Sandler 2004); physical strength translates into greater gains in the drug trade (Levitt and Venkatesh 2000); the prospects of violence shape individual decision to invest in skills and capital (Bates 2001); and the Holocaust shaped economic development in Russia in the 1990s (Acemoglu et al. 2011).

Contemporary Russia is prime fodder for the topic. In the 1990s, case studies and surveys explored the role of private protection rackets, particularly among small businesses, in Russian economic life (Frye and Shleifer 1997; Hendley et al. 2000; Frye and Zhuravskaya 2000; Volkov 2002; Varese 2002). Other studies used sharply drawn narratives to account for episodes of economic violence (Freeland 2000; Klebnikov 2000; Hoffman 2003; Barnes 2006). Some of the best insights came from well-informed novelists, such as Yulia Latynina in her now classic *Okhota Na Iziubra* (*Hunt for Siberian Reindeer*).

In the last decade, scholars have turned their attention from private forms of economic coercion to collusion between economic agents and state-backed wielders of violence (Sakwa 2011; Gans-Morse 2012; Markus 2012; Kapeliushnikov et al. 2013; Rochlitz 2014). Treisman (2007) writes of the rise of the "silovarchs" who have a career background in the *siloviki* (security forces) and have become oligarchs on Mr. Putin's watch.

One of the most prominent ways in which the marriage of violence and wealth shape Russian economic life is the hostile corporate raid or *reiderstvo* in Russian. In standard corporate takeovers in developed economies, firms in economic distress transfer control to takeover specialists who reform the firm and sell what is left to outside investors. In theory, the goal is to create from the rubble of the assets of the distressed firm a more efficient firm that will be economically viable (Romano 1992; Tirole 2006). As with hostile takeovers in the United States, the goal of *reiderstvo* is the transfer of property rights from one entity to another (Sakwa 2011; Hanson 2014). Yet, in Russia the process typically follows a far different pattern. Sakwa

(2011) observes that "raiding entails the hostile attack of a corporate entity against another, often accompanied by physical raid by state organs." Hanson (2014) adds that this attack occurs with the intent of gaining ownership of at least some portion of the firm. *Reiderstvo* is different from simple renationalization as firms often end up in the hands of other private sector firms (Yorke 2014). It also differs from a "hostile takeover" in market economies as *reiderstvo* typically involves state agents applying coercion or threats of coercion against one or both parties.

It is this mix of threats of coercion with an attention to legal details that distinguishes corporate raiding in Russia. Thomas Firestone, a former US Department of Justice official in Moscow and Assistant Attorney General in the United States (2008: 1218), notes: "*reiderstvo* relies on criminal methods, such as fraud, blackmail, obstruction of justice and actual and threatened physical violence. At the same time, it is not just simple thuggery. In contrast to more primitive criminals, Russian '*reideri*' rely on courts, resolutions of shareholders and boards of directors, bankruptcy proceeding and other 'ostensibly legal' means as a cover for their criminal activity." Common tactics for corporate raiding include forced bankruptcies that allow creditors to take control of healthy firms with minimal debts. This form of raiding gained steam with a new Law on Bankruptcy introduced in 1998 designed to make it easier for loss-making firms to enter bankruptcy. At the time, relatively few firms had undergone bankruptcy despite having amassed large debts that they had little hope of repaying, but the 1998 law had the perverse effect of empowering raiders by dramatically lowering the bar for creditors to begin the process of bankrupting debtor firms. The 1998 law allowed any creditor who amassed a debt of roughly $5000 that went unpaid for three months to initiate bankruptcy proceedings. Small creditors often acting on behalf of economic competitors would institute court proceedings in far-flung regional courts where judges had the power to order reorganizations that typically involved replacing the managers of the "debtor" with a new team. Judges also had the power to freeze assets, a particularly powerful step in a volatile economic market like Russia. Volkov (2004) suggests that roughly 30 percent of bankruptcies between 1998 and 2002 when the law was changed were so-called "contract bankruptcies" that were part of hostile takeover efforts. The 1998 Law on Bankruptcy has been amended twice, but still grants strong powers for creditors and is vulnerable to abuse by predatory state officials and business rivals.

Other common tactics include the creation of fraudulent titles, company charters, and powers of attorney that allow raiders to transfer control to front companies. In turn, these front companies then quickly sell the assets to a third party just before the front companies go out of business. Russian law is quite protective of third-party buyers who buy assets in "good faith." Once the transfer of assets has occurred to a good faith purchaser, the raid is "practically irreversible" (Firestone 2008; Skidanova 2010). Moreover, the penalties for providing false evidence in court are rather mild compared to the possible economic gains of taking over another company.

Prior to a hostile takeover attempt, corporate raiders often become minority shareholders who then use their knowledge of the company and decision-making power to drive down the value of the firm so that it can be taken over at lower cost. One hostile takeover specialist with close ties to the security services (Shvartsman 2007) noted: "These are not raids. We do not take enterprises away. We minimize their market value by means of various instruments. As a rule these are voluntary-coercive methods ... [using] various administrative levers. However, people usually figure out where we come from ..."[5]

Using their status as minority shareholders, they initiate frivolous lawsuits, typically in distant regions before friendly judges that seek injunctions to stop the operations of the firm. An "arrest" order from a judge can freeze outstanding shares and remove the decision-making power from the company board, which effectively paralyzes the company. The raiders hope to drive down the value of the stock, force the company into bankruptcy, and then take over the firm at a drastically lower price. For example, the Samara-based Russian telecom company SMARTS Group found itself facing multiple identical lawsuits in a range of regions.[6] The minority shareholders gained jurisdiction in

---

[5] Shvartsman (2007) characterized the ownership structure of his firm: "These are no presidential administration members, but their relatives, high placed people. There are individuals among them, all relatives, from the FSB or SVR." The FSB is the successor to the Soviet-era KGB, while the SVR is the Foreign Intelligence Service.

[6] See "Calling a Friend," *Kommersant'*, December 20, 2005 at www.kommersant. com/page.asp?id=636951. SMARTS hired a law-school classmate and friend of President Putin as part of its legal defense team.

these regions by entering into false contracts with local companies and the legal proceedings dragged on for years.[7] With court cases languishing, raiders turned to another common tactic: bringing charges against shareholders. Gennadii Kiriushin, a major shareholder in SMARTS was put under investigation for fraud, money laundering, and illegal entrepreneurship – charges that many saw as linked to the takeover attempt (Bush 2008).

SMARTS Group is hardly alone as raiders often in collusion with state officials bring criminal charges against economic rivals.[8] State agents of coercion play a key role in corporate raiding. Until the practice was outlawed under the Medvedev Presidency, the Investigative Committee had the authority to investigate claims of tax fraud even without authorization from state tax authorities. (This power was returned to the Investigative Committee after President Putin replaced President Medvedev in 2012). Given the vagaries of Russian tax law, this gave Investigative Committee officials great leverage. Firestone (2008: 1218) notes that "corruption in law enforcement is a major cause of raiding" and concludes that "state charges play an extraordinarily important role in raiding schemes."

Closely related to corporate raiding is the use of the legal code and judicial institutions to extort businesspeople with the goal of taking over their business. It is often difficult to identify whether a raid has been initiated by private competitors or state officials. This type of extortion may be used as a part of a raiding scheme initiated by a corporate rival or a state official intent on acquiring property for himself. Officials from the Police, the Investigative Committee, and the Federal Security Agency (FSB) have frequently used the threat of pre-trial detention or jail for economic crimes as a powerful lever to pry property from the current owners. The problem was even recognized by Minister of Justice of the Russian Federation Konovalov who noted: "It is well known that over the past years, the threat of a prison sentence in particular has become a widespread source of corruption. ... Cases for those types of crimes hardly ever go to court, but are actively used as a means to pressure businessmen" (Mulders 2011). To give some sense of the scope of the problem, Petr Skoblikov, a professor at

---

[7] For a brief history, see http://knowledge.wharton.upenn.edu/article/ hostile-takeovers-russian-style/

[8] See also Myers (2006) on the curious case of Yuri Chichvarkin.

the Academy of the Ministry of Internal Affairs, points out: "In 2007 out of 211,000 criminal cases involving economic crimes only 16 percent were brought to court. It is obvious. These cases were used as a means of blackmail" (Mulders 2011). Even President Putin has called for getting tough on "extortion masquerading as state service."[9]

Scholars examining the nexus of law and economics in Russia have criticized the use of the criminal code for economic repression (Nazrullaeva et al. 2013). One problem is that many activities treated as civil offenses in other countries are seen as criminal in Russia. This gives state agents the power to impose much heavier sanctions – including jail time for many offenses. In addition, legislation surrounding economic crimes is notoriously flexible. Novikova (2011) notes that "the formulation of fraud (*moshenichestvo*) is too broad and used by the security organs not for fighting against real crimes, but for dividing property. Even businesspeople who experience bad luck and cannot pay their debts are considered con men." Similarly, the legal code allows cases to be heard under more than one statute, which can give prosecutors multiple attempts to convict a businessperson for engaging in the same act. Finally, investigators have great leeway to leave cases open and revisit them in the future. The possibility of re-opening cases of alleged economic crimes can give investigators powerful leverage over businesspeople.

The threat of pre-trial detention is perhaps the most powerful stick held by investigators. Despite several efforts to reduce the activity, judges are reluctant to deny pre-trial detention, especially in significant cases. Perhaps no case brought to light this aspect of the Russian legal system more clearly than the death of Sergei Magnitsky, the 37-year-old Russian lawyer working on behalf of foreign investors for the Moscow-based law firm Firestone-Duncan. His death, under the very harsh conditions of pre-trial detention, led the then President Medvedev to dismiss more than 20 officials working in various parts of the penal system, and ultimately resulted in the passage of the Magnitsky Act by the US Congress, which bars Russian officials involved in the Magnitsky case from traveling to or holding assets in the United States.[10]

---

[9] *Moscow Times*, March 5, 2013 available at www.themoscowtimes.com/ sitemap/free/2013/3/article/putin-gets-tough-on-extortion-masquerading-as-state-service/476542.html. For an engrossing account of intra-agency rivalry on economic crime, see Yaffa (2015).

[10] Browder (2015) provides a deeply personal account of the Magnitsky affair that also provides rich detail on the tactics of a corporate takeover in Russia.

While a particularly stark example, the threat of pre-trial detention and jail is a common feature of corporate raids and bureaucratic predation in Russia. Iana Iakovleva, the co-owner of Moscow chemical distributor Sofex Co., was reportedly approached by an official from the Federal Agency for Investigating Narcotics (SKRIN) who offered kickbacks in exchange for the sale of diethyl ether, a chemical often used to produce illegal drugs. When she refused, she was charged with illegal entrepreneurship for allegedly selling the chemical without the required licenses with a charge of money laundering tacked on for good measure. She spent seven months in jail before a court removed this form of ether from the list of controlled substances (White 2009; Meyer 2011). After her release, she founded Business Solidarity, a public interest organization that defends businesspeople who claim to have had their rights violated.[11]

The case of Dmtrii Malov provides another example. Mr. Malov bought a Soviet-era milk processing plant in Kostroma in the 1990s and restructured the business largely using reinvested funds and a bank loan. He soon bought two dairy farms and the business grew rapidly thanks to Russia's massive increase in consumer spending in the 2000s. In 2009, he was approached by an official from the Federal Security Service (FSB) and was told to sell his firm at a knock-down price. Mr. Malov's factory sat on valuable real estate that the city wanted, according to two reports (Safford 2011). When he refused, he was arrested on charges of not using his bank loan for its stated purpose with a charge of stealing state subsidies thrown in on top. He was sentenced to five years in jail. Fortunately, his case was taken up by "Business Russia," an organization of state officials and private businesspeople that defends the rights of private entrepreneurs.[12] They obtained his release, but he is free only on parole.

---

[11] See Pomerantsev (2014: 79–104) for a gripping account of the affair from Iakovleva's point of view.

[12] Boris Titov, the head of Business Russia tells the story: "Dmitrii Malov built a milk factory in Kostroma (a city of 270,000 in central Russia), and he was accused of stealing 1,500,000 rubles worth of state subsidies, subsequently being jailed for five years. This was an obvious incursion on part of the local government, as they needed land in the center of Kostroma, which was owned by Malov's firm. After our investigation, the corrupt FSB (Committee of State Security) official who conducted the case was fired, and Malov was released. Although he was released on parole, we're trying to get all charges dropped."

By some measures, the means and targets of corporate raiding have evolved over time. Rochlitz (2014) conducted an exhaustive search of national and regional newspapers over the period 1999 to 2010 using a strict definition of corporate raiding that required at least two sources to report on the incident and identified more than 300 cases of *reiderstvo*. While the research design by his own admission understates the extent of corporate raiding in Russia, there is less reason to doubt the trends over time. He reports that raiders were more likely to target mining and manufacturing firms with roots in the planned economy in the first half of the decade, while service sector and retail firms created after 1990 were likely targets after 2005. By his accounting, the involvement of state officials in corporate raiding increased consistently throughout the decade.

The problem reached such a scale that policy-makers could not ignore it. President Medvedev, himself a lawyer without strong ties to the security services, made protecting the legal rights of businesspeople a key theme during his presidency from 2008–2012. In December 2009, the then President Medvedev signed legislation banning the use of pre-trial detention for first-time offenders for many types of economic crime, including tax evasion. In April 2010, he penned amendments that reduced the number of economic activities that fell under criminal law. The following month Medvedev lowered the number of economic crimes that could place businesspeople in pre-trial detention, thereby reducing the leverage of the security services over businesspeople. Yet, these efforts did little to assure businesspeople, as judges were reluctant to take advantage of this new legislation and continued to rely heavily on pre-trial detention according to Valerii Borshchov, head of the Moscow Public Oversight Commission.[13]

Fears of legal repression by state officials were certainly understandable despite the steps taken by the then President Medvedev. According to the Ministry of Internal Affairs, more than 3 million economic crimes were registered in Russia between 2000 and 2010. Taking into account the total number of registered legal entities, individual entrepreneurs, and private farmers during this period, 15 percent of

Accessed on June 14, 2014 at http://istigechev.wordpress.com/2012/07/10/
boris-titov-corruption-economic-growth-and-a-wine-making-success-story/
[13] "Spate of Suspect Deaths Casts Spotlight on Moscow's Remand Prisons,"
Radio Free Europe/Radio Liberty, October 26, 2011, www.rferl.org/content/
spate_of_suspect_deaths_casts_sp/24371715.html.

all businesses in Russia had some criminal charges levied against them
between 2000 and 2009 (Novikova 2011). Many of these crimes were
undoubtedly real, but many were likely to have been initiated as part
of efforts by rivals and state officials to extort owners. The rate at
which crimes are closed prior to going court is much greater for economic crimes than for other types of crime – circumstantial evidence
that state officials have brought charges only to drop them, perhaps
due to bribery. Yet, the threat of prison time for being found guilty of
economic crimes in Russia is all too real. In 2011, more than 100,000
businesspeople were in jail for economic crimes.

Following his return to the Presidency in 2012, President Putin
reversed many of the Medvedev-era policies on economic crimes. In
2013, the Investigative Committee was given back the power to conduct investigations without prior approval from the tax authorities.
In addition, while Putin publicly backed a bill to grant amnesty to
entrepreneurs jailed for economic crimes, the scope of the amnesty for
entrepreneurs in jail for economic crimes was greatly reduced after he
returned to power. It was limited to first-time offenders who nonetheless had to reimburse injured parties for any damages that their crimes
may have caused. Despite hopes that tens of thousands of entrepreneurs serving time for economic crimes would be released, several
months into the program less than 50 jailed entrepreneurs had been
set free (Kramer 2013).

Legal Defense against Corporate Raiding and Bureaucratic Predation

Victims have rather weak legal tools to defend against corporate raiding and predatory use of economic law by state officials. Courts in
Russia are divided into two types.[14] State courts of arbitration hear
civil cases between economic entities, and administrative cases involving economic entities and state officials. Courts of general jurisdiction
hear criminal cases. By almost universal acclaim the state courts of
arbitration work much better than the courts of general jurisdiction
(Hendley et al. 2000; Titaev 2012).

Raiding cases suffer from unclear jurisdiction. State arbitration
courts do not hear criminal cases and arbitration court judges are

[14] I discuss these differences in Chapter 4 in much more detail.

quite reluctant to risk hearing cases that may not fall squarely within their legal purview. Similarly, judges from the courts of general jurisdiction, which are most often the proper venue for these cases, have been known to view "raiding" cases as economic in nature, which would leave them in arbitration courts.

To fend off the criminal charges associated with raiding and predation by state officials, victims must largely rely on the courts of general jurisdiction, the courts that hear most administrative and all criminal cases. Yet, pity the businessperson whose fate is tossed to the courts of general jurisdiction.[15] Acquittal rates for the courts of general jurisdiction consistently run well below 1 percent for the average defendant, a rate that applies equally to entrepreneurs (Novikova 2011; Paneyakh 2014).[16] Given their greater means, education, and status than the average defendant, one might have expected entrepreneurs to be acquitted at higher rates than a typical defendant but this is not the case. Paneyakh (2014) attributes these low acquittal rates in large part to the system of incentives by which police, investigators, and judges are rewarded and promoted. Across these different elements of the legal system, state officials face extremely high quotas, with little leeway to alter them, and little incentive to pursue cases that will not end in easy conviction.

In addition, courts of general jurisdiction are especially vulnerable to political pressure. Titaev (2012) and his colleagues reviewed more than 10,000 randomly selected cases of economic crimes that went to court between 2007 and 2011 and found that in administrative cases in the state courts of arbitration roughly 28 percent of cases are overturned by higher-level courts, but this figure was only 6 percent for cases in the courts of general jurisdiction. Since the same administrative agencies go to court in both systems, it would be odd for them to be less professional in cases involving the courts of general jurisdiction than in the state courts of arbitration. This suggests that entrepreneurs

---

[15] In the last decade, justices of the peace have played an increasing role in handling minor administrative and criminal disputes (Hendley 2011). See Solomon (2003) for an early assessment.

[16] Prosecutors in the United States frequently have conviction rates well above 90 percent (Gordon and Huber 2002). Given greater legal protections in the United States, for all its flaws the process by which cases are selected to end up in court provide greater respect for individual rights than in the Russian criminal system. Data from Novikova (2011).

have greater possibilities for defense in state courts of arbitration than in courts of general jurisdiction.

However, Titaev also adds that the state courts of arbitration are much less effective when economic disputes can be recast as criminal disputes, and thereby end up in the courts of general jurisdiction, and this "recasting" is common. In this respect, state courts of arbitration are only as effective as the courts of general jurisdiction where there is a strong bias in favor of the prosecution. Volkov et al. (2011) report that in Russia in 2008 of those cases that end up in the courts of general jurisdiction only 3 percent resulted in a not guilty verdict.

In an April 2011 interview, Iana Iakovleva, the head of Business Solidarity, a prominent anti-raiding public interest group at the time, argued that it is the criminal justice system rather than the arbitration courts that is the main channel for seizing businesses: "It used to be arbitration courts, but the quality and independence of the judges increased there" (Ruvinsky 2011).

Formal legal institutions are not the only recourse available to firms who end up in the crosshairs of state officials and corporate raiders. Businesspeople in Russia rely on many of the same tactics used by their counterparts in more mature market economies who are facing a hostile takeover. They appeal to the media, lobby state officials, mobilize workers to vote or protest, court "White Knight" investors who will offer better terms, and build alliances with various politically influential groups. A number of scholars in recent years have examined how businesses in Russia use social organizations and business associations to protect their property rights more generally. Using data from a 2000 survey of 500 businesspeople, Frye (2004) finds that members of business organizations express greater confidence that they can use the state courts of arbitration to protect their rights in disputes with state officials. Based on a large survey of firms and business associations in Russia conducted in 2003, Pyle (2011) finds that property rights for firms in business associations are better protected in regions with less competitive governments. Markus (2012) uses survey data from 516 firms in Russia and Ukraine to document how business managers create strategic alliances with foreign investors, international financial institutions, and labor organizations that raise the costs to state officials of engaging in bureaucratic predation. Using data from the 2002 Business Environment and Economic Performance Survey (BEEPS), Duvanova (2012) finds that firms facing petty corruption from bureaucrats are more likely to join business associations as a means to protect their rights.

One shortcoming in studies of the impact of firm strategy on property rights protection is the possibility of endogeneity as the unobserved factors that promote a certain strategy, such as membership in a business association, may also be directly associated with the protection of property rights. Moreover, there are clear limits to the extent to which organizations can defend firms against state predation via corporate raiding. Yakovlev et al. (2014) describes two attempts of businesspeople in Russia to create collective organizations to guard against corporate raiding. Business Solidarity was formed by the aforementioned Iana Iakovleva and by firms in the chemical industry. While Business Solidarity received much media attention at its opening, it soon floundered, in part due to its reliance on a single founder and a lack of ties to influential state officials. Business Against Corruption (BAC) on the other hand was created in close (too close) cooperation with the state and the Kremlin-friendly business association, Business-Russia (*Delovaia Rossiia*). Board members of BAC include high-ranking officials of the government, the judiciary, and the President's office, and while BAC's monthly meetings are often covered in the media and it is an important repository of data on corporate conflicts, its capacity to protect firms from hostile takeover is limited in part by its reputation for being so close to the state. Yakovlev et al. (2014:190) note that BAC "can be regarded as an important element in the creation of collective mechanisms of restricting violence. However, BAC's success in protecting businessmen against corruptive pressure and criminal prosecutions has been limited to date. During its two years in operation, the BAC managed to achieve the release from prison and acquittal of only a few unlawfully convicted people."

Corporate Raids and Property Rights

Academic literature on the topic of hostile corporate raiding is not especially large, which is not surprising given the novelty of *reiderstvo*. Yet scholars have begun to explore how firms vary in the extent to which they perceive threats of a hostile takeover. Volkov et al. (2011) discount the importance of economic factors in accounting for the pattern of legal repression by state agents against entrepreneurs. They find that crimes against entrepreneurs declined significantly from

2000–2003, increased at a high and stable rate from 2004–2008, then declined again from 2009–2010. They note that the pattern of charges levied against entrepreneurs does not vary over time with standard economic cycles or with changes in the policies of the security forces. In contrast, the pattern of change over time in the volume of economic crimes is better accounted for by political dynamics. In the period 2000–2003, the new Putin administration pursued policies that encouraged entrepreneurship (Berglof et al. 2003; Frye 2010). However, after the arrest of leading oligarch Mikhail Khodorkovsky in the *YUKOS* case in late 2003, the number of crimes against entrepreneurs increased dramatically.[17] President Medvedev came to power in 2008 and backed a number of legal measures designed to decriminalize various forms of economic activity, reduce the use of pre-trial detention against businesspeople, and increase the use of fines rather than jail time for economic crimes. These changes in policy in turn led to a decline in economic repression against businesspeople. This suggests the underlying political roots of variation over time in the level of legal repression of economic agents in Russia.

Grigorev et al. (2011) take an even more indirect route to discount economic and social explanations for the pattern of economic crimes over time. They argue that if anti-social behaviors such as murders, suicides, and economic crimes have common economic or social roots, then we should see a fairly high correlation among these behaviors over time. However, they find that while suicide and murder rates have declined dramatically in recent years, the number of reported crimes against entrepreneurs has increased. This implies that the dynamics of economic crimes and other forms of anti-social behavior are not driven by common economic or social factors.

Nazrullaeva et al. (2013) use data on economic crimes across regions of Russia and find that turnover in the head of the regional Ministry of Internal Affairs is associated with a decline in economic crimes. They argue that the incentive system used to evaluate officials in the Ministry of Internal Affairs gives new appointees the power to renegotiate down the base level of economic crimes that will be used to judge their performance. Schultz et al. (2014) find that convictions for economic crimes are related to the strength of informal ties between Regional Prosecutors and Chairmen of the Courts in the region based

---

[17] For more on the *YUKOS* case, see Thompson (2005) and Sakwa (2009).

on data on convictions for economic crimes between 2006 and 2010. These studies are quite valuable, but also take an indirect route to identifying the sources of raiding activity. Moreover, they are informative for this study primarily to the extent that economic crimes serve as a proxy for corporate raiding, a claim that is difficult to evaluate.

Others scholars have focused on more firm-specific factors to account for variation in the perceived threat of a hostile takeover. Indeed, three survey-based studies offer more direct evidence of corporate takeovers in Russia and merit more attention. These studies have several advantages in that they provide individual-level evidence and need not rely on data about economic crimes. As such they can more directly measure perceptions of the threat of corporate raiding. Gans-Morse (2012) does not analyze the determinants of corporate raiding per se, but rather deftly explores the breadth of informal and formal strategies that firms use when disputes arise using evidence from 90 interviews with businesspeople, administrative data, and a close reading of the local popular press and academic writings. In a survey of 300 businesspeople in Russia in 2010, he finds that 20 percent had turned to state bureaucrats informally to resolve a problem and 17 percent had used informal contacts with law enforcement officials to resolve a problem in the last three years. As Gans-Morse (2012; 2017), notes these figures likely understate the use of such contacts given respondents' incentives to hide this activity.

Markus (2012; 2015) makes a very useful contribution by unpacking the panoply of threats that businesspeople face – from threats of corporate raiding by market rivals to extortion by tax officials. He argues that firms have a variety of means to ward off takeover attempts including alliances with foreign owners, community organizations, and business associations. He uses data from about 500 industrial firms in Russia and Ukraine to identify the determinants of perceived threats from private and state agents. In the Russian sample, he finds that firms that manage to create alliances with foreign companies and firms that report "very significant" levels of support from the community perceive significantly lower levels of threat of corporate takeover from private agents. In addition, firms that report "very significant" levels of support from the community also report lower threats from state agents. The import of the results is tempered somewhat in that only 3 percent in the sample are able to create alliances with foreign firms and only 7 percent of firms report "very significant" levels of support within the community, which suggests the limits of using the stakeholder strategy. Nonetheless, Markus (2012: 2015) helps us better understand the threats facing firms in Russia and Ukraine.

Like Markus, Kapeliushnikov et al. (2013) focus on the institutional and economic determinants of the perceived likelihood of various forms of corporate raiding. Their study relies on evidence from a representative sample of 957 manufacturing firms across Russia conducted in early 2009 at the nadir of the global financial crisis. They asked respondents about the likelihood of their firm (1) being included in a state-owned company, (2) being the target of a takeover by a larger private company, (3) experiencing a raider attack, (4) falling under the control of local/regional authorities, and (5) having conflict among shareholders. In an extensive analysis including fixed effects for regions and sector, they find that state-owned, smaller, and more poorly performing firms perceived a greater threat to their property; that evaluations of the performance of courts are poor predictors of the perceived likelihood of takeover; and that market competition increases the perceived likelihood of threats to property. Moreover, they find that the perceived likelihood of raiding dampens investment activity even controlling for a host of factors. This is an important step that demonstrates the economic importance of perceived threats to takeover.

In this work, I explore many of these economic and firm-specific factors as well, but also take a slightly different approach by focusing on three factors: (1) asset mobility, (2) firm size, and (3) various forms of political connections, such as the firm's property type, the manager's personal ties with the governor, partisan affiliations, and prior experience in government. This approach permits an assessment of the claim that corporate takeovers, particularly those motivated by state agents, are the result of political activity rather than just economic, institutional, or firm-specific factors.

Asset Mobility

I begin with the assumption that raiders examine the costs and benefits of engaging in a hostile takeover. One potential consideration for corporate raiders is asset mobility (Williamson 1985; Boix 2003; Acemoglu and Robinson 2006). Immobile firms, that is, firms that face high costs in shifting their product lines away from their current use or in moving their physical location may be especially vulnerable to corporate raiding. Faced with a threat of a hostile takeover more mobile firms can either physically move their operations without facing great costs or shift to product lines that are less vulnerable to takeover – an option not easily available to highly immobile firms. This suggests that raiders may be likely to target firms in heavy industry and in the energy and natural resource sectors more often than more mobile sectors, such as retail and wholesale trade, construction, real estate, or transportation. This insight may ring true to observers of Russia as some of the most high profile takeovers (YUKOS, Bashneft', etc.) have occurred in precisely these sectors. By examining a broad range of firms, we can begin to assess the relative importance of asset mobility on property rights.

Asset mobility has been linked to a variety of politically important firm behaviors. In the broader literature on political economy, Frieden (1991) argues that firms with high asset mobility are adept at lobbying the state for protection. Bates (1989) links asset mobility to predation by the government in his study of economic policy-making in Kenya, while Acemoglu and Robinson (2006) and Boix (2003) argue that the holders of immobile assets are often a bulwark of support for autocratic rule because they fear expropriation by the poor under democracy as a result of higher rates of taxation preferred by the median voter. This work extends the literature on asset mobility by examining its impact on the perceived security of property rights.

Size

Managers of larger firms with more employees may have more power to defend themselves against a hostile corporate takeover by outsiders. Such firms may be better able to mobilize workers in public demonstrations in support of existing management. These mobilizations may take the form of street demonstrations as in the case of Togliattiazot mentioned in the opening of this chapter. Alternatively, it may take the form of votes for incumbent politicians. One study from the 2011 parliamentary elections in Russia found that one in four firms in Russia mobilized their workers to go to the polls in one way or another (Frye et al. 2014). Firms with more workers were especially likely to mobilize their workers during this campaign. These forms of mobilization can be valuable for managers and politicians alike.

At the same time, larger firms may be a more valuable prize for corporate raiders. In addition, larger firms may be simply more visible to corporate raiders and may also attract the attention of takeover specialists and government officials. In this view, managers of larger firms may view their property rights as less secure because they are more likely to be the target of a hostile takeover.

Yet, the relationship between size and perceptions of property right could be subtler. Large firms may resist a corporate takeover with even greater ferocity than small firms and this heightened resistance may raise the costs of a hostile takeover. In addition, very small firms may be safe from predation in part because the rewards of victory may be small and they may fly below the radar of corporate raiders. Taking these two statements together suggests a "u"-shaped relationship between firm size and corporate raiding.[18] Both small and large firms would have secure property rights while moderately-sized firms would be most vulnerable.[19]

Political Connections: Unpacking the Concept

Raiders may also consider the defense mechanisms available to firms. One such tool is having political ties to powerful figures within the state. Raiders may avoid targets with better political connections as a hostile takeover attempt risks a costly struggle that would require resources and ultimately reduce the value of the firm. In the broader literature, political connections have been shown to influence stock prices, the distribution of government spending, the death rates of workers, and property rights more generally (Fisman, 2001; Haber et al. 2003; Faccio et al. 2006; Fisman and Wang 2015). Moreover, this theme is familiar to Russia-watchers as well: many argue that politically connected firms have enriched themselves tremendously at the expense of the tax-paying public (Hellman 1998; Guriev and Rachinsky 2005; Frye 2010). Galina Krylova, a lawyer specializing in defending against corporate raiding notes: "the only real preventative measure (against corporate raiding) is to have very good political connections" (Carbonell et al. 2009).

---

[18] This debate is similar to Blattman and Miguel's (2010: 20–14) discussion of contest models in the civil war literature.

[19] Ideally, raiders identify potentially profitable but underperforming firms, but this is a difficult task for both raiders and academic observers.

Political connections are often rather broadly defined in the litera-ture. I try to refine the concept by distinguishing among four types of political connections, each of which captures a different dimension of the relationship between firms and the state. First, consider property-based connections. State-owned firms have much easier access to state officials, and to the extent state-owned firms provide important politi-cal benefits to these officials, they can expect their state patrons to have an incentive to protect them. At the same time, property connec-tions also provide information about the manager to potential raid-ers in the state and thereby increase the certainty about whether the manager will resist a takeover or not. Potential raiders in the state may know that the manager is a "weak" type that can easily be bought off once pressured to give up control of his firm. Similarly, raiders within the state may have better access to the financial condition of state firms than private firms, which may increase the attractiveness of the former as a target of a corporate raid. Perhaps most important, state owners may use their positions as minority shareholders to undermine the rights of other shareholders by instigating conflicts among the share-holders. In this view, state-owned firms should be especially vulnerable to corporate raiding.

Second, consider "institutional" connections here defined as rela-tively recent work experience within the state (Fisman and Wang 2015). In this account, managers who have previously worked in local or regional government are more likely to have allies within the state who can protect against corporate raids. This would suggest a posi-tive relationship between prior work experience within the state and the perceived security of property rights. But knowing that a man-ager recently left the state administration tells us little about whether he left on good terms or bad. If the latter, which seems more likely, we might expect to find a negative relationship between institutional connections as measured here and the perceived security of property rights. While previous work experience in the state is often treated as evidence of good political connections, the opposite may be the case.

Third, consider "personal" connections here seen as a personal relationship with a governor or mayor. The literature on clientelism, Soviet politics, and the politics of transition in Russia emphasizes the importance of personal ties between economic agents and state officials (Scott 1972; Willerton 1992; Ledeneva 2013). These ties may generate the types of trust necessary to engage in the political exchange of favors for support where these "political exchanges" cannot be enforced by a third party such as a court (Berliner 1957; Ledeneva 2006). The "old boys" network of those who have personal relations with influential government officials is a second type of political tie that may be used to protect property rights. Firm managers who have a personal relationship with the governor may view their property rights as less vulnerable to a hostile takeover than those who do not.

A fourth potentially important form of political connections might be called "partisan" connections. We might expect that firm managers who are United Russia members would receive protection from the threat of raiding in exchange for their political support, while politically non-aligned firms would not. Managers who are members of United Russia may be able to deter raiders by using their party membership to signal that any takeover attempt would be met with a vigorous defense. This "exchange" theory of business state relations makes intuitive sense (Frye 2002). Of course, partisan affiliations are not randomly assigned to firm managers and in some cases may be endogenous to the security of property rights. And the sources of partisan affiliations may have little to do with the perceived likelihood of a corporate raid. Nonetheless, due to the possible endogeneity between partisanship and secure property rights, the results here should not be seen as causal.

Conditional Effects of Political Connections

These arguments cited above explore the direct effects of political connections on perceptions of property rights, but it is helpful to consider the conditional effects of political connections as well. Political connections may be especially important for holders of immobile assets who are particularly vulnerable to corporate raiding. Holders of mobile assets may have multiple options to address the threat of a hostile takeover, such as moving jurisdiction or changing product lines to an item that is less attractive to the raider. For these managers, political connections may not be as important as a means to protect against corporate raiding. In contrast, holders of immobile assets have fewer options to protect themselves and may rely more heavily on political connections within the state. In this case, we would expect to find that holders of immobile assets who have good political connections view their property rights as significantly more secure than holders of immobile assets without political connections.

Similarly, political connections may be important for small firms who are more susceptible to a corporate raid than for larger firms who can rely on their size to fend off potential raiders. In these cases, the political connections of firms have important conditional effects on perceptions of the security of property rights.[20]

This is not the first study to focus on a possible link between politics and the risk of corporate takeover. In her study of renationalizations among 153 listed and non-listed companies in Russia between 2000 and 2004, Chernykh (2011: 1237) concludes: "Contrary to commonly held beliefs, there is little evidence that renationalizations in Russia are driven by economic factors: the government neither systematically 'cherry-picks' best performers nor addresses market failures by rescuing underperformers." She finds that formerly privatized firms in strategic sectors were especially likely to be renationalized and notes that her results provide "new firm-level evidence on the importance of political rationale in the government's decision to intervene into the corporate control structures." In her work, politics is reduced to whether or not a firm is characterized as "strategic" or not. This captures an important dimension of politics, but "strategic" firms might also have great economic importance, which muddies the interpretation.

Lambert-Mogiliansky et al. (2007) find the fingerprints of politicians on one particular form of corporate raiding. In a study of bankruptcies that went to court between 1998 and 2002 in Russia, they find that judicial decisions were deeply politicized as powerful regional governors subverted the bankiruptcy process to reward local constituents at the expense of the federal government and Moscow-based banks. It is not clear whether these results extend beyond bankruptcy or have survived changes to the Law on Bankruptcy in 2002.

In his study of reported examples of corporate raiding between 1999 and 2010, Rochlitz (2014) observes a positive correlation between the share of the vote for United Russia in the most recent parliamentary elections in a region and the number of raider attacks in a given region in a given year. One interpretation of this result is that the Kremlin is

---

[20] I focus on the conditional effects of personal and institutional connections on property rights. There are too few firms to understand the conditional effects of full state ownership and membership of United Russia.

willing to countenance economic raids by their allies within the state and society in exchange for electoral support. With its reliance on aggregate-level data, however, Rochlitz's study lacks empirical confirmation at the firm level.

The analysis that follows is novel in that it examines how different types of political connections may influence perceptions about becoming the target of a hostile takeover. Moreover, it is a rare study that measures the partisan preferences of businesspeople directly rather than only inferring them from the size, sector, asset-specificity or competitiveness of the firm, which is common practice in this literature (Frieden 1991).

The Data

Gathering data on how state officials and their allies in the private sector threaten and use violence against rivals in the economy is no easy task. State officials who abuse their authority have little incentive to advertise their activity. Fearing retribution, many victims are reluctant to go public with their tales. Moreover, state officials and private agents who threaten violence do not like to leave paper trails. Given the prevalence of nuisance lawsuits over corporate raiding, examining court documents would likely yield much noise. Case studies of particular takeover battles have provided much insight into the topic, but may miss cases where corporate conflicts did not occur (Sakwa 2009; Adachi 2010; Gustafson 2012; Yorke 2014; Markus 2015). This work takes a different approach. To identify the covariates associated with perceptions of corporate raiding, I hired two public opinion companies in Russia to conduct two surveys. I begin with the larger effort, which surveyed managers from 922 firms from 23 sectors and 15 regions in Russia in November and December 2011.[21] Given the sensitive nature of the topic, it is difficult to measure the extent of fears of corporate raiding. To reduce anxiety among the respondents, we asked a prospective question that did not inquire about past experiences with corporate raiding. This strategy follows Kapeliushnikov et al. (2013), who asked a very similar question. Interviewers asked: "About how likely is it that your firm will experience one of the following in the next two to three years?"

---

[21] See Data Appendix for survey details.

Table 2.1 *Perceived Threats of Hostile Takeover, 2011 Survey*

	Very Likely	Unlikely	Very Unlikely	Hard to Say
1) Become the target of hostile takeover	3	36	53	8
2) Fall under the de facto control of the regional or local government	8	36	47	9
3) Fall under the de facto control of the federal government	5	36	50	9

Answers in percentage. Data from 2011 Survey.

These figures are about half as large as those found in Kapeliushnikov et al. (2013), who asked the same question, although with slightly different response categories.[22] That their study took place in 2009 during a severe recession and included only manufacturing firms likely accounts for much of the difference in the level of the responses between the two surveys. A survey of roughly 500 industrial firms conducted via mail in February through May 2007 reveals higher levels of concern with corporate raiding using a somewhat different question (Markus 2012). Similarly, a survey of 500 firms conducted in 2008 that is discussed below offers slightly higher figures as well.

The figures reported in Table 2.1 have greater import than their relatively small numbers would suggest, in part because even a small probability of the catastrophic event of a corporate raid can change behavior. Taken together, 12 percent of firms answered that at least one of these three forms of corporate raiding was "very likely" in the next two to three years.[23] Roughly 40 percent of firms (those who responded unlikely) considered it possible that their firm could be

---

[22] Results are not directly comparable with Kapeliushnikov et al. (2013) or Markus (2012; 2015) due to differences in sample construction, question wording, and timing.

[23] This figure is lower than the 16 percent reported in column 1 in Table 2.2 as some firms saw more than one of these types of threat to be "highly likely."

taken over by raiders, regional authorities, or the federal government. About 50 percent of respondents believed that such an attack was "very unlikely." That roughly one in eight firms in Russia expect some form of corporate raid to be "highly likely" in the next two to three years suggests the great scale of the practice.

Modeling Perceived Property Rights

I begin by focusing on the impact of asset mobility, firm size, and various measures of political connections on the security of property rights. To measure the security of property rights from takeover by private sector or state agents, I created a simple three-category index by combining responses to the three questions in the survey about the likelihood of a hostile takeover reported in Table 2.1. The index equals one for the 12 percent of respondents who answered that at least one of the three types of hostile takeovers were likely in the next two to three years; two for the 46 percent of respondents who reported that at least one of the three types of corporates raids was "unlikely"; and three for the 42 percent of respondents who reported that all three types of hostile takeover were very unlikely in the next two to three years. Higher scores indicate that property rights are more secure and the mean response is 2.30.[24]

The main challenge to identifying what drives perceptions of the security of property rights is endogeneity. For example, firm managers who are members of United Russia may perceive their property rights as stronger, but firm managers may join United Russia in hopes of strengthening their property rights. A significant correlation between United Russia membership and stronger perceived rights may mean that the latter is driving the former, but the reverse cannot be ruled out. Firms that build relations with foreign owners may view their property rights as more secure, but firms with more secure property rights are more likely to attract foreign investors. Firms that join business organizations

---

[24] The average inter-item covariance of the index is .63 and the scale reliability coefficient is .84, which indicates that that these individual components can be analyzed in a single index. The results are essentially unchanged using a simple additive index that ranges from zero to six, where zero equals a respondent who viewed all of the three as highly likely and six equals a respondent who said that all three types of corporate raid were highly unlikely. Because few responses are in the zero to two range I prefer the simple trichotomous variable used above.

may view their property as more secure, but firms with more secure property rights may be more willing to join business associations.

There are no easy solutions to this problem. Yet, the threat of endogeneity bias may be greater with some variables than with others. I begin with a set of variables of theoretical interest that can be taken as plausibly exogenous at least in the short-run, such as asset mobility and firm size. While it is possible that over time firms may manipulate their sector or hiring patterns to avoid raiding, in the short run the costs of doing so are likely prohibitive.

I measure asset immobility as a dummy variable that equals one for firms in the energy, electricity, heavy industry, and natural resource sectors, and zero for other sectors. I measure size as the log value of the number of employees in the firm at the time of the survey. I use an ordered probit regression and also control for economic sector (dummy variables for construction, trade, transport, communications, finance, and real estate with wholesale/retail trade as the excluded category) and region-specific factors. This initial model has the advantage that independent variables are plausibly exogenous and there are relatively few missing observations.[25]

The results in column 1 in Table 2.2 indicate that managers of firms in immobile sectors view their property rights as significantly less secure than managers in trade as indicated by the negative and significant coefficient on *Immobility*. Among other sectoral variables, light industrial firms, such as textile firms, also view their property rights as less secure. Among other differences, light industrial firms are far less mobile than firms in retail trade.

Firm size is also an important determinant of perceptions of property rights. Managers of larger firms view their property rights as significantly more secure than managers of smaller firms. This result echoes Kapeliushnikov et al. (2013). There does not appear to be a "u"-shaped relation between firm size and perceptions of the security of property rights.[26] The effect of firm size on property rights appears

---

[25] The results for the main variables of theoretical interest are unchanged using a sample that excludes firms with fewer than ten employees.

[26] I also explored whether medium-sized firms, that is, those that lie in the 25th to 75th percentile of the sample in terms of size (17 to 170 employees), viewed their property rights as especially vulnerable but this does not appear to be the case. While the coefficient on this dummy variable is negative it falls short of statistical significance.

Table 2.2 *Power and Perceptions of Property Rights, 2011 Survey*

	Model 2.1	Model 2.2	Model 2.3	Model 2.4
Immobile	−.30**	−.35**	−.54**	−.43**
	(.14)	(.16)	(.18)	(.16)
Size (log # employees)	.08**	.09**	.10**	.09**
	(.03)	(.03)	(.04)	(.03)
State Ownership		−.48**	−.52**	−.52**
		(.20)	(.20)	(.19)
Government Experience		−.44***	−.44***	−.58**
		(.22)	(.17)	(.19)
KnowGovernor		.19	.06	.20
		(.13)	(.14)	(.13)
UR member		.27	.25	.27
		(.28)	(.28)	(.28)
Immobile* GovernmentExperience			.52** (.23)	
Immobile* KnowGovernor				.52 (.34)
Cutpoints	−.75 (.21) .74 (.21)	−.62 (.23) .93 (.24)	−.63 (.23) .93 (.23)	−.62 (.23) .94 (.24)
Test of significance of diff of interaction terms			Prob> chi = .00	Prob> chi = .02
N	771	638	638	638
Wald	92.70	86.03	86.51	87.53
Prob >F	.0000	.0000	.0000	.0000
PsuedoR^{sq}	.06	.07	.08	.07

* = p<.10, ** = p<.05, *** = p<.01, Dependent Variable: Secure Property Index, 1–3. Ordered Probit Estimation. Dummy variables for 15 regions, the construction, financial, real estate, communications, and transport sectors included. Trade sector excluded. Robust standard errors. Higher scores indicate more secure property rights, that is, the less likely the respondent perceived a hostile takeover. Data from 2011 survey.

to be linear as smaller firms, those in the smallest quartile of firms (less than 17 employees) view their property rights as significantly more vulnerable than do large firms (more than 170 employees).

Model 2.2 introduces variables for political connections, but departs from much of the existing literature by decomposing political connections into four parts. I begin with "property-based" political connections by looking at firms with full or partial state ownership. Eight percent of the sample (81 firms) falls into this category. Many firms have had state ownership for some time. Seventy-five percent of state-owned firms had this status in 2003, which suggests that state ownership is rather sticky. Indeed, about 40 percent of state-owned firms were founded as such prior to 1991. State-owned firms are broadly distributed across sectors, which helps to ensure that the effect of state property is not masquerading as sector in the analysis. Heavy and light industrial firms are well represented among state-owned firms (46 of 81), but so are firms in construction, transportation, banking, food processing, and retail trade (probably pharmacies).

"Institutional" connections are measured by a dummy variable which equals one for firms with a top manager who worked in the local or regional government in the last decade (*GovernmentExperience*). Twelve percent of respondents fall into this group. This variable is measured well before the time of the survey, which may reduce some concerns of reverse causality. Whether or not a manager has prior work experience in the state is not randomly assigned, but it would not be easy to manipulate this variable in order to provide protection against a corporate raid.

"Personal" connections are again a dummy variable equaling one for respondents who know the governor personally (*KnowGovernor*). Twenty-eight percent of respondents fit this category. Governors may be a useful ally in a corporate takeover attempt, but many threats of corporate takeover come via powerful allies in federal organs, such as the FSB, the police, or the Investigative Committee, over which the governor may have limited control. Endogeneity concerns may be greater with "personal" connections than with the two preceding measures of political connections because managers may seek a personal relationship with the governor precisely because they want to improve the security of their property rights. It is difficult to know whether personal relations with the governor are strategically created to protect property rights or occur due to factors unrelated to concerns for property rights. To the extent that the latter is the case, estimates of the impact of personal connections on perceptions of property rights will be less biased.

"Partisan" connections capture a respondent's relations with United Russia (*URmember*). Four percent of respondents are members, 26 percent are sympathizers, and 70 percent do not support United

Russia.[27] With so few members of United Russia in the sample, it is difficult to identify the impact of party membership on perceptions of property rights. This variable is especially prone to endogeneity concerns as firm managers who are United Russia members may perceiver their property rights as stronger, but firm managers may seek to join United Russia as a means of warding off a potential hostile takeover. Similarly, respondents who view their property rights as less secure may blame United Russia and therefore reduce their level of support. This possibility would also bias estimates.

These measures of political connections are not highly correlated with each other, which suggests that each springs from a different source, but correlation tables may not be informative because the measures are all dichotomous. In the analyses that follow, I add these variables in a single model, but introducing them one at a time does not change the results. Decomposing political power into these four dimensions is helpful, but does not capture all types of political connections. Managers may have personal connections in the security services, police, or judiciary; they may have family ties to high officials; or they may be large donors to state officials and each of these types of connections may be valuable assets in a corporate takeover battle, but they are not measured here.

Model 2.2 finds again that firms with immobile assets and with fewer workers view their firms as more likely to be the subject of a hostile takeover. In addition, managers of state-owned firms view their property rights as less secure than do private firms. This is surprising given that one might expect state-owned firms to be protected by their patrons within the state, but it appears that having closer relations with the state makes a firm more vulnerable to predation via a hostile takeover. In this case, familiarity breeds predation and private firms view themselves as better able to avoid corporate raids. This finding

---

[27] We asked respondents: "Which of the following statements best captures the relationship of the head (*pervoe litso*) of your firm?"
   1) A member of United Russia
   2) Supports United Russia, but is not a member
   3) Supports another party or movement
   4) Does not support any party or movement.
The large group of non-United Russia supporters includes 9 percent UR opponents, 38 percent independents, and 24 percent either did not respond or found it hard to answer.

accords well with research documenting the high degree of fragmentation and rivalry within the Russian state (Taylor 2011; Easter 2012; Yaffa 2015). Kapeliushnikov et al. (2013) also find that managers of state-owned firms perceive themselves as more likely to experience a hostile takeover.

Respondents who had worked in the state apparatus in the last decade view their property rights as significantly less secure than managers without this experience as indicated by *GovernmentExperience*. This result is also surprising as scholars have often used past work experience within the state as an indicator of good political connections, but it may indicate that managers leave state positions on bad terms with their former employers and thereby make them more vulnerable to attack, but this interpretation requires more research.

Respondents who know the governor personally viewed their property rights as more secure than those who did not, but the coefficient lies just beyond standard levels of significance in this model (p = .14). However, analyses reported in Appendix 2.2 indicate that personal connections are associated with much stronger defense against two of the three forms of corporate raiding studied here. Managers who know the governor personally viewed their firms as significantly less likely to be taken over by the regional government or to fall under the control of the federal government in the next two to three years. In contrast, they viewed their firm as no more likely to be taken over by another private firm. This result underscores the importance of personal connections for protecting property rights from takeover by state officials.

Finally, United Russia members view their property rights as no more secure from a hostile corporate takeover than do non-members. The small number of United Russia members in the sample, however, suggests that caution is warranted in interpreting this result.

In general, these results indicate that managers of firms with low asset mobility, with fewer employees, or with some state ownership view their firms as especially vulnerable to corporate raiding. In addition, personal connections can protect against takeovers by state agencies.

Impact of Institutional and Personal Connections

Previous analyses examine the direct effects of political connections on property rights, but the impact of political connections may depend on features of the right-holder. Political connections may be more important for firms with low asset mobility who perceive themselves as especially vulnerable to a corporate raid. I focus on the conditional impacts of institutional connections (prior work experience in the government) and personal connections (knowing the governor personally). Property-based connections and partisan connections are too scarce in the sample to be useful in this analysis.

In Model 2.3, I create an interaction term by multiplying *Immobile*, a dummy variable that equals one for heavy industry, natural resource, and energy sector firms, by *KnowGovernor*, a dummy variable that equals one for respondents who personally know the governor. I include controls for firm size, sector, and region, along with controls for other types of political connections. The results indicate that managers of immobile firms who do not know the governor personally view their property rights as significantly less secure, as indicated by the negative and significant coefficient on *Immobile*. However, managers of immobile assets who know the governor view their property rights as significantly more secure, as indicated by the significant and positive coefficient on the interaction term *Immobile*KnowGovernor*. Moreover, a test of the difference of coefficients indicates that managers of immobile assets who know the governor view their property rights as significantly more secure than do managers who do not know the governor (p = .00). Personal connections to the governor are associated with much stronger property rights for holders of immobile assets.[28]

In Model 2.4, I explore whether institutional connections can shape perceptions of the holders of immobile assets by creating an interaction term between *Immobile* and *GovernmentExperience*. The results are similar to the preceding analysis, but somewhat less precisely estimated. As before, holders of immobile assets without institutional connections view their property as less secure, as indicated by the negative and significant coefficient on *Immobility*, while holders of immobile assets with institutional connections viewed their property rights as more secure, as revealed by the positive coefficient on the interaction term, although this estimate falls short of statistical significance

---

[28] In unreported analyses, I show that personal relations with the governor of small firms can also significantly improve perceptions of the security of property rights from hostile corporate takeover.

(p = .14). A test of the difference between the two coefficients is statistically significant (p = .02) which indicates that holders of immobile assets with and without institutional connections have vastly different perceptions of the likelihood that their firm will be the subject of a corporate raid. This result again points to the importance of political connections in the perceptions of holders of immobile assets about the likelihood of a corporate raid.

Size of these Effects

The coefficients reported above are based on ordered probit estimations, which make it difficult to estimate the magnitude of their effect. To gain some sense of the substantive importance of the findings, I turn to Figure 2.1, which predicts the likelihood that managers will view their firm as a "very likely" target of at least one type of corporate raid in the next two to three years. These are firms that score one on the three-point Secure Property Rights index cited above. The results here are based on Model 2.3 in Table 2.2 and indicate that managers of immobile firms who do not know the governor are about 8 percentage points more likely to see themselves as a "very likely" target of a hostile takeover, while managers of immobile assets who do not know the governor perceive their firms as 9 percentage points less likely to fall into this category. As the confidence intervals between the results reported in the top and bottom lines of Figure 2.1 do not overlap, we can be quite confident that the difference in these responses is not due to chance.

Managers of state-owned firms are about 8 percentage points more likely to see their firm as being in the "very likely" takeover category. Managers with prior government experience also view their firms as about 8 percentage more likely to answer "very likely" to the hostile takeover question. Managers of small firms, here measured as those in the bottom quarter of the sample (<18 employees) are about 6 percentage points more likely to place themselves in this group.[29] The confidence intervals for these three variables do not cross the mid-point of zero, which indicates that these results are statistically significant at the .05 level. Managers of medium-sized firms, those between the 25th

---

[29] Given the difficulty of interpreting logged values of the number of employees, here I create dummy variables for small and medium-sized firms.

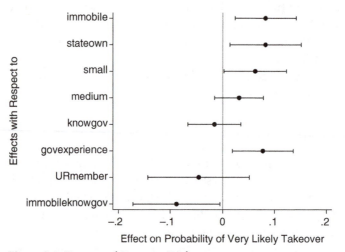

Figure 2.1 Power and Property Rights

and 75th percentile of the sample (between 18 and 170 employees) are more likely than large firms to fall into the "very likely" takeover category, but this result falls short of statistical significance at the .05 level. United Russia members are less likely to report that their firm is a "very likely" takeover target, although this relationship is imprecisely measured. This imprecision is likely due to the small numbers of managers of firms who are United Russia members.

Other variables cited in the literature are not strongly correlated with perceptions of the likelihood of corporate raiding. In analyses reported in Appendix 2.2, I find that members of business organizations and members of financial-industrial groups perceive the threat of takeover just as strongly as do non-members, suggesting that membership in these organizations provides little relief from this challenge to property rights. Exporters view their firms as just as likely to be a target of corporate takeover as non-exporters. Neither the manager's age nor level of education is associated with perceptions of the security of property rights in this analysis.

Managers whose firms had attracted foreign investment in the last two years saw themselves as more likely to be the target of a raid in the coming two to three years, but divining the direction of causation between foreign investment and the perceived quality of property rights is typically difficult due to concerns for endogeneity. For example, it is likely that firms that are performing well may be more attractive to both corporate raiders and to foreign investors, which raises the possibility that an observed relationship between foreign investment and corporate raiding is spurious. Here, however, we find the opposite: foreign investments in the past are associated with a heightened perceived threat of a hostile takeover, which suggests that raiders may be targeting firms that attract foreign investment. Untangling this relationship more precisely is a topic for future research.

Given the sensitivity of asking respondents about the likelihood of a corporate raid, I also explored whether non-responses may be influencing the results. In all regressions I control for covariates that are likely to be associated with non-response, such as size, sector, and region, which should reduce potential bias due to non-response. In Appendix 2.3, I explore this further by creating a dummy variable that equals 1 for respondents who answered all three questions in the Index of Secure Property Rights. Respondents who answered "don't know" or who did not answer equal zero. Eleven percent of respondents fell into the latter category. I then ran a probit model including the independent variables of theoretical interest as well controls for sector and region. The size of the firm is significantly related to non-response, while state ownership and membership in United Russia are marginally significant (p = .08 and .09, respectively). This is a crude test, but suggests that firms that did and did not answer this question are relatively similar in their observable features. If non-response indicates a fear of corporate takeover, this suggests that, if anything, the results presented above may understate the impact of size on perceptions of secure property rights.

One Final Robustness Check

Of course, surveys are able to capture only a snapshot in time and unobserved contextual factors that are specific to a particular time and place may limit the extent to which results can be generalized. One way to check the robustness is to compare results across surveys conducted in different periods. With the help of the Levada Center, I conducted a survey of the top managers of 500 firms in 8 regions

Table 2.3 *Perceived Threats of Hostile Takeover, 2008 Survey*

	To a Great Degree	Somewhat	Not at all	Hard to Say
Likelihood of hostile takeover for firm like theirs	6 n = 28	44 n = 222	36 n = 192	14 n = 72

Answers in percentage, n = number of observations. Data from 2008 survey.

in Russia in 2008 that asked a number of questions about corporate raiding. The question used to measure threats of hostile takeover differs slightly from that used in the preceding analysis so the results are not directly comparable, but to the extent that the two analyses produce roughly similar results we can be more confident in the findings. To measure perceptions of the likelihood of a corporate raid in our 2008 survey, interviewers asked managers:

Sometimes the press writes about attempts to illegally take over the property of a firm using administrative pressure. What do you think, do firms like yours in your region face a threat of this form of takeover?

Six percent of respondents believed that such hostile takeovers were "to a great degree likely"; 44 percent said "somewhat likely"; 36 percent said "not at all" likely, and 14 percent of respondents found it hard to answer. This question is less direct in that respondents were asked about firms "like theirs" rather than about their firm. This may introduce some noise into the measure, but also may increase veracity. Coding the responses on a scale where 1 = "to a great degree," 2 = "somewhat likely," and 3 = "not at all," yields a mean response of 2.36 with a standard deviation of .60.

Immobile firms are measured using the same sectoral categories as in the preceding analysis and again the size of the firm is captured by the log number of employees. To measure the partisan preferences of firm managers, we asked respondents whether they voted in the parliamentary elections of December 2007, and if so, for which party did they vote. Just over two-thirds of managers reported voting for United Russia. This measure captures partisan affiliation less directly than the question posed in the 2011 survey which focused on party

Table **2.4** *Power and Perceptions of Property Rights,*
2008 Survey

	Model 2.5	Model 2.6
Asset Mobility	–.39**	–.38**
	(.18)	(.19)
Size (log #employees)	.04	.04
	(.04)	(.05)
State Ownership		–.37*
		(.21)
UR Voter		.20
		(.13)
Constant or Cutpoints	–1.46 (.27)	–2.29 (.69)
	.33 (.26)	–.48 (.40)
N	432	408
Prob >F	.0121	.0111
R^{sq}	.04	.05

* = p<.10, ** = p<.05, *** = p<.01, Ordered Probit
Estimation. 8 region and 7 sector dummies included, robust
standard errors. Higher scores indicate more secure property
rights. That is, the less likely the respondent perceived a
hostile takeover. Data from 2008 survey.

membership.[30] To reduce the possibility for "fishing," that is, manipulating the inclusion or exclusion of specific variables to produce more favorable results, I repeat the model specification reported in Table 2.2 as closely as possible using this new data (Humphreys et al. 2013). As above, I control for factors specific to the firm, sector, and region, as well firm size and property type. See the appendix for details on these variables. I run an ordered probit estimation and report the following results.

Model 2.5 indicates that firms in the immobile sectors viewed their property rights as significantly less secure – a result that is consistent with the previous survey. In this analysis, however, size is not related to perceptions of property rights. Model 2.6 adds a dummy variable for a firm with full or partial state ownership and a dummy variable

[30] We did not ask respondents about their party affiliations in this survey.

for managers who voted for United Russia in the 2007 Parliamentary elections. Again, state ownership is negatively correlated with perceptions of the security of property rights as measured by the likelihood of a corporate raid. Managers who did and did not vote for United Russia in the 2007 parliamentary elections viewed their property rights as equally secure.

The regression in the results of Tables 2.2 and 2.4 reported above should not be seen as causal given the observational nature of the data (Kramer 1983). In addition, there is a very long debate in political science about the merits of treating individual-level partisanship as exogenous from other traits in accounting for political attitudes and behavior (Campbell et al. 1960; Fiorina 1981; Jackson and Gerber 1993). Moreover, with some variables it is difficult to identify the direction of causation. Rather than making strong causal claims, the analysis here merely intends to identify some patterns in the perceived threat of takeover and to link these threats to political factors.

Conclusion

While exploring the broad theme of the relationship between violence and property rights, this chapter has examined three specific topics. First, it examined a particularly nefarious threat to property rights in contemporary Russia – corporate raiding by private actors in collusion with state officials. One important result focuses on the importance of asset mobility as a means of protection from corporate raiding. In analyses from surveys conducted in 2008 and 2011, managers of firms in sectors with low asset mobility, such as natural resources, industry, and energy, perceived a greater likelihood of being the victim of a corporate than those in trade – a sector where assets are much more mobile. This finding is consistent with popular perceptions about corporate raiding, which are heavily informed by the most high-profile corporate takeovers in Russia from the natural resources sectors, such as the *YUKOS* and *Bashneft'* cases in 2004 and 2014 respectively.

One contribution of this chapter to the broader literature is the unpacking of political connections into more discrete components, including property-based connections via state ownership; institutional connections via prior work experience within the state, personal connections via relationships with powerful individuals within the state, and partisan connections via membership in United Russia.

By measuring partisan allegiances directly, this work hopes to advance discussions on the political roots of the economic behavior of firms. Rather than inferring managers' partisan preferences from their economic sector or class, this work measures their political affiliations directly (Frieden 1991, but see Dickson 2003).

Indeed, it is interesting to note that personal connections to the governor provide some relief against the perceived threat of corporate raiding. Moreover, managers of immobile assets who have personal connections view their property rights as far more secure than those who do not have these connections.

And a manager's recent experience working in state bodies appears to provide little defense against corporate raiding. Indeed, I find a negative relationship between prior work experience in the state apparatus and perceptions of security from a hostile takeover. Thus, by decomposing political connections into different elements we find that not all forms of political connections are equally effective in reducing perceptions of insecure property rights. Taken together, the results indicate that the relationship between "political connections" and property rights is rather nuanced.

More generally, the work points to the centrality of violence and exclusion to property rights and economic development. Corporate raids Russian style may increase demand for accountants and lawyers, but behind the pen is always the sword and the threat of coercion. It is the police, prosecutors, and security services wielding the forces of violence who are integral to the rise in corporate raiding in recent year as they collude with private agents to engage in hostile takeovers. In this respect, the work echoes North et al.'s (2009) call to refocus the question of economic development in lower- and middle-income countries toward the means by which countries control the agents of violence.

Appendix 2.1: Unpacking Property Rights: Different Threats

Here I analyze the individual components of the Secure Property Rights Index, including the perceived likelihood of being taken over by the local or regional government (Model A2.1.1), of being taken over by the federal government (Model A2.1.2), and of experiencing an attack by a raider (Model A2.1.3). These three categorical variables range from 1 to 3. Personal connections appear to provide greater perceived

Table A2.1 *Unpacking Property Rights: Different Threats*

	Model A2.1.1	Model A2.1.2	Model A2.1.3
Immobile	−.17	−.44***	−.16
	(.16)	(.16)	(.17)
Size (log # employees)	.08**	−.00	.02
	(.04)	(.03)	(.03)
State Ownership	−.32	−.30	.00
	(.19)	(.20)	(.20)
Government Experience	−.38***	−.60***	−.19
	(.17)	(.16)	(.16)
KnowGovernor	.26**	.43***	.12
	(.13)	(.13)	(.13)
UR member	.11	.46	.24
	(.29)	(.29)	(.24)
Cutpoints	−1.17 (.24)	−2.20 (.27)	−1.39 (.25)
	.30 (.23)	−.49 (.25)	−.33 (.24)
N	671	677	679
Prob >F	.0000	.0000	.0000
R^{sq}	.06	.09	.07
Model Type	Oprobit	Oprobit	Oprobit
Dependent Variable	Regional Govt Takeover (1–3)	Federal Govt Takeover (1–3)	Private Firm Takeover (1–3)

* = p<.10, ** = p<.05, *** = p<.01, Ordered Probit Estimation. Dummy variables for 15 regions and the construction, financial, real estate, communications, and transport sector included. Trade sector excluded. Robust standard errors. Higher scores indicate more secure property rights. Data from 2011 survey.

security from a takeover by the federal and the regional government than against other forms of corporate raiding and managers with less mobile assets view state threats as greater than private threats. Overall one is struck by the different political dynamics of corporate raiding depending on the nature of the attack (Markus 2012; 2015).

Appendix 2.2: Alternative Specifications

Membership in a business organization or a financial industrial group, export status, presence of a foreign owner, competition as an obstacle and manager age are unrelated to perceptions of property rights. Firms with recent foreign investment perceive their property rights as less secure but divining the direction of causation is difficult.

Table A2.2 *Perceptions of the Security of Property Rights from Takeover*

	Model A2.2.1	Model A2.2.2	Model A2.2.3	Model A2.2.4	Model A2.2.5	Model A2.2.6	Model A2.2.7
Business Org Member	-.07 (.16)						
Industrial Group Member		-.11 (.16)					
Exporter			-.10 (.17)				
Foreign Owner				.00 (.25)			
Foreign Investor in last 2 years					-.63*** (.19)		
Competition as Obstacle						-.03 (.04)	
Manager Age							.00 (.00)
Constant or Cutpoints	-.63 .93	-.61 .94	-.58 .99	-.56 .99	-.55 1.01	-.77 .79	-.45 1.10
N	638	638	611	519	629	633	625
Prob >F	.0000	.0000	.0000	.0000	.0000	.0000	.0000
R^{sq}	.08	.08	.08	.08	.08	.08	.08

$*$ p<.10, $**$ = p<.05, $***$ = p<.01, Dependent Variable Security Index, 1–3. All independent variables from Table 2.3 included in the model, but not reported. Robust standard errors. Higher scores indicate more secure property rights. Data from 2011 survey.

Table A2.3 *Missing Observations*

	Model A2.3.1
Immobile	.02
	(.23)
Size (logged # of employees)	−.13**
	(.04)
State Ownership	.41*
	(.23)
Government Experience	.03
	(.20)
Know Governor	.00
	(.16)
UR Member	−.79*
	(.47)
Constant	−.95***
	(.30)
Wald chi	23.7
N	730
Prob >F	.0000
R^{sq}	.12

* = p<.10, ** = p<.05, *** = p<.01. Probit Model.
Dependent variable is binary and measures non-
response to any components of the Secure Property
Rights Index. Robust standard errors. Data from 2011
survey.

Appendix 2.3: Missing Observations

Because the responses to the question on the likelihood of corporate raiding are not likely to be missing at random, it is difficult to detect possible sources of bias in the non-responses. As a very rough first cut, I estimate a probit model that predicts non-response to any of the questions in the Secure Property Rights Index and include the theoretical variables of interest as well as the controls from previous analyses reported in Table 2.3. The size of the firm is related to non-response, and state ownership and membership in United Russia are marginally significant (p = .08 and .09, respectively).

3 | Autocratic Elections and Property Rights

Yes, as through this world I've wandered
I've seen lots of funny men
Some will rob you with a six-gun
And some with a fountain pen.

Woody Guthrie, The Tale of Pretty Boy Floyd

Hostile corporate raiding in Russia suggests an addendum to Woody Guthrie's categories of theft: Some men will rob with you a six-gun **and** with a fountain pen. Rather than simply stealing a factory via armed seizure or taking control via a legal purchase of shares in a market, corporate raiders in Russia typically rely on some mixture of the two. Indeed, it is the union of threats of coercion and the use of formal legal institutions, courtrooms, share registries, and state regulatory bodies that make hostile corporate takeovers in Russia so worthy of investigation. Raiders may take physical control of a factory, but their rights are greatly enhanced via documentation of formal transfer of the rights from the raided to the raider.

The previous chapter helped to untangle the relationship between bargaining power and property rights at least as measured by the likelihood of a hostile corporate takeover. Managers of larger firms, private firms, and firms with more mobile assets saw their property rights as more secure from a hostile corporate takeover, while managers without personal connections to the governor were far less sanguine about this prospect. The strategy in the prior chapter was to hold constant the bargaining power of the ruler while exploring variations in the amount and types of power held by the right-holder. By unpacking political power and political connections into more discrete components, the last chapter aimed to provide a more nuanced treatment of the impacts of power on perceptions of property rights.

This chapter adopts a different strategy by taking advantage of an exogenous shift in the bargaining power of the ruler – the unexpectedly poor performance of the ruling United Russia party in the December 2011 parliamentary elections – and traces how it shaped the perceptions of right-holders about the likelihood of a hostile corporate takeover.

Fortunately, in the survey analyzed in the preceding chapter, about half of the firm managers were interviewed just prior to the elections and half the managers were interviewed just after the elections. Because there is, on average, little difference in the groups of managers interviewed before and after the elections, I can treat managers interviewed prior to the election as a "control" group and managers interviewed after as a "treatment" group akin to a natural experiment (Dunning 2012). Assuming that the two groups are statistically identical in all respects, differences in the perceptions of property rights between these two groups can be attributed to the electoral shock.[1]

This chapter finds that the electoral shock had important consequences for some types of firm. Managers of firms with immobile assets or with state ownership perceived the chances of a corporate raid to be significantly lower after the elections than before, while managers of large firms viewed their property rights as more vulnerable after the election. In this way, a shock to the bargaining power of the ruling party helped to level the playing field for vulnerable firms.

The shock to the bargaining power of the ruling party had little impact on managers with personal connections to the governor or had prior work experience within the government. Because the political shock to the ruling party took place in a federal, rather than a local election, it may be that the results of the election did not have a strong impact on political connections to local and regional officials.

It is surprising that the electoral shock to United Russia shaped perceptions of property rights. While the results of the Duma election reduced United Russia's seat share and shook public confidence in the President and Prime Minister, it did not cause a turnover in government.[2] Nor did it change expectations that the then Prime Minister Putin would return to office as President a few months hence. Nor did the shock occur in the most powerful policy-making branch of the

---

[1] See Garcia-Ponce and de Pasquale (2014), Frye and Borisova (2015) and Frye and Yakovlev (2016) for a similar strategy of causal identification.

[2] See Malesky and Samphantharak (2008) on the importance of political turnover for changing property rights and firm–state relations.

Russian government – the Presidency. While this relatively small shock produced some important effects on perceptions of property rights, an even larger shock might produce even stronger effects.

Bargaining Power and Property Rights

That more powerful rulers strike better bargains with right-holders over the distribution of property is a tenet of the literature on property rights. In *Of Rule and Revenue* Margaret Levi (1988) argues that rulers with greater bargaining power and longer discount rates are better able to structure property rights to maximize their revenue. She defines (1988: 2) bargaining power as the "degree of control over coercive, economic, and political resources" and emphasizes control over resources, the dependence of rulers on constituent groups for revenue and labor, and the possibilities of collective action on the part of the ruled (1988: 17–22). Rulers with more resources are better able to shape property rights to their advantage.

Levi is not alone in recognizing that the discount rate of the ruler may shape property rights. It is a standard result of bargaining theory that players who have longer time horizons can be more patient and obtain a greater share of the spoils (Rubinstein 1982). With respect to property rights, Olson (1993) formalizes this insight in his treatment of the "roving bandit" as an autocratic ruler who protects private property rights in exchange for tax revenue. The ruler's incentive to protect rather than seize property depends on his time horizon. Rulers who expect to lose office in the near term have little incentive to protect property rights as they will not stay in office long enough to reap the gains from the right-holder's investment.

Similarly, North (1981) argues that rulers seek to maximize revenue but only if doing so will not jeopardize their hold on office. He emphasizes how changes in political competition can alter the bargaining power of rulers. Treating rulers as analogous to firms in a market, he notes (1981:26) that "where there are no close substitutes [for the ruler], the existing ruler is a despot, dictator or an absolute Monarch. The closer the substitutes, the fewer the degrees of freedom the ruler possesses and the greater the percentage of incremental income that will be retained by the constituents." Other things equal, heightened political competition reduces the ruler's yield from property rights.

Some scholars trace the bargaining power of rulers to the mobilization capacity of their political base (Bates 1981), while others link the bargaining power of the ruler to personal characteristics, such as their charisma, leadership style, and personal popularity or ethnicity (Caro 2002; Kasara 2007; McGregor Burns 2010).

Yet because many of these sources of bargaining power are likely shaped by the property rights held by the ruler, it becomes difficult to identify the direction of causation between bargaining power and property rights. A ruler who increases his control over property rights (for whatever reason) may extend his time horizon, reduce political competition, increase his popularity, and expand his base of constituent support, all of which may lead back to even stronger property rights for the ruler. That the security of property rights and these features of bargaining power are often so tightly interwoven presents an empirical challenge.

Recognizing this problem, scholars have focused on more exogenous sources of changes in bargaining power to better identify their impacts on property rights, but these are often difficult to find. North and Thomas (1973) note that exogenous changes in prices can be an important source of shifts in property rights. In their view, the exogenous shock of the "Black Death," which killed up to half of the population in Europe in just five years in the mid-fourteenth century, raised the price of labor, and thereby reduced the bargaining power of rulers, which resulted in a vastly more productive structure of property rights and, ultimately, *The Rise of the Western World* (North and Thomas, 1973).[3]

In their extensive study of natural-resource-rich countries in the second half of the twentieth century, Guriev et al. (2011) find that changes in oil prices heightened incentives for rulers to renationalize the property of privately owned oil companies. It is hardly a surprise that the boom in oil prices in 2006 was accompanied by renationalizations of energy firms in Algeria, Bolivia, Chad, Dubai, Ecuador, Senegal, Russia, and Venezuela (Frye 2014).

Fisman (2001) pioneered the strategy of examining how shocks to the health of the ruler shape the prices of stocks of firms with strong and weak ties to the ruler, first using data from Indonesian ruler

---

[3] See Haddock and Kiesling (2002) on the impact of the Black Death on property rights.

Suharto before turning to the impact of Vice President Dick Cheney's various health scares on firms with ties to him. Fisman (2001) finds sharp declines in the share prices of firms with Suharto family members on their board after announcements about President Suharto's ill health and, in research with co-authors, finds no effect on the share prices of companies related to Vice-President Cheney during his various bouts of ill health (Khurana et al. 2012).

Goriaiev and Sonin (2005) probe how the stock price of state-owned and privately owned firms reacted to the announcement of various legal actions taken against YUKOS in 2004. Others look at how election results that produce unexpected shifts in the party in power shape share prices of firms with distinctly partisan economic profiles (Bernhardt and Leblang 2006). In all these works, the authors look for plausibly exogenous sources of variation in the bargaining power of rulers.

These shocks to the bargaining power of the ruler are unlikely to be caused by the distribution of property rights, which gives hope that it is possible to identify the direction of causation in the relationship between bargaining power and property rights. In this spirit, I examine a different type of exogenous shock to the relative bargaining power of the ruler: a surprising election result that weakened the bargaining power of the ruling party. Before exploring the relationship between this shift in bargaining power and perceptions of property rights using survey data, I provide background on the election that helped to shift the ruling party's bargaining power.

Elections Russian Style

On December 4, 2011, Russian citizens went to the polls to elect a new Duma. This was Russia's sixth parliamentary election since the fall of communism and while elections in the 1990s invariably produced surprising results, elections had become increasingly predictable and dull in the 2000s. Elections in 2003 and 2007 had produced large majorities for the ruling United Russia party, and United Russia had in turn used its political power to greatly reduce the ability of opposition parties to compete in elections.

By the 2011 elections, the official landscape was dominated by United Russia and the three so-called "systemic opposition" parties. On the left was the Communist Party of the Russian Federation headed by its longstanding and anti-charismatic leader, Gennadii Zyuganov, on the nationalist front was the incongruously named Liberal Democratic Party led by the colorful and ineffectual Vladimir Zhirinovsky, and in the nondescript center-left was the Just Russia Party led by long-time government functionary, Sergei Mironov.[4] These parties may have occupied somewhat different parts of the political spectrum but were united in their willingness to cooperate with United Russia and enjoy the spoils of office without exercising much real power.

"Non-systemic" opposition parties, such as Yabloko, Patriots of Russia, Right Cause, and others also competed, but the deck was stacked against them. Informally barred from appearing on television and harassed with nuisance lawsuits and petty obstructionism, these opposition parties also faced formal rules that drastically reduced their chances of winning seats.[5] To obtain access to the ballot, parties had to have at least 45,000 members with 450 members in at least half of Russia's then 83 regions and at least 150 members in the other half. In addition, any party needed to receive 5 percent of the vote to obtain one guaranteed seat in the Duma and 7 percent of votes to take part in the distribution of seats according to share of votes. This high electoral threshold was especially important as any party seeking to nominate a candidate for the presidency that did not have representation in the Duma had to collect 2 million signatures – a daunting task in an autocracy. Russia's elimination of the single-member districts that previously comprised half of the mandates in the Duma and the switch to a fully proportional system for allocating votes into seats further increased the importance of clearing the electoral threshold and weakened non-systemic opposition parties. The government also hindered vote monitoring groups. Most importantly, they clamped down on the vote-monitoring agency GOLOS by closing the main office on the eve of elections (Vasilyeva 2011).

Other factors too contributed to the prevailing view that United Russia would have a smooth sailing in the parliamentary election.[6] Russia had experienced a long period of economic growth from 2000

---

[4] The "Just" in Just Russia refers to social equality rather than to nativism.
[5] For details, see www.iss.europa.eu/publications/detail/article/
state-duma-elections-2011-and-the-marginal-role-of-russian-parties-part-1/
[6] For an overview of pre-election expectations, see Udensiva-Brenner 2011, which includes comments by Nikolai Petrov, Konstantin Sonin, Alena Ledeneva, Yulia Latynina, and Masha Lipman three weeks prior to the election.

to 2008 when the global financial crisis hit Russia very hard, but the economy was recovering rapidly at the time of the elections. Annual economic growth in 2010 and 2011 achieved an enviable 4.5 and 4.3 percent, respectively. Moreover, President Medvedev and Prime Minister Putin had approval ratings in the mid-60s – down from their previous peaks by about 20 points, but still high.[7]

Ominous notes sounded too, many of which were more apparent in retrospect. On September 24, Prime Minister Putin announced his intention to run for the presidency in elections slated for March 2012, but his announcement was met with indifference at best. Two months later in a pre-election appearance at a mixed martial arts match, Putin was greeted with whistles, boos, and catcalls by a crowd that was expected to be favorable.

A research team led by Belanovsky and Dmitriev at the Center for Strategic Research caught this sentiment through a series of focus groups in several provinces. Their report from March (2011:1) began: "The period of political stability in Russia is coming to an end. If the trends presented in this report continue and nothing is done in response, the country will be headed toward political cataclysms comparable to the crises of the late 1980s and early 1990s." They also noted: "a critical mass of the opposition majority in Moscow and other big cities will be reached by the beginning of autumn, that is, before the parliamentary elections. In turn, the big cities, being centers of information, will actively spread opposition sentiments through-out the country speeding up the growth of opposition sentiments in the provinces." This report, which later earned Dmitriev the title of "Russia's Nostradamus," was met with little note at the time of its publication.

Most public opinion organizations predicted that United Russia would win a comfortable majority in the election. One question was whether United Russia would use falsifications to obtain a constitutional majority in the Duma, but it was difficult to find much enthusiasm for these elections either from voters or state officials.

Yet on December 4, United Russia performed poorly as its vote share fell from 64 percent to 49 percent and it seat share fell from 315 to 238 of the 450 seats. Vote shares for United Russia fell in almost

---

[7] See Volkov (2011).

every region with the most precipitous drops occurring in the Far East, the large urban centers of Central Russia, and Moscow. Turnout nationally also fell from 64 percent in 2007 to 60 percent in 2011, perhaps an indication of declining enthusiasm for United Russia. In addition, the number of spoiled ballots increased from 1.1 percent to 1.6 percent of all ballots. Taken together this was quite a defeat for a dominant party.

Many argued that the vote totals for United Russia would have been much lower were it not for extensive fraud.[8] Enikolopov et al. (2013) show that voting for United Russia in Moscow was about 11 percentage points higher in polling places not monitored by independent observers. Forensic methods also revealed many suspicious patterns in the voting. An abnormally large number of polling places reported vote totals of just over 50 percent for United Russia and an abnormally high number of "round numbers" in their last digit which suggests tampering (Kobak et al. 2012). Roughly one in four workers experienced some form of political pressure from their employers to vote in the parliamentary election (Frye et al. 2014). And this is all without mentioning the traditionally suspicious 90-plus percent vote shares received by pro-regime parties in the republics of the North Caucasus.

Whether vote fraud was more extensive than in past elections was a matter of debate, but the visibility of fraud was certainly greater in 2011 than it had been previously. Videos of voting carousels, ballot-box stuffing, and voter intimidation became a staple of public commentary in the wake of the election. Major newspapers published numerous accounts of fraud as well. In an appropriately titled report "An Exciting End to a Dull Election," Nikolai Petrov (2011) noted that the elections were not more fraudulent than past elections, but they were more scandalous.

In the wake of the elections, protestors took to the streets in Moscow. On December 5, about 3000 protestors called for new elections and clashed with police. Held on a Monday night without much publicity, the event included the usual suspects from the "non-systemic" opposition, such as Alexei Navalny, Boris Nemtsov, Vladimir Ryzkhov, Irina Chirikova, among others, but also a large number of

---

[8] For an excellent description of election day tricks, see www.themoscowtimes. com/news/article/live-blog-duma-vote-2011/449143.html

political novices (Greene 2014: 202–219). Several hundred protestors were arrested. More surprisingly, on December 10, roughly 50,000 protestors marched to Bolotnaia Square to demand new elections and call for an end to corruption. This event, the largest political protest in Moscow since the fall of the Soviet Union, brought together opposition groups from across the political spectrum for the first time to oppose United Russia.

The election did not cause a turnover in government, nor did it alter Putin's plans to run for the presidency, yet it significantly reduced the seat share of United Russia in the Duma. More importantly, it demonstrated to all that the ruling party was vulnerable and many speculated that these results would have longer-term impacts on politics in Russia. One opposition-oriented commentator observed that following the elections: "Russians have lost respect for Putin and his team… The last stage of Putin's saga has begun" (Shevtsova and Wood 2011). Dmitri Trenin, a less partisan analyst noted: "Even though Vladimir Putin remains the country's most popular politician by far, his Teflon coating has visibly cracked" (Trenin et al. 2011). The next section examines whether this shift in bargaining power was reflected in perceptions of property rights.

Data and Analysis

In an ideal world, I would have designed the survey of businesspeople cited in the last chapter so that respondents would be randomly selected to be interviewed before and after the elections of December 4, 2011. This random assignment of respondents into a "control" group interviewed before the elections and "treatment" group interviewed after the elections would allow me to attribute any differences in the perceptions of property rights between the two groups to the elections of December 4. Because these two groups would be statistically identical, that is, they would have equal numbers of large and small firms, profitable and unprofitable firms, politically connected and unconnected firms, etc., I could rule out the possibility of these factors accounting for any differences in the responses between the two groups. This is a powerful form of control that resembles an experimental design (Dunning 2012).

This was not the design I used, but I got lucky. The survey was put into the field in late November in part due to end-of-the year budgeting concerns. For idiosyncratic reasons, our research team would have had to fill out much less paperwork if we spent the funds in calendar year 2011 than in 2012. As luck would have it the groups of respondents interviewed before and after the election are well balanced on covariates likely to be associated with perceptions of property rights. As we see in Table 3.1, the groups of managers in the pre-election and post-election samples are statistically indistinguishable in many characteristics. A slightly larger number of light industry firms are found in the post-election sample (.16 versus .23, p = .02) and on average firms are somewhat larger in the pre-election sample, although this difference is only significant at the .07 level (4.16 versus 3.93, p = .07).

One area in which the two samples are not balanced is region. In 7 of the 15 capital cities under study the number of respondents interviewed before and after the elections was roughly balanced, but in two capitals (Voronezh and Ekaterinburg) significantly more of the respondents were interviewed before the election, and in six others (Moscow, Tula, Kursk, Novogorod, Ufa, and Kemerovo) more of the respondents were interviewed after the election. Because regional factors may color perceptions of property rights, it is important to control for these factors. For example, if respondents in regions with weak property rights were interviewed prior to the election and respondents in regions with stronger property rights were interviewed after the election, and we found that property rights were stronger after the election, it would be difficult to determine whether imbalances in the regional composition of firms or the election results were causing this difference. In the statistical analysis, I control for the size of the firm, the region in which the firm was located, and whether or not the firm was in the light industry sector and am able to estimate the impact of the election on perceptions of property rights controlling for other factors in which the samples are balanced.

Regressions

In this analysis, I examine how the political shock of the elections shaped perceptions of the likelihood of a corporate takeover. The dependent variable is the secure property rights index described in Chapter 2 that measured whether respondents believed that their firm was "very likely," "unlikely," or "very unlikely" to be the target of three different types of corporate takeover. Firm managers who answered

Table 3.1 *Balance Statistics*

	Pre-Election	Post-Election	Absolute Difference Post-Election and Pre-Election p-value in par.
Size (log # of employees)	4.16	3.93	.27 (.07)
Light Industry	.17	.23	.06 (.03)
Immobile	.22	.20	.02 (.35)
State Owned	.10	.08	.02 (.25)
KnowGovernor	.30	.32	.02 (.51)
Government Experience	.14	.14	.00 (.79)
Member United Russia	.03	.05	.02 (.38)
Supports United Russia	.27	.23	.04 (.15)
Energy	.01	.02	.01 (.37)
Heavy Industry	.15	.14	.01 (.57)
Communication	.04	.05	.01 (.22)
Transport	.05	.05	.00 (.93)
Construction	.11	.10	.01 (.44)
Financial	.08	.06	.02 (.28)
Real Estate/ Insurance	.08	.07	.01 (.52)
Forestry	.02	.04	.02 (.27)
Retail Trade	.19	.22	.03 (.28)
Foreign Ownership	.06	.07	.01 (.76)
Sell to the State	.43	.46	.03 (.72)
Export	.13	.14	.01 (.86)
Business Organization	.14	.14	.00 (.96)
Competition as Problem	3.46	3.53	.07 (.36)
Investment Index 1–8	3.58	3.49	.09 (.45)
Member of Industrial Group	.16	.17	.01 (.82)

Table 3.1 (*cont.*)

	Pre-Election	Post-Election	Absolute Difference Post-Election and Pre-Election p-value in par.
Major Investment in 2010–12 (1–3)	1.59	1.64	.05 (.37)
Time Horizon (1–4)	1.95	2.0	.05 (.53)
Age of the Director	44	45	01 (.55)
Higher Education	.93	.94	.01 (.72)
Tenure with Firm	18.7	19.4	.07 (.55)

that any of the three types of corporate raid was "highly likely" receive a score of one, those who answered that any of the three types of corporate raid was "unlikely" receive a score of two; while those who view all three types of corporate raid as "very unlikely" receive a score of three. In each model, I include controls for region, firm size, and a dummy variable for light industrial firms.[9]

In Model 3.1, I estimate the impact of the elections on immobile firms by interacting a dummy variable, *PostElection*, with a dummy variable that equals one for firms in the energy, natural resourcs, or heavy industry sectors to create *Immobile**PostElection. The previous chapter showed that on average firms in the immobile sector viewed their property rights as less secure. This analysis determines whether the shock to the bargaining power of the ruler attenuates these perceptions of vulnerability. I also interact *PostElection* with *Size* to examine whether the impact of the elections was conditional on the logged number of employees within the firm.

Managers of firms with immobile assets interviewed prior to the election perceived their firm to be significantly less secure, as indicated

---

[9] In unreported results, I find that the election outcome had little direct impact on the average firm. The coefficient on a dummy variable *PostElection* is not significantly related to perceptions of property rights. This could be because the shock was not especially large. Alternatively, it could be that the political shock strengthened the perceived property rights of some firms, but weakened the perceived property rights of others, which on average leads to a null effect.

by the negative and significant coefficient on *Immobile*, but managers with immobile assets interviewed after the election viewed their property rights as significantly more secure as indicated by the positive and significant coefficient on *Immobile*PostElection*. In addition, larger firms perceived their property rights as significantly more secure prior to the elections and less secure after the elections. This result should be viewed with some caution as firms on average are slightly larger in the pre-election sample (p = .07), which may be causing this difference.

Model 3.2 explores how managers in firms with some state ownership responded to the shock of the parliamentary elections by creating the interaction term *StateOwnership*PostElection*. Managers of state-owned firms viewed their property rights as significantly less secure prior to the elections as indicated by the negative and significant coefficient on *State Ownership*, while they viewed their firm as no less secure than private firms after the election as indicated by the coefficient on *StateOwnership*PostElection*. The difference between these two coefficients is statistically significant, indicating that the elections had a strong impact on the perceptions of managers of state-owned firms. That firms with immobile assets, fewer employees, or some state ownership viewed their property rights as less secure prior to the elections than after indicates that the shift in bargaining power of the ruler helped to level the playing field for these vulnerable firms.

Models 3.3 and 3.4 indicate that the impact of the political shock of the election results on perceptions of property rights does not depend on the respondent's institutional connections as measured by prior work experience in the government or personal connections as measured by whether or not the manager personally knew the governor. These results are not too surprising in that the institutional connections of the manager may not depend on the fate of United Russia. In addition, the parliamentary elections were held at the national level and had little direct short-term impact on governors as these regional executives were not up for election in December 2011. Managers who knew the governor personally could likely still count on the support of the governor's office regardless of the national election result.

More surprising are the results in Model 3.5. Here I create a dummy variable that equals one for managers who are members of

United Russia and another dummy variable for managers who identified as United Russia supporters and then interact both of these
dummy variables with *PostElection*. The election had little effect
on managers who were United Russia members. This may be due
to the small number of United Russia members in the analysis (just
31 firms of 771 in the analysis). Or it may be that these managers perceive themselves as insulated from a political shock of this
magnitude.

Surprisingly, respondents who support United Russia but are not
members view their property rights as more secure after the election
than before. Several possibilities present themselves. Supporters of
United Russia may have expected their party to do even worse than it
did in the election and were positively surprised by the results. Without
knowing their expectations about the elections, however, this is specu-
lation. Or it could be that more vulnerable firms identify themselves as
United Russia supporters in an effort to curry favor with the regime.
In this case, preferences for United Russia are due to the insecurity
of property rights rather than the other way around, and as United
Russia's bargaining position weakens after the election, they view their
previously insecure property rights as more secure. In some respects,
this resembles the common problem of determining the extent to
which political partisanship is endogenous to context (Kramer 1983;
Gerber et al. 2010). In a word, it is very difficult to interpret this particular relationship.

To give a better sense of the magnitude of the results in model 3.2, I
estimate the probability that respondents will place themselves in the
least secure category of property rights on the scale of property rights.
I run the same regression as in Model 3.2, which allows me to examine
how the shift in bargaining power induced by the poor showing of
United Russia in the elections influences the responses of managers of
different types of firm. Managers of firms with immobile assets interviewed before the election are about 8 percentage points more likely
to place their firm in the "very likely" takeover category, while their
counterparts in immobile firms interviewed after the election are about
11 percentage points less likely to place themselves in this most vulnerable group. Managers of small firms (less than 17 employees) interviewed prior to the elections were 12 percentage points more likely to
view their firm as a "very likely" target of a corporate takeover, but
small firm managers interviewed after the electoral shock were about

Table 3.2 *Elections and Perceptions of Property Rights, 2011 Survey*

	Model 3.1	Model 3.2	Model 3.3	Model 3.4	Model 3.5
PostElection	.11	.17	.10	.09	.03
	(.23)	(.23)	(.24)	(.23)	(.23)
Immobile	−.46**	−.40**	−.44**	−.50***	−.45***
	(.16)	(.16)	(.17)	(.16)	(.16)
Immobile* PostElection	.47**	.45**	.39*	.50**	.46**
	(.22)	(.22)	(.24)	(.29)	(.22)
Size	.09**	.12***	.11***	.10**	.09**
	(.04)	(.04)	(.04)	(.04)	(.04)
Size* PostElection	−.06	−.08	−.05	−.06	−.06
	(.05)	(.05)	(.06)	(.06)	(.05)
State Ownership		−.66***			
		(.21)			
State Ownership* PostElection		.13			
		(.35)			
Government Experience			−.18		
			(.19)		
Gov'tExperience* PostElection			−.45		
			(.28)		
KnowGovernor				−.12	
				(.16)	
KnowGovernor* PostElection				.16	
				(.20)	
UR Member					−.10
					(.36)
UR Member* PostElection					.36
					(.49)
UR_ Supporter					−.34**
					(.13)
UR Supporter* PostElection					.39**
					(.10)
Cut Points	−.66	−.59	−.57	−.60	−.73
	.81	.90	.97	.88	.74
N	771	771	671	723	771
Prob >chi2	.0000	.0000	.0000	.0000	.0000
R^{sq}	.05	.06	.06	.05	.05

* = p<.10, ** = p<.05, *** = p<.01. Ordered Probit Estimation. 15 region and 1 sector Dummy not reported. Robust standard errors. Positive coefficient means more secure property rights. Data from 2011 survey.

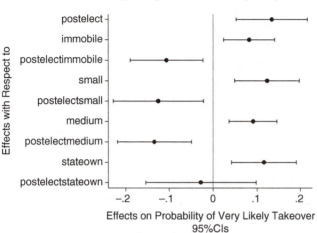

Figure 3.1 Elections and Property Rights

13 percentage less likely to hold this view. The effects for medium-sized firms are roughly the same.

Managers of state-owned firms interviewed prior to the political shock were 12 percentage points more likely to view their firm as a "very likely" target of a corporate takeover, while their counterparts in state-owned firms interviewed after the elections were 3 percentage points less likely to place their firm in this category, although the latter result is very imprecisely estimated. Taken together these results indicate that vulnerable firms (immobile, state owned, fewer employees) viewed their property rights as very insecure prior to the electoral shock to the ruling party, and, and in most cases, significantly more secure after the poor showing of United Russia. These results are displayed graphically in Figure 3.1.

The results are robust to the employment of dichotomous or continuous measures of property rights. Dropping very small firms with fewer than 10 employees for whom hostile corporate takeovers may be less of an issue also produces little change in the results.

The results also rest on the assumption that the economic environment did not change after the elections in ways that might have influenced perceptions of property rights for specific groups. It is difficult to discern any economic shocks coterminous with the elections that would have had this effect. In addition, I assume that responses to questions unrelated to property rights, such as questions about partisanship, past foreign investment, and political connections were not influenced by the election results. If, for example, respondents were more reluctant to admit support for United Russia after the election than before, then it would be difficult to estimate the impact of the election conditional on the partisanship of the respondent. However, as noted above, there seems to be little difference in the pre-election and post-election samples in terms of United Russia membership or United Russia support, incidence of foreign investment, or presence of immobile assets.

In addition, to the extent that respondents anticipated the poor showing of United Russia in the elections, it should be more difficult to find a significant relationship between the shift in bargaining power and a change in perceptions of property rights.

This chapter analyzed one type of political shock in one specific setting, which makes it difficult to generalize these results to other contexts. Moreover, because interviews were conducted shortly after the election it is difficult to know whether these effects lasted beyond the survey. While the analysis found some important short-term effects on perceptions of property rights, it has little to say about the duration of these effects.

Conclusion

Many have noted that the surprisingly poor showing of United Russia tarnished the teflon of President Putin and brought large demonstrations to the center of Moscow, but the economic consequences of this shock have been less frequently explored. I found that this political shock had important short-term effects on perceptions of the property rights of some firm managers. Managers of firms with immobile assets or state ownership viewed their property rights as less vulnerable after the election, while larger firms viewed their property rights as more vulnerable after the election. These results indicate that shifts in the bargaining power of the ruler had tangible effects on perceptions of property rights for some groups of firms. The shock to the bargaining power of the ruler appears to have leveled the playing a field for the most vulnerable firms in the sample, those with immobile assets, few employees, or state ownership.

For theories of property rights, these results suggest the value of finding an exogenous source of variation in property rights. Because the bargaining power of the ruler typically influences and is simultaneously influenced by property rights, it is difficult to identify whether the bargaining power of the ruler drives property rights or property rights drive the bargaining power of the ruler. By taking advantage of the plausibly exogenous timing of interviews of right-holders, I can make some progress toward overcoming this problem.

The results also add to the growing literature on elections under autocracy. They provide some evidence in support of the importance of autocratic elections at the level of the individual. In recent years, scholars have argued that elections under autocracy are far more than a façade; they generate useful information for rulers about the strength of the opposition and the performance of subordinates (Boix and Svolik 2013; Gehlbach and Simpser 2014). Others have noted that authoritarian elections have impacts on the likelihood of turnover in the leadership (Pop-Eleches and Robertson 2015), public spending, and social policy (Magaloni 2006; Lust-Okar 2006; Blaydes 2011). Some of these studies rely on aggregate level data in which it is difficult to identify the impact of elections on outcomes. In contrast, this work provides evidence at the level of the individual about the impacts of elections under autocracy.

For Russia watchers, these results indicate that the dominance of United Russia and its satellite parties is perceived to be an important barrier to the creation of stronger property rights, especially for the most vulnerable firms. Weakening the bargaining power of the ruling party helped to improve perceptions of the security of property rights among firms with immobile assets, some state ownership, and fewer workers. In the case of Russia, and likely elsewhere, the challenge of creating stronger protections against corporate raiding is not just technical or economic, but is deeply rooted in politics.

Chapters 2 and 3 examined existential threats to businesses in Russia as managers weighed the prospect of their firm succumbing to a hostile takeover (with a possible prison term added for good measure). In the next chapter, I turn from the existential to the everyday by focusing on how state institutions resolve mundane disputes involving run-of-the-mill firms. These analyses begin to identify how formal and informal institutions can constrain powerful rulers and right-holders.

Appendix 3.1

Table A3.1 *Balance by Region*

Regions	Pre-Election Before 12/4/11	Post-Election After 12/4/11	Difference Between Post-Election and Pre-Election p-value in par.
Moscow	.03	.10	.07 (.00)
Tula	.03	.12	.09 (.00)
Smolensk	.05	.08	.02 (.07)
Voronezh	.10	.04	.06 (.00)
Kursk	.03	.09	.06 (.00)
Nizhnii Novgorod	.06	.07	.01 (.96)
Novgorod	.03	.11	.08 (.00)
Ulyanovsk	.05	.06	.01 (.83)
Rostov	.05	.08	.03 (.02)
Ufa	.02	.12	.10 (.00)
Ekaterinburg	.11	.02	.09 (.00)
Omsk	.06	.07	.01 (.56)
Kemerovo	.02	.15	.14 (.00)
Irkutsk	.07	.05	.02 (.20)
Khabarovsk	.07	.06	.01 (.64)

4 | Courts and Connections

Who's The Boss: We or the Law? We are Masters over the Law, not the Law over Us – so we have to change the law; we have to see that it is possible to execute these speculators.

Nikita Khrushchev, 1961 (Simis 1982: 30)

Political scientists, economists, and sociologists disagree on many things, but they agree that capable public institutions such as police and courts are central to strong property rights and economic development. For Tilly (1992), the relationship between state agents of coercion and private agents of capital largely determined the economic fate of states in Europe over the last millennium. For North (1981; 1990), capable state institutions, such as courts and bureaucracies, that constrained rulers from arbitrary seizures of property, boosted trade between private entities and created a more level playing field, drove the industrial revolution and the rise of the West. For Rauch and Evans (2000), meritocratic bureaucracies distinguished the leaders from the laggards among lower- and middle-income countries over the last quarter century. This chapter focuses on one state institution: the courts. As arbiters of disputes over property, courts are a key public institution whose performance has shaped economic development for better and worse from Japan to Egypt and Argentina to China (West 2005; Moustafa 2008; Helmke 2005; Landry 2008).[1]

The conventional wisdom is that courts and other state institutions responsible for protecting property rights in Russia are notoriously corrupt, inefficient, and weak. This view is prevalent not only in the media and popular commentary on Russia, but is also held by some academics as well (Burger and Sorokina 2003; Holmes 2003;

---

[1] See Shapiro (1981; 1988) for seminal works on comparative courts.

Satarov 2003; Ledeneva 2006; Lambert-Mogiliansky et al. 2007).[2] In the absence of reliable courts, this conventional wisdom suggests that Russian businesses rely heavily on informal practices, such as turning to personal contacts within the state, bribing court officials, or paying the security forces to resolve economic disputes.

As I detail later in the chapter, however, some academic studies have put the courts in a more favorable light. These scholars tend to emphasize Russia's legal dualism – a legal system that works passably for routine cases, but is little help in high-stakes or politically charged cases. Most prominently, Hendley (2002: 2007a; 2007b; 2009; 2012b) argues that the "law works" in Russia for firms in everyday disputes, that the low level of trust in courts does not lead to lower use, and that Russians make use of the law far more frequently than the popular press suggests. For example, she finds that courts work serviceably well in everyday cases of debt collection and tax disputes, but are little help when the political stakes are high (Hendley 2011). While still recognizing the obvious warts in the Russian legal system, other scholars have documented that businesspeople and citizens use the state courts of arbitration frequently and that these courts provide a measure of security for property rights holders, even as other parts of the systems are quite dysfunctional (Titaev 2012; Trochev 2012; Shvets 2013; Gans-Morse 2014). In earlier periods, scholars found that the Soviet and Tsarist legal systems were also quite dualistic (Feifer 1964; Burbank 2004; 2012).[3]

Assessing claims about the quality of Russian courts is a challenge due to the great heterogeneity in effectiveness within the system. Scholars may find that criminal courts work less well than state arbitration courts, arbitration courts work better in mundane cases than in high-stakes cases, corporate takeover cases are fraught with

---

[2] This chapter deals primarily with state courts of arbitration, which handle the bulk of business disputes and do not hear cases involving human rights or political rights – an area where the Russian court system is very weak.

[3] Anton Chekhov's brilliant short story, *Chameleon*, depicts this bias well. In a provincial Russian town, a petty merchant is nipped by a puppy and seeks redress from a policeman who immediately asks the gathering crowd who owns the dog. Upon hearing that the owner may be General Zhigalov, the policeman turns and accuses the merchant of provoking the attack, which he denies. The General's cook passes and says the offending dog is not the General's and the policeman threatens to have the dog killed. After some consternation, the cook says that the dog is owned by the brother of the General and the policeman lets the cook take the dog home without punishment.

difficulties, debt collection cases are resolved without incident, but much of this nuance gets drowned out by headline-grabbing cases of spectacular violations of property rights.

In addition, performance is a relative measure and it is important to compare the Russian judicial system to real world counterparts in other middle-income countries rather than to idealized versions of legalized systems in advanced democracies. Many middle-income countries struggle to enforce judicial decisions, insulate judges from political pressure, and to root out bribery and corruption and such problems are far from unknown in wealthy democracies (c.f. O'Brien and Li 2004; Japelli et al. 2005; Magaloni 2008; Ingram 2011).

Finally, as many have noted, analyzing the impact of courts by using examples of litigation is helpful, but this approach can be problematic because only a small number of cases end up in court (Macauley 1963; Hendley et al. 2001). Drawing inferences from a sample of court cases can produce insightful analyses of cases that end up in court, but are less useful for making general claims about the impact of courts on behavior in other cases because we miss exchanges in which both sides hold up their end of the contract. This selection problem also leads us to miss cases in which contracts are violated but the aggrieved party does not turn to the courts.

By examining how businesspeople perceive the use of courts and other strategies for resolving disputes in their daily economic life, I try to address these challenges. In doing so, I aim to identify when the conventional wisdom of Russia's failed legal system fits the data and when it misleads. For example, respondents in surveys conducted in 2005, 2008, and 2011 report relying heavily on informal institutions, such as negotiations with partners to prevent and resolve disputes – a view consistent with the conventional wisdom on Russia. This finding is hardly confined to Russia as a long line of research on economic disputes in a variety of settings stresses that businesspeople frequently try to resolve disputes informally and that state courts are often only a last resort (Macauley 1963; Bernstein 1992; Greif 1994; West 2005).

While businesspeople in Russia often turn to informal ties, they also use courts more frequently than some other options that grab the headlines, such as using criminal organizations or the state security services to resolve everyday disputes.[4] Moreover, once an everyday

---

[4] This is consistent with Hendley et al. (2000); Titaev (2012), and others.

dispute arises, businesspeople often see courts as more effective than informal institutions such as negotiating with business partners, turning to protection rackets, or calling in the security forces. These results come with some caveats, but complicate the popular view of a wholly ineffectual legal system in Russia.

Most importantly, the chapter uses survey-based experiments to address the difficult question of the relative importance of political power and connections for protecting property rights in everyday disputes. The use of survey experiments is especially important due to the presence of hard-to-measure variables such as corruption that may be influencing perceptions of property rights. While it is difficult to identify precisely how widespread corruption is in Russian courtrooms, it is widely held that judges in Russia often accept bribes to ensure favorable decisions (Satarov et al. 2010). To account for the possible impact of corruption on property rights, researchers using traditional regression-based approaches often have to rely on crude proxies to ensure that bribery is not driving the outcome.

In contrast, the survey experiments used in this work rely on the assumption that perceptions about the impact of corruption are equally distributed across treatment and control groups due to random assignment. Just as in each treatment and control group there are roughly equal numbers of young and old, and rich and poor, there should also be equal numbers of those for whom judicial corruption is a big problem and a small problem. That is to say, because the average level of perceptions about corruption are equal between treatment and control groups due to random assignment, corruption perceptions cannot account for the differences in average responses between groups. Where this assumption is satisfied, we can be confident that perceptions of corruption are not systematically influencing the results that follow. This assumption cannot be tested directly but seems plausible given the large number of respondents in each group and the random assignment of respondents to groups. In other words, the analysis controls, however imperfectly, for the impact of corruption on perceptions of property rights.

Many studies have pointed to the importance of political connections in Russia and elsewhere for the protection of property rights, but fewer estimate the impact of political connections relative to other factors.[5] More specifically, this chapter asks three questions: Do

---

[5] But see Fisman (2001), Faccio et al. (2006), Han and Zhang (2015), Szakonyi (2016), and Hou (2016).

respondents perceive that it is better in court for a disputant to be politically connected or to have the facts of the case on their side? Do they believe that in court it is better to be politically connected or to be a large firm? And once a dispute occurs do respondents believe that formal means, such as courts, or informal means, such as negotiations, are more effective in resolving disputes?

The results indicate that respondents perceive that connections to the regional government are important, particularly when respondents adopt informal strategies to protect their property rights. They also reveal that the quality of the case, the size of the disputants, and other case-specific features influence the perceived capacity of firms to use courts to protect their property rights. In other words, political connections are perceived to be an important consideration, but other factors are relevant as well for protecting property rights in everyday disputes in Russia. Taken together, these results suggest a more nuanced picture of the role of courts in everyday disputes in Russia than is typical.

Description of the Court System

The judicial system of the Russian Federation is based on a civil law tradition in which court officials are seen as agents of the state – an image deeply reinforced in the Soviet period. Formally, the judicial system consists of several types of courts: the Constitutional Court, general courts (or "courts of general jurisdiction"), arbitration courts, appellate courts, justices of the peace, and military tribunals. Two sets of courts are most relevant for this project: state courts of arbitration that hear economic and commercial disputes among legal entities and/or individual entrepreneurs; and general courts that hear non-commercial (e.g. criminal) disputes, among individuals and legal entities.

The state courts of arbitration were reformed in 1992 from their Soviet-era predecessor *Gosarbitrazh*, as a separate forum for resolving business disputes. Arbitration court judges hear disputes between firms, including property and commercial disputes, and between firms and the state, including, tax, land, and administrative actions. The state arbitration courts are organized along regional lines with 81 courts of first instance located in Russia's 83 regions. The jurisdiction of each of the regional courts coincides with the administrative borders of their respective regions. Ten higher-level arbitration courts hear appeals, as, until 2014, did a Supreme Arbitration Court. State arbitration courts heard over 1.4 million cases in 2009 and employ about 3100 judges, who until recently were appointed for life (Solomon 2002).[6] The Ministry of Justice at the federal level provides salaries and budgets for these courts, but in the 1990s local and regional governments often provided additional informal monies to supplement frequent short-falls in financing. Judges are appointed by the executive branch after they have been screened and approved by a corporate organization of judges.

The general courts emerged as the successor to the court system of the USSR and inherited many of the qualities of its predecessor. Judges in the more than 2500 courts of general jurisdiction hear the vast majority of cases including civil, criminal, and administrative cases that are not commercial disputes (Partlett 2014). These include crimes against other individuals, such as theft, fraud, and assault; they also try crimes against the state, such as money laundering, tax evasion, and corruption.

The two courts share some traits. Each is marked by a strict organizational hierarchy with promotion and hiring decisions based heavily on recommendations from a board of judges that is closely monitored by the executive branch. Judges in both court systems face very high workloads and are subject to political pressure, although to differing degrees.

Yet, the differences are also noteworthy.[7] General court judges are paid about 10–15 percent less than judges in the state courts of arbitration.[8] General court judges work especially closely with prosecutors and are often reluctant to cross them (Schultz et al. 2014). These judges are especially vulnerable to political pressure and the most egregious use of courts to punish political dissent has occurred in the general courts, including the cases of Sergei Magnitsky, Alexei Navalny, and Mikhail Khodorkovsky, among others.

These differences are apparent in the professional backgrounds of the two heads of the agencies. The general courts are headed by Viacheslav Lebedev who was born in 1943, graduated law school in

---

[6] See www.Arbit.ru for more information.
[7] In many countries, criminal courts are seen as less prestigious than commercial courts.
[8] RAPSI news December 19, 2012. "Federation Council Approves Law on Increasing Judges' Wages."

1970, and worked in the Moscow City Courts until 1989, when he was named head of the general courts, a position he has held for more than 25 years. His entire professional career has been spent in the general courts. In contrast, the head of the state courts of arbitration, Anton Ivanov, was born in 1965, completed his law degree in 1987 and defended a dissertation on "Property Rights and Commodity-Money Relations" in 1991. He worked as a corporate lawyer for *Soyuzkonstrakt-Uslugi* and Gazprom-Media, and taught at his alma-mater for seven years, before being appointed the head of the Supreme Arbitration Court in 2005. Ivanov is a personal friend and ally of current Prime Minister Dmitrii Medvedev (Novikov 2014).

There is also considerable evidence that businesspeople perceive state courts of arbitration and state courts of general jurisdiction very differently. In surveys of businesspeople that I conducted in eight regions in Russia in 2000, 2005, 2008, and 2011, respondents repeatedly said that state courts of arbitration performed significantly better than state courts of general jurisdiction. As reported in Table 4.1, respondents were asked to rate the performance of the state courts of arbitration and the state courts of general jurisdiction on a scale of 1–5. In each survey, businesspeople rated the state courts of arbitration as performing significantly better than the state courts of general jurisdiction.[9]

Titaev (2012) and colleagues reached a similar conclusion in their analysis of 10,000 randomly selected judicial cases involving economic crimes. They found that even for those cases that end up in court:

State courts of arbitration and state courts of general jurisdiction in Russia push economic development in two opposite directions. State courts of arbitration are fully capable of protecting investors' rights by ensuring the competitiveness and equality of those in court regardless of their ties to the government, while the state courts of general jurisdiction nullify these achievements thanks to their arbitrariness and submissiveness (to state power).

In addition, his reading of judicial decisions indicates that appeals are far more common in courts of general jurisdiction than in the state courts of arbitration. Moreover, appeals of decisions made by

---

[9] The evidence here should not be used to make comparisons of the evolution of the quality the courts over time due to the possible presence of survivor bias in the surveys and the lack of panel data.

Table 4.1 *Perceived Effectiveness of Courts*

	State Courts of Arbitration Mean (sd)	State Courts of General Jurisdiction Mean (sd)	Significance of Difference in Means
2000	3.19 (.93)	2.82 (.82)	t = 5.10
2005	3.22 (.83)	2.87 (.79)	t = 7.03
2008	3.42 (.78)	3.23 (.81)	t = 3.34
2011	3.42 (.89)	3.28 (.91)	t = 2.93

arbitration courts are just as likely to decide cases in favor of private agents as state agents.[10] The relative transparency of the courts of arbitration have also been a boon to anti-corruption activists such as Alexei Navalny, who used evidence of violations of minority shareholder rights presented in arbitration courts to publicly shame members of the political and economic elite (Partlett 2014).

The Evolution of State Courts of Arbitration

The state courts of arbitration have evolved significantly over the last 25 years with major changes moving in line with the bargaining power of the ruler. In the early 1990s, President Boris Yeltsin introduced sweeping changes in legal institutions, including life tenure for judges, and expanded court authority over commercial, constitutional, and administrative disputes. His administration created justices of the peace, which eventually led to significant declines in the caseloads of overworked judges in the courts of general jurisdiction and courts of arbitration (Solomon 2003). In addition, Yeltsin oversaw the transfer of the administration of courts from the executive branch to a judicial body under the authority of the Supreme

---

[10] Partlett (2014) and Pomeranz (2014) provide fairly positive assessments of arbitration courts.

Arbitration Court – a move that was widely seen as increasing the autonomy of the court.[11]

The impact of these reforms, however, was limited in large part by the fraught relationship between President Yeltsin and the Duma and by the weakness of the central government, which faced severe and chronic shortages of funds in the 1990s. Court facilities were in disrepair, pay for judicial officials declined significantly in real terms, and bailiffs often lacked the resources to enforce decisions against state and private parties. With federal support at anemic levels, regional officials often helped to fill the shortfall but typically they did so in exchange for favorable treatment by the courts. Reliance on local officials for unofficial financial support, housing, and logistics drastically limited the reach of central organs of power in Russia's regions in the 1990s (Stoner-Weiss 2006).

President Vladimir Putin came to power vowing to establish "a dictatorship of the rule of law," and thanks to the ruble devaluation of 1998 and the boom in oil prices, the Russian state had the financial resources to support judicial reform. Moreover, President Putin had much stronger support within the Duma, and over time his approval ratings soared, which strengthened his position among the elites and the masses. This increase in bargaining power helped the Putin administration to pass a new criminal code (2002) and civil code (2003). While far from ideal, these new procedural codes helped to establish legal rules of the game.

The Putin administration sought to increase the technical capacity of the courts by compelling courts to create websites to post their decisions and to improve physical infrastructure such as their buildings.[12] It also dramatically increased funding for the courts. The Plan for the Improvement of the Courts for 2002–06 called for 44 billion rubles in new spending, and additional monies were made available in the Plan for 2007–11. Judges' base salaries increased significantly. In the early

---

[11] Solomon (2003: 66). Hendley (2007b: 245–249) discusses changes to the Civil Code that defined the power of arbitration court judges. Solomon (2004) also reviews the evolution of judicial authority in Russia.

[12] In addition, on President Putin's watch, jury trials expanded to all regions in Russia (except Chechnya) despite opposition from the prosecutor's office and many judges. Win rates of citizens against state officials are roughly 80 percent, which suggests the possibility of selection bias in the cases that citizens bring to court (Solomon 2002).

2000s, they were about $1000 per month, which was fairly high for many Russian cities (Solomon 2003: 68). By late 2013, this figure had increased to over $4000 per month.[13] Even an otherwise highly critical Council of Europe report from 2009 on judicial institutions in Russia noted that the "strong improvement in the social status of judges and prosecutors in recent years have all but eliminated their dependence on executive bodies for housing and other basic needs."[14]

Yet, while the Putin administration stressed improving the technocratic efficiency of the court, it also made the courts increasingly subservient to the executive branch, using both formal and informal measures. Legislation passed in Putin's second term allowed non-judges to hold one-third of the seats on the Judicial Qualifications Commissions that hires and fire judges. Previously only judges served on this important commission (Solomon 2008: 68). One Moscow city court judge noted that this effort will "weaken the foundation of judicial authority and erase the notion of separation of power," while a second noted "the judiciary is already under the Kremlin's influence" and added that "if this terrible bill is approved, it means that we will lose any hope of seeing an independent judiciary system in Russia, since it will be completely in the hands of the Kremlin" (Mereu 2004). In addition, in 2002, judges lost strong protections against criminal prosecution and faced new disciplinary measures short of firing. Court Chairs, who have tremendous influence over judges in their jurisdiction, have become keenly dependent on local political and economic figures (Solomon 2008: 69). As Chairs largely control promotion decisions, they are an attractive target for political and economic elites intent on influencing the judicial process (Mereu 2004).

In 2008, the head of the Supreme Arbitration Courts traced the trajectory of the arbitration courts: "In the early 1990s, a public meeting style of democracy prevailed (*mitingovaia demokratiia*) which allowed the courts to develop as an autonomous branch of power, but then

---

[13] http://rapsinews.com/legislation_news/20121219/265832014.html.

[14] Parliamentary Resolution 1685 (2009). "Allegations of Politically Motivated Abuses of the Criminal Justice System in COE Member States." http://assembly. coe.int/nw/xml/XRef/Xref-XML2HTML-en.asp?fileid=17778&lang=en. See also Jordan (2009). Solomon (2008: 70) notes: "the majority of cases are processed more quickly in Russia than in Western countries, and only a small share of cases became victim of overly complicated procedural norms." See also Solomon (2010).

executive power was strengthened, and because of this judicial power wavered." He added that proposals to limit the immunity of judges under discussion "were a dangerous path. Given the current condition of the security forces, this would lead to complete subjugation ... and judges would fall onto a black list" (Butorina 2014).

President Medvedev came to power in 2008 and sought to stem encroachments on the authority of judges by, among other things, ordering the Justice Minister to monitor law enforcement agencies and report annually on the execution of court decisions. He also pushed efforts to post court proceedings on the internet and to empower judges to issue fines rather than jail time for economic crimes (Novikov 2014). The impact of these reforms was limited, in large part by the power of the security services and President Medvedev's dependence on the then Prime Minister Putin.

Shortly after returning to the presidency in 2012, President Putin reversed many of Medvedev's efforts to humanize the legal system and strengthen the position of judges (Panin and d'Amora 2013). Most importantly, in the summer of 2013, President Putin proposed a merger of the Supreme Court of Arbitration and Supreme Court of General Jurisdiction into a single Supreme Court comprising 170 judges to oversee lower general and arbitration courts.[15] The authorities argued that the change would reduce inconsistencies in court rulings, but critics saw it is an effort by the Kremlin to further centralize a judicial system that was already widely viewed as beholden to the president (Hille 2013; Partlett 2013). One view suggested that the arbitration courts were being weakened to prevent further leaks of information about violations of minority shareholder rights that had drawn the ire of those involved in hostile corporate takeovers (Partlett 2014).

The proposal to merge the top tiers of the two court systems surprised many and provoked an atypical outcry from the legal community and investors. Before President Putin announced this plan publicly at the St. Petersburg Economic Forum, Anton Ivanov, the head of the Supreme Arbitration Court was critical: "There is not a single country where an entire federal system would link to one court – not with such a large number of disputes and regions." He predicted that it would be difficult for a single court to manage and expected that courts would

[15] http://rapsinews.com/trend/court_merger/.

"lose influence on the proceedings." Even government owned RIA-Novosti reported:

The reform was met with unusually outspoken, but unsuccessful resistance from some quarters of the judicial community. A number of Supreme Arbitration Court judges stepped down in recent months. Russia's judiciary is routinely accused of corruption and dependence on the executive. The Supreme Arbitration Court had generally been recognized as an exception to that rule, with lawyers and businessmen alike praising it for its effectiveness, fairness and transparency.[16]

This proposal provoked the resignation of more than a dozen Supreme Arbitration Court judges and an outcry from the business community.[17] On behalf of the Supreme Arbitration Court, Ivanov wrote a very critical 15-page comment on the merger legislation that was sent to the Duma for discussion (Yarkov 2013; Ivanov 2014).

In February 2014, new legislation created the Supreme Court, which merged the top tiers of the two court systems.[18] An Economic Collegium within the Supreme Court oversees lower level arbitration courts, but many view the merger as a loss of autonomy for the arbitration courts. Underscoring the subversion of the courts of arbitration, Viacheslav Lebedev, the head of courts of general jurisdiction, was named leader of this new body. It is too soon to judge the impact or fate of these changes in policy.[19] Yet the timing and shape of the merger drives home two broader points. Changes in the broad contours of the legal system depend in part on shifts in the bargaining power of the ruler. In addition, this evolution shows that formal and informal legal institutions, and the property rights that flow from them, are largely politically contingent.

---

[16] http://russialist.org/ria-novosti-putin-signs-contentious-courts-merger-into-law/ . For further critiques by Russian lawyers, see Balmforth (2013).

[17] See Novosti.ru, October 10, 2013 and also *Vedemosti* October 23, 2013. www.vedomosti.ru/politics/articles/2013/10/23/ v-otstavku-poprosilis-uzhe-22-sudi-vas

[18] Rumors have long circulated that the creation of this unified Supreme Court was done to prepare a soft landing for Dmitrii Medvedev should President Putin dismiss him.

[19] Protégés of Ivanov also apparently lost out on key posts in the merged courts. See *Vedomosti*, May 29, 2014. www.vedomosti.ru/newspaper/articles/2014/05/29/ predsedatel-iz-byvshih and *Vedomosti*, May 20, 2014 www.vedomosti.ru/politics/ articles/2015/05/20/v-arbitrazhnoi-sisteme-prodolzhaetsya-kadrovaya-chistka

Evaluating Court Performance

One imperfect means of evaluating court performance is to explore court use over time. In the 2000s, Russian firms were rather willing to take disputes with private firms and state agencies to court (Hendley 2004; 2007a). As depicted in Figure 4.1, the years 2004 and 2005 saw increases in cases against state bodies in part due to tax and social benefit reforms and 2009 saw an increase in disputes between private firms, likely in response to the global financial crisis, which hit Russia hard.

While the number of court cases increased by 96 percent between 2001 and 2012, the size of the Russian economy increased by more than 60 percent. With a larger economy and more transactions one might expect to find greater court use even if the quality of the legal systems remains constant. This is particularly so because court decisions are required to implement bank orders in cases of default and insurance claims. Increased use of courts does not necessarily indicate that courts have become more capacious – disputes may have become more likely.

Another possible benchmark is court use, speed, and quality in other countries. These comparisons are inevitably very rough as laws, legal institutions, including the power and structures of the courts, vary tremendously across countries in ways that are likely to influence court use.[20] Filing fees in Russian courts are very low relative to other countries, which may contribute to greater court use. Russian courts issue rulings relatively quickly. Arbitration courts are required to issue a decision within two months from the date of filing. This requirement is met in more than 95 percent of cases (Hendley 2007b: 245). Chemin (2012:466) finds that India's lower court judges in the early 2000s had backlogs on average of between 500 and 1000 cases. Using subnational data in Italy, Jappelli et al. (2005) find that an average trial on financial matters in the early 1990s was about 44 months. Not surprisingly they find that districts with slower courts experience lower levels of bank lending and higher percentages of non-performing loans. Djankov et al. (2003) survey lawyers in 109 countries to gain measures of legal formalism in courts and find that higher scores on this index is associated with lower performance, especially in developing countries. They also find that Russia's degree of procedural formalism is slightly below the

---

[20] On the inefficiency of courts in Brazil to battle corruption by state officials see Higino and Gico (2010). On the performance of courts in China, see O'Brien and Li (2004). On courts in Mexico, see Ingram et al. (2011).

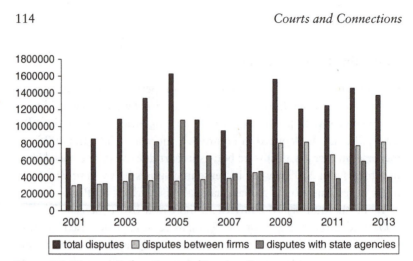

Figure 4.1 Disputes Before States Arbitration Courts

global mean (3.39 versus 3.53) and that court rules for handling tenant eviction and check collection cases are lower than global averages (130 versus 347 days and 160 versus 327 days, respectively).

With some exceptions, academic studies have been more charitable than the conventional wisdom in their evaluation of the performance of state courts of arbitration.[21] Scholars have tended to focus on the everyday transactions of Russian firms, while more popular accounts have probed more high-profile cases of the politically motivated use of courts, which may account for the more positive evaluations made by academics. Most prominently, Hendley et al. (1999; 2000) report that courts in Russia work better than the conventional wisdom suggests. Based on a survey of 328 firms conducted in 1997, they argue (2000: 628) that "contrary to conventional wisdom, Russian enterprises do not reject the use of law and legal institutions when disputes arise. Many enterprises use the courts. This is not to say that a legalistic strategy is preferred, but merely that such a strategy is considered feasible." Elsewhere (1999: 1), they conclude "that law works in Russia because our results show that the economic and institutional environment rewards enterprises that invest effort in constructing contracts, that possess superior legal knowledge, and that orient legal work to new opportunities."[22] This insight runs through much of Hendley's work

[21] Lawyers are well paid, but it is unclear whether this is related to their skill as a legal mind or as a facilitator of corruption.

[22] A later version of this chapter appeared as Hendley et al. (2001).

on judges, courts, and bailiffs (cf. Hendley 2002; Hendley 2004).[23] For example, using two national surveys of the mass public from the first half of the 2000s, she finds that while Russians distrust courts, this does not prevent them from using courts in a dispute as litigants' behavior is motivated more by material concerns than by attitudes about the legal system (Hendley 2012b). Similarly, her research using focus groups finds that the reasons that Russians are reluctant to turn to courts are not driven by "telephone law" or legacies of the Soviet past, but rather mirror the determinants of court use in other countries (Hendley 2009).[24]

Using administrative data from 1996 to 2002, Shvets (2013) finds that the quality of courts shapes an important economic outcome – the willingness of banks to lend to firms. She measures the independence of state arbitration courts across regions in Russia using the appeal rate of lower-level court decisions by appellate courts and finds that banks are more willing to lend to firms in regions in which the arbitration courts have more independence from local political elites.

Titaev (2012) studied more than 10,000 randomly selected decisions by state arbitration courts and found that firms located in the capital city of a region (where arbitration courts are located) are no more likely to win their cases than firms located outside the capital city, which suggests that close connections to those in the capital are not a good predictor of success in courts. Based on this research, he argues that the court system is an "effective and modern mechanism for resolving disputes in the economic sphere," but also that "beyond the economic sphere, the court system does not facilitate the defense of civil rights, and serves as an instrument to defend political elites from competitors." Using the same data, Dmitrieva (2013) finds that in administrative cases the courts have a slight bias in favor of the government, but in civil cases they have tended to favor business.[25]

In separate work with these data, Titaev et al. (2014) show that cases vary tremendously in size. The average size of a case in the arbitration court is about $100,000, but the median case is quite small – roughly

---

[23] For a critique, see Gustaffson (2013) and Hendley and Murrell's (2015) reply.
[24] Ledeneva (2013: 150–178) finds that various forms of "telephone law" are perceived by the public to be quite common. Ledeneva's (2013) interview with a former judge, Olga Kudeshkina, provides riveting details of how political elites pressure judges in criminal cases.
[25] See also Solomon (2004).

$3,000. Courts do handle large cases, but are overwhelmed with relatively small matters. Administrative cases brought by the government are much smaller with an average size of about $25,000 and a median size of $100 – often lower than court costs. They also find that private plaintiffs win cases against private firms at a rate of 47 percent and against the government at a rate of 40 percent, and that the win rate for the government in administrative cases brought by the government is well over 60 percent. They conclude their study by noting that "one cannot say that there is a clear pro-government bias in all category of cases ... government agencies are somewhat weaker than the average businessperson in civil cases ... but in some situations (for example, routine cases emerging from administrative investigations) the court is clearly on the side of the government."

Trochev (2012: 22) finds that courts are friendlier to private citizens and firms in cases of administrative law – those involving wrongful actions by government officials – than in criminal law. Using data on administrative law cases in Russia, he finds that between 2007 and 2011 private citizens and firms brought roughly 500,000 lawsuits per year against state officials and agencies and won these cases at close to a 90 percent success rate. These cases often involve tax authorities, pension funds, and various types of administrative fines. In addition, businesses brought between 80,000 and 100,000 lawsuits per year against government officials and agencies (mostly tax cases) and won between 48 and 60 percent of these cases. Moreover, the Finance Ministry set aside increasingly larger sums (around 15 billion rubles or $500 million in 2009) to pay compensation for damages caused by the wrongful actions of government officials. One key distinction is that prosecutors are rarely present in administrative cases, which likely gives judges greater freedom to rule against the state.

Popova (2006) relies on data from appeals to courts about violations of the electoral law in the parliamentary elections of 1999 and finds that courts in Russia are vulnerable to pressure from regional authorities; that litigants "forum shop" to find more friendly venues, and that candidates with prior experience with the legal system tend to use them less. However, she also notes (2006: 391) that "scathing journalistic accounts of judicial corruption, inefficiency and total subservience to politicians seem to be exaggerated. Both the courts and the Central Election Commission were acceptable appeal venues since opposition candidates used them to defend their electoral rights more often than all other groups of candidates."

Focusing on bankruptcy cases, Lambert-Mogiliansky et al. (2007) find that the quality of judicial systems across regions influenced post-bankruptcy-firm performance, but also that courts were strongly influenced by regional governors, often at the expense of federal agencies and Moscow-based creditors. Their findings are "consistent with the view that politically strong governors subverted enforcement of the 1998 bankruptcy law." With some exceptions, scholars using more qualitative methods have been more critical of the courts of arbitration in Russia (Ledeneva 2006; 2013; Volkov 2002; Varese 2002).

Yet, for all its strengths the literature leaves open some important avenues for research. For example, the literature does not always distinguish between types of disputant, but this distinction is quite important as perceptions of the performance of courts depend on whether the disputes are with private or state actors (Frye 2004). Moreover, much of this literature focuses on the 1990s and early 2000s when Russian politics was much more politically polarized, but also more competitive. Less research has been conducted on how businesspeople have used Russia's courts since the autocratic turn in politics in the Putin era (but see Ledeneva 2006; Hendley 2007; Trochev 2012). Here I am able to extend the analysis until 2011.

Background Data on Disputes

Survey data from 2005 and 2008 indicates that respondents reported using a range of strategies to help resolve disputes. In Figure 4.2, I report the frequency with which respondents used different strategies for resolving disputes with the regional/municipal government and with private firms.

Data from a 2005 survey indicate that 88 percent of respondents said that they used negotiations with a business partner in the private sector, but 71 percent said that they had used the courts to resolve a dispute with a private business partner in the last two years. Sixteen percent of respondents who experienced a dispute with a business partner said that they had turned to the security forces, while 19 percent said that they had used an "influential business person" for this purpose. The results are roughly similar for surveys of businesspeople conducted in 2008 and 2011 cited in the preceding chapters. They are

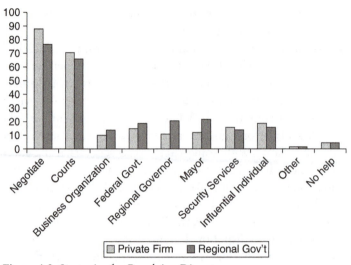

Figure 4.2 Strategies for Resolving Disputes

also quite consistent with data collected by Hendley et al. (2000) from surveys conducted in 1997 and 1999, which also show that negotiations and courts are the most common strategies for resolving disputes. This comparison indicates the slow progress in reforming the legal system in Russia over this period.

Of the 26 percent of respondents who reported having had a dispute with the local or regional government, more than three-quarters used negotiations, and two-thirds used courts to help resolve the dispute. Thirteen percent reported that they had contacted the security forces to assist in their dispute (this figure is likely understated given disincentives to report the use of the security forces in helping to pacify a dispute) and 16 percent said that they had turned to an "influential individual, such as a businessperson or head of another firm."[26]

Moving beyond the frequency with which firms used different dispute resolution mechanisms, interviewers also asked respondents who had experienced a dispute to evaluate the effectiveness of different strategies in recouping their losses during a dispute. One

---

[26] To reduce the bias of reporting on one's own behavior, interviewers also asked respondents how frequently other firms used these methods and the results were largely unchanged.

Table 4.2 *Rough Return Rates for Disputes with Private Firms*

Percent of damages returned on average	Method Used in the Dispute Percent Reporting			
	Negotiations N = 360	Court N = 324	State Security Forces N = 218	Influential businessperson N = 210
1. Almost nothing 0%	21	14	67	46
2. About 25%	16	13	16	24
3. About 50%	19	25	9	17
4. About 75%	19	22	6	8
5. Almost everything 100%	24	27	3	6
Mean response on 1–5 scale	**3.11**	**3.35**	**1.62**	**2.04**

"When you have had a conflict with a business partner what steps did you take and how effective were these steps?" The scale measures the amount of damages returned where 1 = 0, 2 = 25 percent, 3 = 50 percent, 4 = 75 percent, and 5 = 100 percent. Data from 2005 survey. N = number of respondents using this method.

must be careful in interpreting these results because respondents very likely choose their strategy based on the difficulty of the case. Respondents may only use the security forces for the most difficult cases. If so, then the difficulty of the legal case rather than the effectiveness of the security forces may be driving the rate of returned losses.

Table 4.2 indicates that once a dispute occurs with a private firm respondents perceived courts to be more effective than other means of recouping losses. The mean return reported by those who used courts is significantly higher than that reported by those who used negotiations (3.35 versus 3.11, t = 2.2). Moreover, the reported return rates for those who turned to the security forces and to influential individuals are much lower.[27] About 50 percent of respondents were able to recoup about 50 percent of their losses using courts.

---

[27] Using data from nine regions from 1997 to 2000, Hendley (2002) finds that in tax cases in which the firm initiated the case, taxpayers received about 70 percent of the amount sought.

Table 4.3 *Rough Return Rates for Disputes with the Regional Government*

	Method Used in the Dispute Percent Reporting			
Percent of damages returned on average	Negotiations N = 161	Court N = 143	State Security Forces N = 95	Influential business-person N = 90
1. Almost nothing 0%	52	22	82	63
2. About 25%	14	18	5	11
3. About 50%	10	20	8	9
4. About 75%	10	14	3	11
5. Almost everything 100%	14	29	1	6
Mean response on 1–5 scale	**2.20**	**3.11**	**1.36**	**1.84**

"When you have had a conflict with the local or regional government what steps did you take and how effective were these steps?" The scale measures the amount of damages returned where 1 = 0, 2 = 25 percent, 3 = 50 percent, 4 = 75 percent, and 5 = 100 percent. Data from 2005 survey. N = number of respondents using this method.

This figure is high relative to other means of resolving disputes, but whether this is an impressive figure in absolute terms is in the eye of the beholder.[28]

Disputes with the regional government present a somewhat similar pattern. Table 4.3 reveals that respondents were able to recoup significantly greater sums in disputes in which they used courts compared to other methods. More than 80 percent of respondents who reported using the security forces to help resolve a dispute with the regional or local government report getting almost nothing in return, while 60 percent of respondents report recouping at least half their losses in a dispute with the local or regional government. It is best not to put too much weight on these results as the choice of strategy is surely endogenous to features of the case. In addition, these tables report only the evaluations of those businesspeople who experienced

[28] I repeated these questions in a 2008 survey with a smaller sample and found similar results, but also an increase in the returns achieved by using the security forces and influential individuals. For more on debt collection, see Hendley (2004).

conflicts in the last year, which is a non-random subgroup of the firms in the survey. Yet, the large differences between the perceived effectiveness of different dispute resolution methods gives one to pause about the conventional wisdom about legal institutions in Russia.

To minimize the selection bias caused by only examining respondents who experienced disputes, interviewers asked all respondents a hypothetical question about the perceived effectiveness of using courts against various entities. Doing so generates responses from all businesspeople in the survey rather than only those who had used a particular means of resolving a dispute. Interviewers asked: "What do you think, in the event of an economic dispute (conflict) with the regional or city government can your firm protect its legal interest by using the courts?" They then substituted "the federal government" and "business partners" for the "regional government" before repeating these three questions, but in these cases also asked whether firms could protect their legal interests using negotiations without turning to courts. This approach can reveal whether respondents believed that once a dispute arises courts can protect their legal interests better than negotiations without use of the courts.

The responses in Figure 4.3 indicate that in a dispute with the regional or city government, 59 percent of respondents said that courts could protect their legal interests, while only 51 percent of respondents said that negotiations alone could protect their rights in such a dispute. Respondents report similar differences in the effectiveness of courts and negotiations alone in disputes with the federal government and with business partners. In each of these three types of dispute, these differences in the perceived effectiveness of courts and negotiations alone are statistically significant at the .05 level.[29]

Figure 4.3 also indicates that respondents consider the state courts of arbitration to be more effective in resolving disputes with private firms

---

[29] Respondents who used courts in a dispute with a business partner are no more likely than those who did not to believe that they can use courts against a business partner ($t = 1.43$), while those who used courts against the state are significantly more likely to believe that they can use the courts against the state ($t = 2.2$). These differences, however, have two shortcomings. First, it is a non-random sample of respondents who use courts. Those who do and do not use courts may differ in ways that are related to their perceptions of the performance of courts. Second, it is not clear that the experience of actually being in court is what is driving the higher ratings of courts among those who used them.

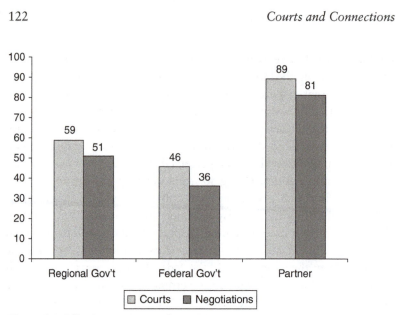

Figure 4.3 Effectiveness in Resolving Disputes

than with state agents. Comparing results in columns 1 and 3 reveals a more than 30 percentage point difference in the perceived effectiveness of courts in disputes with the regional government and with other private firms. Previous work has found that the ability of businesspeople to use courts to defend their legal interests in disputes with the local or regional government is an important predictor of investment rates (Frye 2004).

Courts and Connections

The raw survey data indicate that courts in Russia are perceived to be a common and relatively effective tool, but have not identified under what conditions they are effective. What features of a dispute make courts more or less effective? The next section focuses on this question with special attention to the role of political connections. A central problem of political economy is how to minimize the negative economic impacts of political connections. Where politically powerful firms use their connections to weaken more efficient competitors, markets become distorted. Absent a level playing field, more efficient, but politically weaker firms have little incentive to innovate or invest. This case is often overstated because of the prevalence of judicial bias in favor of well-connected firms in developing and developed countries (Galanter 1975; Ramseyer 1994; Posner 2008). However, the core point – that limiting the impact of political connections on the legal system can improve economic performance – carries great weight, particularly in developing and transition countries. The influence of powerful firms on state policy and judicial decisions has been a central theme in Russian politics since the 1990s (Hellman et al. 2003).

Better to be Right or Connected?

I begin by exploring the impact of political connections on the perceived performance of arbitration courts. Measuring political connections is difficult given incentives to under-report connections where they may provoke a backlash and over-report them when the goal is to intimidate or claim credit. I use an indirect method in which I manipulate information given to respondents about disputants' political connections. I examine whether respondents perceive having good political connections or a strong legal case is more important in a dispute before the court. I randomly assigned one of four versions of the question to respondents and manipulated whether the case was easy or difficult to prove in court and whether or not their counterpart had good political connections. I also examined whether political connections were perceived to have a greater impact when firms used only negotiations than when they used courts to resolve a dispute by simply asking about both instances.

More specifically, interviewers asked:

Let's say that your firm placed a large order to obtain a product that you needed and that you prepaid 100% of the price of the good. However, after receiving the product a defect was found that would be [easy/difficult] to prove in court. [XXX[30]/In addition, it turns out the seller has close relations with the regional government.]

What do you think, can your firm defend its legal interests by negotiating with this company, without turning to courts?
1) no   2) likely no   3) likely yes   4) yes   5) hard to say

What do you think, can your firm defend its legal interests by turning to the state courts of arbitration?
1) no   2) likely no   3) likely yes   4) yes   5) hard to say

---

[30] The XXX indicates that respondents received no information about the seller's relations with the regional government.

Table 4.4 *Better to be Right or Connected: Using Only Negotiations*

	No information (C1)	Good Connections (C2)	Difference (C1-C2) t-test (se)
Easy to Prove (R1)	3.17 (.66) n = 103	2.77 (.91) n = 113	.40*** (.11) t = 3.67
Hard to Prove (R2)	2.69 (.82) n = 112	2.46 (.97) n = 123	.23** (.11) t = 1.96
Difference (R1-R2) T-test (se)	.48*** (.10) t = 4.70	.31*** (.12) t = 2.68	

* p<.10, ** p<.05, and *** p<.01. Mean response to each of the four conditions where 1 = no, 2 = more or less no, 3 = more or less yes, 4 = yes. Standard deviation in parentheses. n = number of observations. Differences report standard errors in parentheses. Data from 2008 survey.

If we compare responses among the four conditions in Table 4.4, we find that political connections have a powerful impact on the perceived effectiveness of negotiations, especially when it would be easy to prove the case in court. Take Row 1, for instance. Respondents who were told that it would be easy to prove the case in court and received no information about the political connections of their counterpart were significantly more confident that they could use negotiations to protect their property rights than when they were told that their counterpart had good connections with the regional government (3.17 versus 2.77, t = 3.7). A mention that the other party had good connections reduced the respondent's confidence in the ability of negotiations to protect their property by 40 percentage points. Connections also had a strong impact on the perceived ability of respondents to use negotiations when it would be hard to prove the case in court (2.69 versus 2.46).

To give some more concrete sense of the of the size of the differences in responses, it is worth noting that 89 percent of respondents who answered the questions answered either "yes" or "more or less yes" that if the case was easy to prove in court, then they could use negotiations to protect their legal interests. However, only 71 percent held this view if the company was well connected with the regional government – a drop of 18 percentage points. If the case was hard to prove in a court, 65 percent said that they could more or less use negotiations to protect their legal rights, but this figure is only 51 percent if their counterpart is well connected. Taken together, these results indicate that the perceived impact of negotiations on the defense of property rights is highly conditional on the extent to which one's counterparty is connected to the regional government.

Somewhat surprisingly the quality of one's case also influences the perceived effectiveness of using only negotiations to resolve disputes. Comparing responses in the "easy to prove" and "hard to prove" rows when respondents receive no information about their counterparts' political connections in column 1 reveals sharp differences (3.17 versus 2.69, t = 4.7, p = .00). Similarly, comparing the "easy to prove" and "hard to prove" cases when counterparts are well connected with the regional government in column two reveals significant differences in the extent to which respondents believe that they can use negotiations to protect their property rights (2.76 versus 2.46, t = 2.4, p = .02).

When respondents are given no information about their counterparty's level of political connections, but are told that it would be easy to prove the case, 89 percent of respondents believe that negotiations could protect their property rights, but this figure declines by 24 percentage points if the respondent is told that it would be difficult to prove one's case in court. When respondents are told that their counterparty is well connected to the regional government and that their case would be easy to prove in court, 65 percent of respondents more or less believed that they could use negotiations to protect their interests. This figure falls by 14 percentage points when respondents are told that it would be difficult to prove one's case in court. Having explored respondents' perceptions of the effectiveness of negotiations in protecting property, I next analyze their perceptions of the effectiveness of state courts to resolve the same dispute (Table 4.5).

Interviewers also asked respondents whether they believed that they could use the courts to protect their property rights in these same four scenarios. The mean responses in row one reveal significant differences depending on whether respondents were told that their counterpart had good political connections or not (3.35 versus 3.13, t = 2.0,

Table 4.5 *Better to be Right or Connected: Using Courts*

	No Information (C1)	Good Connections (C2)	Difference (C1-C2) t-test (se)
Easy to Prove	3.35	3.13	.22**
(R1)	(.78)	(.81)	(.09)
	n = 101	n = 120	t = 2.0
Hard to Prove	2.96	2.99	.03
(R2)	(.75)	(.89)	(.10)
	n = 117	n = 120	t = .18
Difference	.39***	.14	
(R1-R2)	(.10)	(.09)	
t-test (se)	t = 3.93	t = 1.2	

*p<.10, ** p<.05, and *** p<.01. Mean response to each of the four conditions where 1 = no, 2 = more or less no, 3 = more or less yes, 4 = yes. Standard deviation in parentheses. n = number of observations. Differences report standard error in parentheses. Data from 2008 survey.

p = .04). However, when respondents thought it would be difficult to prove their case in court political connections seem to have little influence as indicated by the responses in the row two (2.96 versus 2.99, t = .18). Respondents perceive the political connections of the defendant to be important when the injured party has the facts of the case on their side, but of less use when they do not.

The quality of the case seems to be quite important in respondents' evaluations of the ability of courts to protect their property when the respondents have little information about the political connections of their counterpart (3.35 versus 2.96, t = 3.8, p = .00). More concretely, when a case is easy to prove and respondents have no information about their counterpart's political connections, 93 percent of respondents indicated that they could more or less use courts to protect their interests, while this figure is 78 percent when respondents are told it would be hard to prove their case in court. These overall numbers are high and possibly inflated by the structure of the responses. Because respondents were given no middle category, they were forced to choose between "more or less yes" or "more or less no." But the important point is not the level of the responses, but rather the differences in responses between different conditions. While this approach permits strong claims about the precision of the estimates of the differences among responses, it can make only weak claims that the level of the responses are representative of the population given the relatively small number of responses in each scenario.

Because respondents were asked to rate the effectiveness of using only negotiations and using courts to resolve the same dispute, I can compare the two sets of esponses.[31] Comparing responses in Tables 4.4 and 4.5 demonstrates that businesspeople perceive the courts to be better able to protect their rights. In each of the four conditions, respondents gave significantly higher scores to the courts than to negotiations. Looking at the upper-left quadrant in each table, when the case is easy to prove and respondents receive no information about the other firm's connections with the regional government, to the regional government, respondents rated negotiations as 3.17 and courts as 3.35 on a scale of 1–4, a difference of 18 percentage points.

In this section I focused on the impact of the quality of the case and the political connections on the capacity of negotiations and courts to protect property rights. In this next section I explore the impact of political connections and the size of the firm.

Better to Be Big or Connected?

To gain additional leverage on the importance of political connections for property rights, I also created a hypothetical scenario that explored whether respondents believed that state courts of arbitration were more biased in favor of large or politically connected firms. I am especially interested in whether respondents believe it is better to be big or politically connected.

Interviewers asked:

Let's say that your firm fulfilled a large order worth about 10 percent of your annual revenue for a [small company with about 100 employees/a

---

[31] This comparison between courts and negotiations does not take advantage of randomization to control for unobserved heterogeneity. I simply compare the responses to the two questions asking about the perceived effectiveness of negotiations and courts to resolve the same dispute.

large company with about 3,000 employees]. The buyer paid 50 percent in advance, but is now refusing to pay the rest of the bill because it claims that the product is defective. You are sure that the product is in good working order. [XXX[32]/In addition, the buyer firm has close relations with the local regional government.]

What do you think, can your firm defend its legal interests by negotiating with this company, without turning to courts?
1) no   2) likely no   3) likely yes   4) yes   5) hard to say

What do you think, can your firm defend its legal interests by turning to the state courts of arbitration?
1) no   2) likely no   3) likely yes   4) yes   5) hard to say

First, I discuss the impact of firm size and political connections on perceptions of property rights in this dispute when the respondent uses only negotiations. Looking across row one in Table 4.6 suggests that respondents perceive political connections as having a strong impact on the usefulness of negotiations for protecting property rights when the firm is small. The difference in responses in disputes with "small" partners who are well connected and with "small" partners who are not is 32 percentage points (t = 2.8, p = .01). There is a 15 percentage point drop in row two when respondents are told that the large firm has good political connections with the regional government (t = 1.57, p = .12). This drop is large, but not quite statistically significant.

The size of the firm also matters, but only when respondents are not given information about the political connections of the other firm. In column one, when respondents face a large firm rather than a small firm they are about 18 percentage points (2.70–2.52) less likely to believe that negotiations can protect their property rights but this effect vanishes in column two when comparing responses when the small and large firms have good political connections with the regional government (2.38 versus 2.37).

The raw data behind these responses indicate that 60 percent of respondents said that they could use negotiations to defend their legal interests if the opposite party was small, but this figure fell by 14 percentage points if this small firm was also well connected with

---

[32] The XXX indicates that respondents received no information about the firm's relations with the regional government.

Table 4.6 *Better to be Big or Connected: Using Only Negotiations*

	No Information (C1)	Good Connections (C2)	Difference (C1-C2) (se) t-test
Small Firm	2.70	2.38	.32**
(R1)	(.60)	(.89)	(.10)
	n = 106	n = 103	t = 2.81
Large Firm	2.52	2.37	.15
(R2)	(.78)	(.75)	(.11)
	n = 109	n = 106	t = 1.57
Difference	.18*	.01	
(R1-R2)	(.10)	(.12)	
t-test (se)	t = 1.72	t = .09	

$*$ p<.10, $**$ p<.05, and $***$ p<.01. Mean response to each of the four conditions where 1 = no, 2 = more or less no, 3 = more or less yes, 4 = yes. Standard deviation in parentheses. n = number of observations. Differences report standard error in parentheses. Data from 2008 survey.

the regional authorities. Forty-nine percent of respondents said that they could protect their rights using negotiations without turning to courts if their counterparty was big, but this figure falls by 6 percentage points if the big firm is perceived to be well connected with the regional government.

Responses about the perceived effectiveness of courts in a dispute present a similar but more precisely drawn picture. Rows one and two in Table 4.7 indicates that telling respondents that the other firm had good connections with the regional government induced a drop of 21 percentage points in their confidence that courts could protect their property rights (3.28 versus 3.07) and a 19 percentage point drop if the firm was large (3.07 versus 2.87). Looking down columns one and two reveals that moving from a small to a large firm induces a change of 21 percentage points when no additional information is provided about the rival's political connections (3.28 versus 3.07) and a 20 percentage point drop when they are told that the other firm has good relations with the regional government (3.07 versus 2.87).

It is not surprising that firms on good terms with the regional government are expected to get better treatment. More interesting is the

Table 4.7 *Better to be Big or Connected: Using Courts*

	No Information (C1)	Good Connections (C2)	Difference (C1-C2) (se) t-test
Small Firm (R1)	3.28 (.60) n = 106	3.07 (.68) n = 101	.21** (.10) t = 2.36
Big Firm (R2)	3.07 (.67) n = 104	2.87 (.77) n = 108	.19* (.10) t = 1.91
Difference (R1-R2) t-test (se)	.21** (.09) t = 2.39	.20* (.09) t = 1.89	

*p<.10, ** p<.05, and *** p<.01. Mean response to each of the four conditions where 1 = no, 2 = more or less no, 3 = more or less yes, 4 = yes. Standard deviation in parentheses. n = number of observations. Differences report standard error in parentheses. Data from 2008 survey.

perceived size of the improvements, which are substantial, particularly in disputes with small firms. For example, when businesspeople were told that the disputant had only 100 employees, 81 percent of respondents said that the courts could protect their rights. However, when told that the disputant also had good relations with the regional government, this figure declined by nine percentage points. To put the size of this nine-percentage point decrease in perspective, it is equal to the change produced by being a firm with 3000 workers rather than 100 workers.

Finally, comparing responses to similar questions in Tables 4.6 and 4.7 indicates that under these conditions, respondents perceive courts as better able to protect their property rights than negotiations. When told that the opposing firm was small and had good connections with the regional government, respondents rated courts 69 percentage points higher than negotiations (3.07 for courts versus 2.38 for negotiations). When respondents were told that the firm was large and were given no addition informational, they rated courts 55 percentage points higher than negotiations (3.07 versus 2.52). Similar differences are reported in the other two conditions as well.

At least in this simple comparison of responses, respondents perceived using courts to be more effective than using only negotiations to resolve this particular type of dispute.

Several conclusions follow from these analyses. Political connections to the regional governor are perceived to be an important asset during a dispute, but the facts of the case also matter. As in other countries, larger firms are also perceived to do better in court (Galanter 1975). Respondents appear to believe that having the facts on your side or having greater resources can offset the importance of political connections, particularly in court. Respondents appear to have greater faith that courts can protect their property rights than negotiations alone.

Types of Connection

Previous analyses have focused on perceptions of connections with regional governors as a means of protecting property rights, but certainly governors are not the only source of political connections in Russia. As noted in the first two chapters, the security services (*siloviki*), including the Investigative Committee, the FSB, and the police are important economic players as well. The next two survey experiments explore how ties to the security services shape perceptions of property rights.

In the first scenario, interviewers asked firm managers whether they would be willing to accept an offer from a firm with which they had not worked before and varied the political connections of the seller firm. Twenty five percent of respondents were randomly selected to receive no additional information about the seller. Interviewers told another quarter of randomly selected respondents that the seller firm had good relations with the security forces. In a similar fashion, interviewers told the final two groups that the seller had good relations with the governor of the region and with influential business elites in the region. I am interested in learning whether having good ties with the security services gave firms an advantage in everyday trading whether or not a dispute occurred.

More specifically interviewers asked:

Let's say that your firm received an offer for a product that you needed whose price was 10 percent less than the market price from a company that you had not worked with before from another region in Russia.

1) No additional information
2) In addition, it is well known that the head (owner) of the other firm is well connected with the governor of your region.
3) In addition, it is well known that the head (owner) of the other firm has good relations with the representatives of the security forces (*siloviki*) in your region.
4) In addition, it is well known that the head (owner) of the supplier company has good relations with influential businesspeople in your region.

On a scale of 1–5, about how likely is that you would accept this offer?
1) Very unlikely (0%)
2) Unlikely (25%)
3) Fifty-fifty (50%)
4) Likely (75%)
5) Very likely (100%)

In the first version of the question, respondents received no additional information about the supplier and the average response was 3.15, indicating that respondents were just about as likely to accept as reject the offer. When told that the supplier was well connected to the security services, the average response was essentially the same (3.09). This suggests that in the course of ordinary "trucking and trading" the perception of having ties to the security forces is not especially valuable.

Telling respondents that the supplier firm had good ties with the governor had essentially no impact on the likelihood of accepting the offer (3.25). Only telling respondents that the supplier firm had good relations with an influential businessperson had a marginally significant impact on the acceptance rate. The average response to this version of the question was 3.35 (t = 1.91). When compared to the responses of those who received no additional information about the seller, this response is significant at the .10 level. This difference suggests the importance of informal relationships for ordinary firms in Russia engaged in everyday transactions.

However, ties to the security forces emerge as an important consideration once a conflict ensues. In the second experimental question reported in Table 4.9, I describe a typical business conflict and varied the characteristics of their trading partner. In the first condition, one quarter of the respondents were randomly chosen to receive no

Table 4.8 *The Value of Connections Before a Dispute*

	Mean (s.d.) N	Difference compared to no information case t-stat
No additional information	3.15 (1.14) n = 204	
Seller has good ties with governor	3.25 (1.15) n = 189	.10 t = .95
Seller has good ties with *siloviki* (security forces)	3.09 (1.04) n = 203	–.06 t = .46
Seller has good ties with influential businesspeople in your region	3.35* (1.11) n = 199	.20* t = 1.91

* p<.10, ** p<.05, and *** p<.01. Mean Response to question "How likely would you be to accept the offer on a scale of 1–5?" where 1 = almost zero and five equals almost 100 percent. Standard deviations in parentheses. n = number of observations in each group. Data from 2011 survey.

additional information about the buyer. But in the other cases, I varied whether the seller had good connections with the governor of the region, the security services, or influential businesspeople in the region. More precisely, interviewers asked:

Let's say that your firm (organization) has become involved in a dispute with another firm. Your company received payment for a good or service, but the other firm says that the product was defective. You are sure that the product or service was in good working order. The other firm is threatening to go to court.

1) no additional information
2) In addition, you have information that the head (owner) of the other firm has good relations with the governor of your region.
3) In addition, you have information that the head (owner) of the other firm has good relations with influential businesspeople in the region.
4) In addition, you have information that the head (owner) of the other firm has good relations with the security forces.

Table 4.9 *The Value of Connections During a Dispute*

	Mean (s.d.) N	Difference compared to no information case t-test
No additional information	3.44 (.97) n = 199	–
Buyer firm has good ties with *siloviki* (security forces)	3.22 (1.11) n = 203	–.22** t = 2.11
Buyer firm has good ties with governor	3.26 (1.04) n = 198	–.18* t = 1.77
Buyer firm has good ties with influential businesspeople	3.32 (1.07) n = 196	–.12 t = 1.07

* p<.10, ** p<.05, and *** p<.01. Mean Response to question: "About how confident are you that your company can defend its interests by going to court?" 1 = Very unlikely (0%), 2 = Unlikely (25%), 3 = Fifty-fifty (50%), 4 = Likely (75%), 5 = Very Likely (100%). Standard deviation in parentheses. n = number of observations. Data from 2011 survey.

About how confident are you that your company can defend its interests by going to court?
Very unlikely (0%)
Unlikely (25%)
Fifty-fifty (50%)
Likely (75%)
Very Likely (100%)

In the baseline case where firms received no additional information about their trading partner, most firms were cautiously optimistic that they could use the courts to defend their interests in condition. In this case, the average response was 3.44. When told that the buyer had good relations with the security forces, the average response fell significantly to 3.23 (t = 2.02 versus the baseline). Once a dispute has emerged, having good ties with the security services is perceived to be a valuable bargaining chip. Similarly, when a trading partner has good ties with the regional governor, respondents were far less confident that courts could protect their property. The average response to this version of the question was 3.26 (t = 1.78 versus the baseline condition of receiving no information). Finally, whether or not the buyer had good relations with influential businesspeople in the region had little impact on perceptions of the capacity of the court to protect the respondent's property. To give some sense of the magnitude of these drops, in the baseline condition 45 percent of respondents said that they were at least 50 percent certain they could recoup their losses by using the courts, but this figure falls to 39 percent when respondents were told that the buyer has good connections with the security forces.

Caveats

The responses in these survey experiments can be critiqued for lacking external validity as they are generally asking businesspeople hypothetical questions about their expected behavior rather than directly measuring their actual behavior in a business conflict. These analyses do not explore precisely how respondents believe that they can use courts to protect their rights. Respondents may believe that courts can protect their rights, but only if they pay bribes, but this possibility is difficult to address. The analyses in the survey experiments capture respondents' perceptions rather than objective reality, but these perceptions are important as expectations about the performance of institutions and how other players will respond help to make up the rules of the game for doing business in Russia. Finally, in the survey experiments I examine how businesspeople perceive the effectiveness of negotiations and courts to protect property rights in specific types of dispute between firms. Whether or not these responses generalize to other types of dispute is an open question.

Yet, using survey experiments with hypothetical situations has several appealing qualities. First, it is difficult to measure political connections given incentives to hide these relations. Second, analyzing court cases raises selection bias because only certain types of firm and certain types of dispute end up in courts. The threat of using courts may influence behavior even when courts are not used. Analyzing solely those cases that went to court not only raises selection issues, it also misses the impact of courts on those who have not used them. By asking all respondents about their perception of the court and how it might influence their behavior, we are able to recapture information that is lost when we only analyze firms that have experienced disputes. Finally, these questions are less threatening than asking about personal experiences and may produce greater veracity in the responses.

Conclusion

State institutions, such as courts, are central to protecting property rights, but are very difficult to build. In this chapter, I focused on the arbitration courts and explored the strategies of firms in resolving mundane disputes. These disputes rarely make headlines, but are the stuff of everyday economic life in Russia. Moreover, how businesspeople choose to resolve these disputes will go some way toward determining whether judges or the security services play an expanded role in Russia's economic future.

In the surveys from 2005, 2008, and 2011, businesspeople reported relying heavily on courts and negotiations to resolve disputes, but also turning to state security forces in a not trivial percentage of disputes. In addition, businesspeople reported that when a dispute occurred state courts of arbitration performed relatively well.

In a number of survey experiments businesspeople perceived that political connections to the regional government were valuable tools during disputes. This is hardly news. But the analysis also provides a rough measure of how important political connections are seen to be relative to other factors, such as the size of the firm and the quality of the case. The survey experiments also suggest that respondents perceive the impact of political connections as especially important when disputes are resolved informally. Finally, and in contrast to the conventional wisdom, respondents also perceived that the strength of one's case has an important impact on the capacity of the courts to defend property rights. Respondents perceive that it is important to have the facts of the case on your side as well as to have friends in high places. This view is at odds with much research on courts in Russia, which emphasizes the importance of personal connections with state officials, economic power, and a willingness to pay bribes.

More generally, the results indicate a high degree of dualism in the Russian legal system at least during the period under study. Arbitration courts that handle business disputes are perceived to work better than courts of general jurisdiction that handle criminal cases. Mundane business cases are handled relatively well, while high-stakes political cases are not. If property rights in Russia were primarily a function of a weak state or Russian culture as argued in Holmes (1996) or Newcity (1997), we would not see that great heterogeneity in performance in legal institutions and types of court case. It is easier to understand this legal dualism as a function of politics (Holmes 2003). In this view, politicians may prefer a legal dualism that allows them to intervene selectively in the judiciary to reward supporters and punish opponents when needed, but also gives right-holders some confidence that their rights will be respected in more mundane cases. This allows right-holders to use their assets productively when they do not challenge interests of the ruler, while also generating tax revenue for the ruler.

Moreover, changes in the outlines of the court system and the power of judges over time in Russia provides further support for the political roots of legal dualism. As depicted earlier in this chapter reforms to the courts in Russia have tended to follow the political calendar as each new president sought to leave their trace on the judicial system. This temporal pattern of reform fits poorly with the view that property rights in Russia are merely a "halfway house" between communism and capitalism, a function of a weak state, or a result of Russian culture. Examining the changes in the levels of subservience of courts of arbitration over time, the differences in the relative performance of the arbitration courts and the general courts, and the role of political connections in the survey experiments indicate that the broad patterns of legal dualism in postcommunist Russia stem from changes in the bargaining power of the ruler and the right-holders.

In addition, this legal dualism suggests the value of viewing property rights as a private rather than solely public good. One traditional interpretation of property rights emphasizes that they are a public good produced by rulers to encourage productive economic activity and increase tax revenue (Pejovich 1998). Rulers have an economic incentive to bolster property rights and, over time, rulers who fail to do so will be replaced by more efficient competitors. This is a helpful simplification in many political economy models, but also obscures the political roots of property rights, which are often granted and enforced on political rather than economic grounds. To the extent that rulers can ration property rights in various degrees according to specific features of the dispute and those involved, it is especially helpful to view property rights as private goods.

5 | Reputation and the Rule of Law

Who steals my purse steals trash; 'tis something, nothing;
'Twas mine, 'tis his, and has been slave to thousands;
But he that filches from me my good name
Robs me of that which not enriches him
And makes me poor indeed.

William Shakespeare, Othello, Act Three (3.3.180–186)

I don't give a damn 'bout my reputation.

Joan Jett, "Bad Reputation"

Of course, courts are not the only institution that businesspeople in Russia use to protect property rights. As in all countries, businesspeople rely on a rich array of informal institutions that do not require enforcement by the state to guard their property. Concerns for reputation, ethnicity, cross-cutting social ties, and civic associations can promote stronger property rights without right-holders having to rely on state-backed coercion for enforcement. Scholars of postcommunism have forcefully argued for the importance of informal institutions in protecting property and promoting trade in the region (Gerber and Kharkhodin 1994; Frye 2000; Gaddy and Ickes 2002; Pyle 2005; Ledeneva 2006). Yet, there is still much to learn. What role do informal institutions, such as reputation, and formal institutions, such as courts, play in protecting property?[1] How valuable is a good reputation relative to other forms of protecting property rights? Is word of mouth or press coverage a more potent source for reputation? Does a concern for reputation or confidence in the courts provide stronger incentives to trade? Do informal institutions that promote trade undermine or underpin state institutions?

---

[1] Less benignly, mafia-like private protection organizations are another informal institution used to protect property. See Hendley et al. (2000); Frye and Zhuravskaya (2000); Varese (2002); Volkov (2002); and Frye (2002).

Answers to these questions have important implications for transition and developing countries where many have cited weak institutions – both formal and informal – as a primary obstacle to economic development and political stability. Some argue that informal institutions, such as trust, social networks, and reputations are essential to protecting property (Macauley 1963; DeSoto 1989; Putnam 1993). Even the most capable state lacks the resources to resolve every dispute over property rights, and most states in the developing and transitional world are quite incapable. Informal institutions fill in the gaps where the state does not provide protection, allowing right-holders to protect their property. Others, however, suggest that formal institutions are central to protecting property rights (North 1981; Rauch and Evans 2000). State-backed adjudication and enforcement provides economies of scope and scale that informal institutions simply cannot match.

These questions also inform a central debate on state/society relations. Some argue that trust-based social networks that rely on reputation sap the ability of state agents to collect taxes, deliver justice, and provide public goods (Migdal 1988). Others claim that strong networks based on social trust are the key to improving the quality of governance by state officials (Putnam 1993).

To enter into these debates, I embedded experimental questions in three surveys of businesspeople conducted in Russia and I present four results, each of which has wider implications for the study of development and Russia. First, reputation provides a powerful stimulus to trade. More precisely, a good reputation provides a greater boost to trade than does a 15 percent discount in price. Moreover, the costs of having a bad reputation appear to be much larger than the benefits of having a good reputation. Many studies recognize that informal institutions and good reputations are central to trade in Russia and other developing economies, but this chapter identifies the magnitude of the impact of reputation on the security of property, and thereby more precisely measures the value of this important informal institution. Moreover, many studies of informal institutions fail to control for other factors that may be correlated with both the quality of institutions and the observed behavior. For example, close personal ties may lead businesspeople to engage in trade, but these ties may be correlated with other factors, such as a good reputation or geographic location, that make these businesses likely to trade with each other.

Second, "word of mouth" and the "local press" are equally power-ful in conveying information about a firm's reputation. Many argue that personal networks in Russia are important as a source of cred-ible information about everyday social and business practices, but this finding suggests that businesspeople in Russia perceive the coun-try's oft-maligned newspapers as a valuable source of information (Ledeneva 2006).

Third, state-run courts can improve property rights by promot-ing trade between firms, but the evidence here is mixed. The survey experiments suggest that if firms have used courts successfully in the past, businesspeople expect them to be more likely to take the risky step of trading with a new partner. At least in the run-of-the-mill trades between firms analyzed here, the state courts of arbitra-tion are perceived to work relatively well. However, courts appear to have little direct effect on decisions to give credit to buyers or suppliers.

Fourth, having established the importance of reputation for trade in hypothetical questions embedded in survey experiments, I explore how reputation works in practice by turning to a multivariate analysis of reported firm behavior. In my analyses, a good reputation has a signifi-cant and positive impact on the decision to give credit – an important indicator of the security of property rights. In addition, strong courts amplify the effect of reputation under some conditions. When courts are perceived to work well, some forms of reputation are a more effec-tive means of protecting property, which suggests that reputation and courts are complements rather than substitutes. However, this result from the regression analysis of decisions to give credit is offset by the survey experiments, which find no evidence that reputation and courts are substitutes or complements.[2] Thus, one should be cautious in mak-ing strong claims about the interaction of informal and formal institu-tions based on these results. Perhaps the best one can say is that there is no evidence of a substitution effect between formal and informal institutions, weak evidence of complementarity, but most likely there is no strong interaction between reputation and courts on decisions to trade in the cases at hand.

---

[2] The survey experiments only focus on the perceived ability of the courts and reputation to promote trade prior to a dispute and say nothing about whether courts and reputation are substitutes or complements after a dispute occurs.

Formal and Informal Institutions

The exchange of goods and money invariably creates a problem. Unless goods are exchanged simultaneously and quality can be determined on the spot, the party who gives up control of their assets first becomes vulnerable to breach. Sellers who receive payment may abscond with the funds without delivering the good, while buyers who receive the good before payment may decline to send the money. As each party can anticipate the other's behavior, both sides are likely to decline to trade and miss an opportunity for potential gains.[3] To capture these gains societies have developed a rich variety of formal and informal institutions that sharpen incentives to trade. Countries that create institutions to prevent disputes and promote trade most efficiently have typically been at the frontier of economic development (North 1990; Knack and Keefer 1995; Acemoglu, Johnson, and Robinson 2001). All societies rely on a mix of formal and informal institutions to promote these types of exchange and scholars debate the relative importance of each. Formal institutions have the advantage of economies of scope and scale in organizing the coercion necessary to sanction violators of property rights. Few dispute that the development of capable public institutions such as the state is central to economic development (North 1981).

Because even the best-governed state lacks the resources to resolve every potential dispute, informal solutions to protecting property and promoting trade are widespread (Macauley 1963). Geertz (1978) identifies information relayed through gossip and social sanctions as critical to promoting trade in the bazaars of Morocco. Williamson (1985) argues that private firms have considerable scope in designing bilateral private institutions to support trade without recourse to state institutions. Others point to social networks, business organizations, professional associations, and ethnic networks that provide means to sanction non-compliance and thereby promote cooperation without relying on the state for enforcement (Granovetter 1985; Milgrom et al. 1990; Ellickson, 1991; Ostrom 1990; Bernstein 1992; McMillan and Woodruff 1999).[4]

---

[3] The famous debate over the timing of the payment and receipt of the chair in Ilf and Petrov's classic *Twelve Chairs* highlights this problem. "*Den'gi utrom i stulia vecherom?*" ("Payment in the morning, chairs in the evening?")

[4] Elsewhere in Eastern Europe Stark (1996) and McDermott (2002) emphasize the role of social networks.

Such informal mechanisms may have advantages over public institu-tions, particularly where the latter function poorly. Market participants may have more expertise than judges and they can take advantage of information that cannot be used in court (Charny 1990; Johnson et al. 2002b: 229). Over the long run the state offers economies of scope and scale that informal institutions cannot match, but which is a more potent stimulus to trade in a given setting is not immediately clear.

Observers of Russia have contributed to this debate. Some have identified trading networks based on long-standing social ties and a concern for reputation as key factors in maintaining production and trade (Gerber and Kharkhodin 1994; Sedaitis 1994; Ledeneva 1998; 2006; Hendley et al. 2000; 2001; Frye 2000; Gaddy and Ickes 2002; Pyle 2005; Raiser et al. 2007). Others have found that state courts in Russia are used more frequently and are more effective than is com-monly appreciated (Hendley et al. 2000; 2001; Shvets 2005; 2013; Simachev 2003; Hendley 2004; but see Hellman et al. 2003; Burger 2004; and Ledeneva 2013). As in other settings, however, there is con-siderable debate about which is more important in protecting rights to trade.

Institutions as Substitutes

Another important debate examines the interrelationship between informal and formal mechanisms for preventing disputes and pro-moting trade. One view argues that informal and formal institutions serve as substitutes. A reliance on informal institutions "crowds out" demand for formal state institutions and reduces the resources avail-able to state agents (Frey 1997). When businesspeople in the private sector can overcome the problems that plague trade using informal means, such as reputation or trust, they express less demand for capa-ble state institutions.[5] Rather than devoting resources to develop the state, businesspeople invest in the creation of powerful private organi-zations to support trade. Bernstein (1992) finds that diamond trad-ers in the tight-knit community of Orthodox Jews in New York City

[5] This is a common assumption in models of public goods production that require economic agents to invest in either the formal or informal economy. Investing in the formal economy generates a good equilibrium where firms pay taxes and use courts, while investing in the informal economy leads firms to avoid taxes and use private protection rackets. See Johnson et al. (1997).

opposed state regulation even when offered and instead preferred to rely on private means to resolve disputes. Ellickson (1991) argues that ranchers and farmers in Shasta County California used informal understandings of the law rather than formal institutions to resolve disputes. In this view, powerful social networks reduce demand for state institutions that resolve disputes.

On a macro-level, some argue that countries with strong social institutions that provide many forms of public goods have difficulty developing capable states. Most prominently, Migdal (1988) characterizes these polities as having "strong societies and weak states." States and social organizations consistently compete for the authority to make rules for society and where social organizations are imbued with dense networks of trust they may have advantages over the state. Thus, the micro-level decision studied here may have implications for larger processes at the level of the state and society. The substitution argument suggests that strong informal institutions that support trade should be associated with weak state institutions and vice versa.

Institutions as Complements

A competing argument suggests that informal and formal institutions are complements. That is, strengthening one increases demand for the other. Strong informal institutions and strong formal institutions go hand in hand in promoting trade. North (1990: 46) argues that "public rules can complement and increase the effectiveness of private constraints." More broadly, capable state institutions may make reputation and social trust more effective by sharing information about other social actors (Levi 1998; Frye 2000). Moreover, strong social institutions that rely on reputation may help private agents overcome collective action problems and hold public officials accountable and thereby increase the effectiveness of state institutions (Putnam 1993). Finally, capable private institutions that support trade may ease the burden on state officials by reducing the number of disputes that end up in court. This view suggests that the development of informal and formal institutions should be mutually reinforcing (Putnam 1993).

The relationship between informal and formal institutions has important ramifications for understanding the development of state capacity. If the use of reputation to promote social cooperation underpins state capacity, then it may be worthwhile to use scarce foreign aid to develop social organizations that promote trust and transmit information about reputation. If, however, a reliance on networks of reputation to support trade undermines state capacity, then such strategies require difficult decisions about the trade-offs between strengthening formal and informal institutions.[6]

Given the importance of the issue and the advantages of studying it in a transition setting, it is not surprising that scholars of Russia have begun to explore this topic. Hendley et al. (2000) conducted an innovative study of 328 business managers in six cities in Russia in 1997, which explored their strategies for resolving disputes. Respondents were asked to rate the "importance of each of the following methods for your firm" for resolving disputes on a scale of 1–10 where the rating should "reflect both the frequency of use and effectiveness" of the different mechanisms. Respondents rated negotiations as a 7.39 and arbitration courts as a 5.40 on this ten-point scale. The authors note that three-quarters (76.4%) of firms facing disputes with suppliers used negotiations to help resolve the dispute, and about one-quarter (25.5%) turned to state arbitration courts. In addition, they found little evidence of complementarities among negotiations, private meetings between firm representatives, and the use of courts.[7] Johnson et al. (2002a) in a 1997 study of 1500 medium-size manufacturing firms in five postcommunist countries observe that informal institutions such as personal relationships are a predominant form of contracting, but that courts play a critical role in promoting trade as well. In a related work based on the same survey, Johnson et al. (2002b) found that social networks and gossip substitute for public legal institutions, but that business networks and trade associations complement public legal institutions. Pyle (2005) uses data from the Johnson et al. survey to find that business organizations help resolve contracting problems, particularly when trading partners are located in other regions. In a study of five markets in Moscow in the 1990s, Frye (2000) finds that when state policy lowered the costs of sharing information sufficiently, brokers created organizations that relied on reputation to support exchange and served as substitutes for state courts.

[6] Laboratory experiments also assess the impact of formal and informal institutions on the propensity to trade (Lazzarini et al. 2004).

[7] Hendley and Murrell (2003) repeated this question in a study of 254 companies in Romania in 2001 and, again, found little evidence of complementarities among formal and informal institutions.

The Value of Reputation

Focusing on reputation and courts in Russia is important because, as we saw in the last chapter, businesspeople rely heavily on both bilateral negotiations and courts to help resolve disputes. Indeed, businesspeople in Russia report using these methods far more than any others. I explore the value of a good reputation relative to a deep discount in sale price in a survey of 666 businesspeople conducted in 2005. In this experimental design, I create four slightly different versions of the question and randomly assign respondents to questions. Half the managers were asked whether they would accept an offer to buy a good at a price five percent below the market price, and half were offered the same good at a 20 percent discount relative to the market price. In addition, half the managers were told that the seller had a good reputation and half were given no additional information about the reputation of the seller. This set-up allows us to compare the relative impact of a reputation for honesty relative to not having any information about the reputation of a trading partner. In addition, it permits comparison of the importance of reputation relative to a steep discount in price. More specifically interviewers asked:

Reputation and Price Discounts

Let's say that a firm with which you had not worked before offered to sell you a high quality product at a price [5/20] percent lower than the market price and asked for 50 percent prepayment.[XXX/ **In addition this firm has a good reputation in the region in that it almost always fulfills its contractual obligations.**][8] Would your firm be willing to accept this offer?

1) No   2) Probably No   3) Probably Yes   4) Yes

Table 5.1 reports the percentage of respondents willing to accept the offer under the four experimental conditions.

Having a good reputation is a valuable asset. A seller with a good reputation can increase the percentage of buyers accepting her offer of a 5 percent discount to the market price by 25 percentage points compared to a similar offer made by a seller about whose reputation is little known (3.07 versus 2.82). In addition, with a price 20 percent

---

[8] Here XXX indicates that the respondent does not receive any information about the seller's reputation.

Table 5.1 *The Value of Reputation*

	No Information About Buyer's Reputation C1	Buyer has a Good Reputation C2	Difference (C1-C2) (se) t-test
5 percent discount (R1)	2.82 (.83) n = 107	3.07 (.92) n = 123	.25** (.12) t = 2.04
20 percent discount (R2)	2.78 (.92) n = 103	3.11 (.68) n = 136	.33** (.10) t = 3.19
Difference (R1-R2) (se) t-stat	−.04 (.03) t = .31	.04 (.10) t = .40	

* $p<.10$, ** $p<.05$, and *** $p<.01$. Mean responses where 1 = no, 2 = probably no, 3 = probably yes and 4 = yes,. Standard deviation in parentheses n = number of observations. Differences report standard errors in parentheses. Data from 2005 survey.

lower than the market price, a seller with a good reputation can increase the number of buyers accepting the offer by 33 percentage points (3.11 versus 2.78).

It is interesting that when information about the reputation of the seller is not provided reducing the price from five to 20 percent below the market does not lead to more acceptances of the offer as indicated in column 2 (2.82 versus 2.78). The same result obtains when the seller has a good reputation. Buyers are much more likely to accept the offer, but the difference in price produces almost no difference in response (3.07 versus 3.11). It seems that a discount of 20 percent to the market, if anything, produces skepticism about the credibility of the offer and reduces the likelihood that a buyer will accept. Thus, having a good reputation is a more potent stimulus to trade than is a discount of 15 percent of the market price. Finally that such a steep discount in price even produces such a small change in the acceptance rate even when the seller has a good reputation, suggests that market relations in Russia still leave much to be desired.

Sources of Information on Reputation

There is considerable agreement that reputation is an important factor in promoting trade in Russia and other developing economies, but less is known about how different sources of information about a reputation influence outcomes. To explore this issue, I conducted an experiment that manipulates whether the source of information about a firm's reputation is "the local press" or an "old business acquaintance." Much work on Russia emphasizes the importance of personal contacts for engaging in trade, but we have little evidence comparing the relative importance of these personal relationships with other sources of information. I also manipulated whether the information conveyed led the respondent to believe that the seller had either a good or a bad reputation for abiding by its contractual obligations. More directly, interviewers asked:

Gossip, the Press, and Reputation

Let's say that a company from another region with whom you had not worked before offered to sell you a product that you need for 10 percent less than the market price. Recently you learned [in the **local press/from an old business acquaintance**] that the company had [**always/not always**] fulfilled its obligations to other firms in your region. Would your firm accept this offer?
1) No   2) Probably No   3) Probably Yes   4) Yes

The results from Table 5.2 indicate somewhat surprisingly that "the local press" and "an old business acquaintance" are equally powerful sources of information about a firm's reputation. When the seller has a bad reputation and the source of information about the reputation is the local press, only 16 percent of respondents accepted the offer, but this figure was only 15 percent when the source of information was an old business acquaintance. Similarly, there are only minor differences in the acceptance rate when the seller has a good reputation (67 percent for the local press versus 69 percent for an old business acquaintance).

Regardless of the source, sellers with a good reputation were far more likely to have their offer accepted than sellers with a bad reputation (2.98 versus 1.82 if the source is the local press and 3.06 versus 1.86 if the source is an old business acquaintance). The impact of reputation here is much larger than in the preceding experiment. This may be a reflection of the comparison group. In this experiment, the

Table 5.2 *The Sources of Reputation*

	Bad Reputation (C1)	Good Reputation (C2)	Difference (C1-C2) (se) t-stat
Local Press (R1)	1.82 (.74) n = 112	2.98 (.80) n = 101	1.16*** (.10) t = 11.00
Old Business Acquaintance (R2)	1.86 (.77) n = 114	3.06 (.80) n = 108	1.20*** (.10) t = 11.39
Difference (R1-R2) (se) t-stat	.04 (.10) t = .40	.08 (.11) t = .72	

* p<.10, ** p<.05, and *** p<.01. Mean responses where 1 = no, 2 = probably no, 3 = probably yes and 4 = yes. Standard deviation in parentheses. n = number of observations. Differences report standard errors in parentheses. Data from 2005 survey.

impact of a seller with a good reputation is relative to a seller with a bad reputation, but in the preceding experiment the impact of a seller with a good reputation is relative to a seller having no reputation. This suggests that the costs of having a bad reputation far outweigh the benefits of having a good reputation.

Business Associations, Reputation, and Trade

I also explore the extent to which membership in a prominent business association can increase the propensity to trade. The focus is slightly different than in the preceding examples. If previous questions concerned features specific to a firm, in this case reputation attaches to all members of the business association. In this manipulation, some respondents were told that the buyer is a member of the Russian Union of Industrialists and Entrepreneurs (RUIE), the most prominent business association in Russia, while others received no information about the membership status of the buyer. In addition, respondents were told that the potential buyer was either from the respondent's region or from another region. Pyle (2005) argues that business associations are

Table 5.3 *The Benefits of Membership*

	No information about membership (C1)	Member of Russian Union of Industrialists and Entrepreneurs (C2)	Difference (C1-C2) (se) t-stat
Another Region	2.85	3.12	.27**
(R1)	(.81)	(.78)	(.11)
	n = 105	n = 102	t = 2.44
Firm's own Region	2.73	2.96	.23*
(R2)	(.95)	(.87)	(.12)
	n = 104	n = 117	t = 1.88
Difference (R1-R2)	.12	.16	
(se) t-stat	(.12)	(.11)	
	t = .98	t = 1.42	

* p<.10, ** p<.05, and *** p<.01. Mean responses where 1 = no, 2 = probably no, 3 = probably yes and 4 = yes. Standard deviation in parentheses. n = number of observations. Differences report standard errors in parentheses. Data from 2008 survey.

especially valuable in promoting trade across regions. To assess these arguments, interviewers asked:

Business Associations and Trade
Let's say that a firm from [**your/another**] region is planning to place a large order (about 20 percent of your annual sales) with your firm at the market price and offers to pay 50 percent up front and pay the rest two months after it receives the product. [**XXX**[9]/**The company is a member of the RUIE (the Russian Union of Industrialists and Entrepreneurs**). Would your firm be willing to accept this offer? 1) No   2) Probably No   3) Probably Yes   4) Yes

Table 5.3 indicates that being a member of a prominent business association (the RUIE) significantly increases the likelihood that the respondent will accept the offer. If the buyer is from another region,

---

[9] The XXX indicates that respondents received no information about whether the company is a member of the RUIE.

being a member of the RUIE increases the likelihood that the respondent will accept the offer by 16 percentage points (74 percent versus
58 percent). If the buyer is from the respondent's region, the increase
is 20 percentage points (71 percent versus 51 percent). This indicates
that membership in the RUIE can play a signal role in promoting trade
regardless of whether the trading partner is from a firm's own region.
This result again illustrates the value of private solutions to the problem of trade in Russia.

One would expect that firms would prefer to trade with a partner from their own region to reduce transaction costs and to benefit
from local knowledge, but that does not appear to be the case, as in
this experiment respondents were on average no more likely to prefer
trading with a firm from their region. In column 1, firms were just
as likely to prefer trading with a firm outside their region as with
one from within their region (2.85 versus 2.73). When the potential
trading partner was a member of the RUIE, as reported in column 2,
respondents were slightly more likely to prefer trading with a firm
from another region, although this difference was not statistically significant (3.12 versus 2.96, t = 1.42, p = .16)

Substitutes or Complements

Thus far the experiments have explored how various features of reputation and the specific features of the trade shape propensity to trade,
but have not yet explored whether informal or formal institutions are
substitutes or complements. In experiment 5.4, I explored the relative
impact of reputation and the use of courts on the propensity to trade
by manipulating the reputation of the buyer and the ability of the
seller to use the courts. Interviewers asked each respondent one of the
four versions of the following experiment.

Substitutes or Complements
Let's say that a retail trading company is planning to place a large
order at a large manufacturing company at an acceptable price. The
retail trading company has a [**good reputation in the region in that
it always fulfills its contracts/a bad reputation in that doesn't always
fulfill its contracts**].
What do you think, will the manufacturing firm accept this order bearing in mind that it has almost [**always/never**] been able to use the

state courts of arbitration to protect its interests? If yes, then with what conditions?

1. Refuse the order
2. Accept the order with conditions, such as prepayment or credit check
If prepayment, then how much? ___
Only with credit check
3. Accept the order without conditions

Interpreting the answers requires some clarification given the variance in the size of prepayment requested by the manufacturing firm. I code requests for prepayment greater than 50 percent as equivalent to "refusing the offer" as this indicates that the seller is unwilling to assume the bulk of the risk of engaging in this trade.[10] Requests for prepayment less than 50 percent and acceptances pending a credit check are treated as conditionally accepting the deal as in these cases the seller is vulnerable to breach by the buyer. Table 5.4 reports the raw responses for each of the four different versions of the question. For example, in the best-case scenario reported in condition 1 in which the buyer has a good reputation and the seller has almost always used the courts successfully in the past, 20 percent of respondents rejected the offer outright, while most of the respondents (60 percent) accepted the offer with conditions and twenty percent accepted the offer without conditions. In the worst-case scenario reported in condition 4 in the bottom row of Table 5.4 in which the buyer has a bad reputation and the seller has not used courts successfully in the past, 59 percent of respondents rejected the offer outright; 38 percent agreed conditionally, and only 3 percent of respondents agreed without conditions. These figures highlight the difficulty of doing business in contemporary Russia.

The results in Table 5.4 provide strong evidence that reputation by itself influences the propensity to trade. For example, compare the responses in condition one and condition three. In both cases, the seller has used courts successfully in the past, but in condition

---

[10] Other coding schemes change the raw figures in each cell, but produce substantively similar findings. Coding all prepayments as conditional accepts or coding only 100 percent prepayments as refusals still leads to the conclusion that reputation is a powerful predictor of trade and courts are associated with more trade only when reputation is weak. The responses asking for prepayment cluster around 50 percent and 100 percent

Table 5.4 *The Propensity to Trade*

1. Good Reputation/Can Use Courts	Percent
Refuse	20
Accept with conditions	60
Accept without conditions	20
N = 165	
2. Good Reputation/Cannot Use Courts	
Refuse	25
Accept with conditions	56
Accept without conditions	19
N = 172	
3. Bad Reputation/Can Use Courts	
Refuse	46
Accept with conditions	47
Accept without conditions	7
N = 166	
4. Bad Reputation/Cannot Use Courts	
Refuse	59
Accept with conditions	38
Accept without conditions	3
N = 163	

N = number of observations. Data from 2005 survey.

one the seller has a good reputation and in condition three the seller has a bad reputation. When the buyer has used courts in the past, moving from a bad reputation to a good reputation decreases the outright refusals from 46 percent to 20 percent of responses and increases the "accept without conditions" responses from 7 percent to 20 percent. The impact of reputation on the probability of making the trade is even larger when the seller has been unable to use the courts in the past, as indicated by the responses in conditions two and four. Moreover, the size of these increases is substantial. Moving from a bad to a good reputation when the seller has been unable to use the courts decreases the outright refusals by 34 percentage points – from 59 percent to 25 percent of respondents.

Next, consider courts. Comparing responses in conditions 1 and 2 indicates that when the buyer has a good reputation, the ability of the seller to use courts increases the propensity to trade only at the

Table 5.5 *Reputation and Courts*

	Can Use Courts (C1)	Cannot Use Courts (C2)	Difference (C1-C2) (se) t-stat
Good Reputation	2.00	1.94	.06
(R1)	(.64)	(.66)	(.07)
	n = 165	n = 172	t = .85
Bad Reputation	1.61	1.43	.18***
(R2)	.61	(.55)	(.06)
	n = 166	n = 163	t = 2.80
Difference	.39***	.51***	
(R1-R2)	(.07)	(.07)	
(se) t-stat	t = 5.72	t = 7.66	

* p<.10, ** p<.05, and *** p<.01 Table reports mean responses where the propensity to trade is coded as follows: Refuse = 1, Accept with Conditions = 2, Accept without Conditions = 3. Standard deviations in parentheses. n = number of observations. Differences report standard errors in parentheses. Data from 2005 survey.

margins. For example, moving from condition 1 when the seller has used courts successfully to condition two where the seller has not, increases the outright refusals from 20 percent to 25 percent and has little impact on the accept unconditionally responses (20 percent versus 19 percent). Courts play a more prominent role when the buyer has a bad reputation. In condition four where the buyer has a bad reputation and the seller has been unable to use the courts, 59 percent of responses were outright refusals, 38 percent of responses were accept with conditions, and only 3 percent of responses were accept unconditionally. Moving to condition three where the buyer still has a bad reputation, but the seller has used courts successfully decreases the outright refusals to 46 percent, increases the conditional acceptances to 48 percent and increases the accept without conditions to seven percent.

Table 5.5 provides a different perspective on the same data. In this table, I code the responses as follows: reject the offer equals one, accept with conditions equals two, and accept without conditions as three and calculate the mean of the responses in each of the four versions of the question.[11] This provides information on the changes in the mean response across each of the four experimental conditions. Higher scores indicate a greater propensity to trade and more confidence in the security of property rights.

In the case at hand, a good reputation is a strong stimulus to trade regardless of the quality of courts as revealed in columns one and two. That the impact of a good reputation is not conditional on the quality of courts suggests that reputation and courts in this analysis are neither substitute not complements. Confidence in the courts also has a statistically significant impact on the propensity to trade, but only when the potential trading partner has a bad reputation. When the seller has a bad reputation, moving from a trading partner that cannot use courts to one who can use courts increases the propensity to trade score by 18 percentage points (1.43 and 1.61)., but when the seller has a good reputation courts provide a much smaller boost to trade of just 6 percentage points (1.94 versus 2.00). Again, there is little evidence of a complementarity or substitution effect.

Good, Bad, and No Reputation

I essentially repeated the last experimental question in a survey of 500 firms conducted in 8 regions in Russia in 2008, but rather than telling respondents that a potential trading partner had either "a bad reputation," or a "good reputation" in the region, interviewers told half the respondents that the potential trading partner was "reliable" and the other half of the respondents received no information about the reputation of the potential trading partner. By comparing responses between these two experiments, we can begin to explore the impact of a good reputation relative to a bad reputation and a good reputation relative to receiving no information about a firm's reputation. Doing so may reveal whether the impact of a good reputation has the same magnitude as a bad reputation.

Reputation, Courts, and Trade
Let's say that a firm in retail trade plans to place a big order at a large manufacturing plant in your region at a market price. This retail

---

[11] The responses are not strictly ordinal, but are treated as such.

Table 5.6 *Reputation and Courts, 2008*

1. Good Reputation/Can Use Courts	Percent
Refuse	28
Accept with conditions	53
Accept without conditions	19
N = 98	
2. Good Reputation/Cannot Use Courts	
Refuse	41
Accept with conditions	48
Accept without conditions	11
N = 103	
3. No Information/Can Use Courts	
Refuse	30
Accept with conditions	52
Accept without conditions	18
N = 94	
4. No Information/Cannot Use Courts	
Refuse	48
Accept with conditions	44
Accept without conditions	8
N = 109	

N = number of observations. Data from 2008 survey.

trading firm recently opened [**XXX**[12]**/, but in the region it is considered to be a reliable partner.**]

What do you think, will the manufacturing firm accept this trade given than it has [**rarely/often**] been able to defend its interests in the state courts of arbitration?

1) It will refuse the offer
2) It will accept the offer, but only on condition of a prepayment of _ ___ percent of the order. Please indicate the amount of prepayment
3) It will accept the offer without any prepayment

Table 5.6 reports the results for each of the four scenarios. For example, when the respondent is given no information about the

---

[12] The XXX indicates that respondents received no information about whether the firm is considered a reliabilie partner.

Table 5.7 *No Reputation Versus a Good Reputation*

	Can Use Courts (C1)	Cannot Use Courts (C2)	Difference (C1-C2) (se) t-stat
Seller has Good	1.92	1.69	.23**
Reputation	(.68)	(.66)	(.09)
(R1)	n = 109	n = 94	t = 2.44
Seller has No	1.87	1.60	.27**
Reputation	.68	.64	(.64)
(R2)	n = 103	n = .98	t = 2.90
Difference	.05	.09	
(R1-R2)	(.09)	(.09)	
(se) t-stat	t = .53	t = .96	

* p<.10, ** p<.05, and *** p<.01. Table reports mean responses where the propensity to trade is coded as follows: Refuse = 1, Accept with Conditions = 2, Accept without Conditions = 3. Standard deviation in parentheses n = number of observations. Differences report standard errors in parentheses. Data from 2008 survey.

reputation of the buyer and the seller is not expected to be able to use the courts, 48 percent of the respondents said that the manufacturer would refuse the offer outright, 44 percent said that the manufacturer would request at least 50 percent prepayment and 8 percent said that the manufacturer would accept the trade without preconditions.

To make the results reported above easier to understand, I recoded the responses as in the previous example where Refuse = 1, Accept with Conditions = 2, Accept without Conditions = 3.

The results in Table 5.7 indicate that respondents reported that buyers would be just as likely to trade with sellers with a good reputation as with sellers about whose reputation they have no information. Where respondents were given no information about the reputation of the seller firm and the buyer could use courts, result were not significantly different from when they were told that the seller firm "was considered a reliable trading partner in the region." The responses were 1.92 and 1.87 respectively. A good reputation also had little impact when respondents were told that the buyer had not been able to use courts (1.69 versus 1.60). These results are intriguing in light of the previous experiment that found powerful differences between the impact of a good and a bad reputation. Taking together the results from these two experimental questions, I find that the impact of a good reputation relative to no information about reputation is much smaller than the impact of a good reputation relative to a bad reputation. In other words, the costs of a bad reputation are far greater than the benefits of a good reputation.

Table 5.7 also indicates that respondents believed that courts were a significant promoter of trade. When respondents were told that the seller had been successful using courts in the past, responses were significantly higher than when they were told the seller had been unable to use the courts to defend their rights in the past. These results hold when the respondents received no information about the seller's reputation (1.87 versus 1.60) and when they were told that the seller had a good reputation (1.92 versus 1.69). Finally, as in Table 5.5, there is little evidence that the impact of reputation is conditional on the quality of courts.[13]

Reputation and Giving Credit

The preceding experiments help mitigate an endogeneity problem, but are vulnerable to charges that the responses to the hypothetical scenarios may not be valid measures of actual behavior. In the next section, I examine how expectations that other managers will punish violators influence the probability of giving credit. In addition, I explore whether reputation and perceptions of the quality of courts are better seen as substitutes or complements. Whereas the previous analyses examined how managers responded to hypothetical situations, the next analyses consider how reputation and perceptions of courts have shaped the reported behavior of managers.

Examining the decision to give credit has important theoretical implications (Johnson et al. 2002a; 2002b). Whether firms give credit to other firms is an important indicator of confidence that their rights will be protected. The giver of credit suffers an up-front loss for the prospect of a greater return in the future and is vulnerable to violation of breach by the debtor. In addition, by promoting exchanges that otherwise would not take place, the creation of institutions to support the expansion of

---

[13] Results from Tables 5.5 and 5.7 are not directly comparable as they are conducted in different surveys with different samples, but they do tap similar conceptions of reputations and courts in a similar setting.

Table 5.8 *Measuring Reputation*

Q. What do you think, what steps will other businesses in your region take if it became known that a firm has violated its obligations toward other firms in your region?

	Yes (%)
1) Do nothing	27.5
2) Gradually unwind the relationship	19.5
3) Change terms of relationship, e.g., 100% prepayment	51.4
4) Immediately stop the relationship	1.7
	N = 590

credit plays a critical role in economic development (North 1990; Greif 2006). To explore the determinants of giving credit, I turn to multivariate statistical analysis. The dependent variable here is the probability that a manager had given credit to a supplier or buyer in the last two years. Just under half of respondents (49 percent) had done so.

Measuring reputation is a challenge. Borrowing from MacMillan and Woodruff (1999), I created a variable, *Reputation*, based on the responses to the question reported below in Table 5.8. This question asked "What do you think, what steps will other businesses in your region take if it became known that a firm has violated its obligations toward other firms in your region?"

Just over half the respondents (51.4 percent) said that other firms were likely to insist on 100 percent prepayment, among other means. Only a handful of respondents expected another businessperson to end the relationship immediately, but most expected their counterparts to change the terms on which they traded with a known offender. I create dummy variables for these responses: *WeakReputation* for respondents who said that other firms would "do nothing"; *MediumReputation* for respondents who expected other firms to "gradually unwind the relationship"; and *StrongReputation* for those who said either "change the terms of relationship/demand 100% prepayment" or "end the relationship immediately." I include those who answered "immediately stop the relationship" in *StrongReputation* because there are too few responses for a separate analysis.[14]

---

[14] Measures of reputation often only bear a faint resemblance to the concept. In some cases, it is reduced to long-time horizons, in other cases it is a broad measure of social trust.

I include a variable, *Courts*, which measures whether a respondent rated the quality of the state arbitration court in their region as satisfactory based on a scale of 1–3.[15] Other factors may also influence decisions to give credit. I add dummy variables for state-owned firms; dummy variables for each of eight different economic sectors and each of ten regions in which a firm is located; and a continuous variable (logged) for the number of employees in a firm. To control for the personal characteristics of the manager I also add variables for the age, gender, and education level of the respondent. I estimate a probit model with robust standard errors. The dependent variable in model 5.1 is whether the respondent gave credit to either a buyer or a supplier in the last year and the coefficients report the marginal effects of a one-unit change in the independent variables. The excluded category for the reputation variables is *WeakReputation*.

The results from Model 5.1 in Table 5.9 indicate that when managers perceive that others will "gradually unwind the relationship" they are no more likely to give credit than when they expect managers to "do nothing" as indicated by the coefficient on *MediumReputation*. Managers who expected others to "demand prepayment" or "immediately end the relationship" were about 11 percentage points more likely to give credit than managers who expected others to do nothing. This strong form of reputation has a pronounced impact on the willingness to give credit. Perceptions of the quality of courts is unrelated to the likelihood of giving credit. Managers of firms with more employees were more likely to extend credit to other firms, while managers of state-owned firms were about 20 percent less likely to do so.

Having examined the direct effects of these forms of reputation and courts, I turn to the conditional effects of these variables. In Model 5.2, I also create interaction terms by multiplying the dummy variables for reputation by *Courts*. These interaction terms allow us to examine whether the impact of reputation on the probability of giving credit differs when courts are weak and when they are strong. This variable should help determine whether reputation

---

[15] The original question included a five-point scale ranging from 1, very poorly, to 5, very well, but less than 5 percent of responses fall into either of the two extreme categories. I thus recode *Courts* into three categories.

Table 5.9 *Reputation and Giving Credit*

	5.1 Supplier or Buyer Credit	5.2 Supplier or Buyer Credit
MediumReputation	.04 (.08)	–.46** .(16)
StrongReputation	.11** (.06)	–.00 (.20)
Courts	–.01 (.04)	–.06 (.09)
MediumReputation* Courts		.25** (.11)
StrongReputation* Courts		.06 (.09)
Size	.08*** (.02)	.08*** (.02)
State Ownership	–.21** (.09)	.21** (.09)
Wald Chi2	103	111.30
Prob >chi2	.0000	.0000
Pseudo R2	.18	.19
N	493	493

Data from 2008 survey. Probit Estimation. Eight sectoral dummies, ten
regional dummy variables and manager characteristics are included,
but not reported. Coefficients report effects marginal effect size of a
one-unit change in the independent variables. Data from 2008 survey.

and courts are substitutes or complements.[16] The results indicate
that the impact of *MediumReputation* on the probability of giving credit to a supplier is conditional on the perceived quality of
courts. When courts are perceived to be incapable, having confidence that others will punish violators by gradually unwinding the
relations is associated with significantly lower levels of giving credit
as indicated by the coefficient on *MediumReputation*. Indeed, the
magnitude of this coefficient indicates a 46 percentage point drop in

[16] A three-category dependent variable that measures whether respondents gave
credit to customers, suppliers, or to both yields similar results.

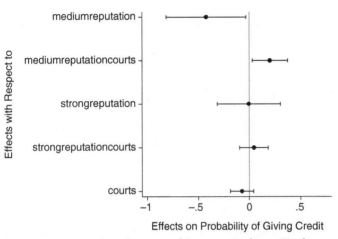

Figure 5.1 Reputation, Courts, and Property Rights to Trade

the likelihood of giving credit. However, when courts are perceived to be even moderately capable, having confidence that others will punish violators by gradually unwinding the relations is associated with sharp increases in credit giving, as indicated by the positive and significant coefficient on *MediumReputation*Courts*. In other words, businesspeople who expect others to "gradually unwind the relationship" perceive reputation and courts as complements rather than substitutes when making decisions to extend credit.

However, there is no conditional effect among respondents who expect others to either "demand prepayment" or "end the relationship" as indicated by the coefficients on *StrongReputation and StrongReputation*Courts*. The coefficients on both these variables depicted below are insignificant as their confidence intervals straddle the zero lines on Figure 5.1.

Caveats

These results are subject to a number of limitations. Like the results of all surveys, the data provide only a snapshot of a fairly dynamic environment. In addition, not all informal institutions are alike. I focus on reputation as a much-theorized phenomenon, but other types of informal institutions may interact differently with formal institutions. Moreover, while courts do not appear to be especially powerful in

shaping decisions to provide credit, they may be more effective in protecting property rights in other ways.

More generally, this chapter answers the call for basic research on
the operation of legal institutions in developing and middle-income
countries, especially those who have been the target of intensive efforts
to promote the rule of law and property rights. Carothers (2006)
rightfully notes that many standard prescriptions to promote the rule
of law have remarkably little empirical support, in large part due to a
lack of basic research. Tellingly, Carothers subtitled a volume of essays
on recent work on rule of law reform: *In Search of Knowledge.*

Conclusion

The quality of institutions – both formal and informal – is a critical
issue for transition and developing countries in general and Russia in
particular. Evidence from surveys of businesspeople in Russia from
2005 and 2008 contributes to these debates. Experimental and cross-
section analyses of survey responses indicate that in Russia a good
reputation is a potent stimulus to trade, while courts have a positive,
but less robust impact on exchange. There is no evidence that a good
reputation and capable courts are substitutes or complements in the
experimental analyses, but there is (weak) evidence that they complement each other when credit decisions are made. That reputation
and courts are mutually supporting is broadly consistent with Putnam
(1993), but not Migdal (1988).

Survey experiments also suggest that firms that are members of the
Russian Union of Industrialists and Entrepreneurs are perceived to be
more reliable trading property rights. The membership in a business
association can also strengthen perceived property rights.

Given the importance of reputation for promoting trade, future
research would do well to analyze precisely how reputations travel.
I found that learning about a firm's reputation via an acquaintance or
in the newspaper has equally powerful effects on the likelihood of trading, but there is still much that we do not know. How do business elites
gain information about contract violations if the disputes do not end
up in court? Why are some business elites better informed about the
reputations of potential trading partners than others? How do managers verify information about a particular dispute absent an impartial
third-party arbiter? These are questions that merit greater attention.

6 | *Social Norms and the Banker's Gold Watch*

This gold watch remains mine only as long as everybody around me agrees that it really belongs to me. If 90 percent of my neighbors should think different, I wouldn't be able to sleep soundly anymore.

Anonymous Russian banker (Yakovlev 2006: 1053)

Property rights define distributions of assets, create economic incentives, and ultimately shape the material base of society. As illustrated by the quote above, however, the security of property rights also has a normative dimension. Social norms that support a given distribution of property rights may reassure right-holders that their property rights will be respected, but where social norms undercut the existing allocation of property rights, right-holders rightly fear expropriations in ways both big and small (Dmitriev 2006; Hoff and Stiglitz 2004). Indeed, right-holders themselves often devote considerable effort to shaping social norms in ways that perpetuate the continued enjoyment of their rights via programs of corporate social responsibility or advertising campaigns. If property rights are broadly viewed as legitimate, then appeals to change them may come to little result.[1]

Social norms about the legitimacy of property rights are often thought to be difficult to change. Denzau and North (1994: 3) emphasize that individual mental models about economic relations are often specific to context and culture and that it may be rational to follow a mental model rooted in culture or myth as long as individuals do not encounter sufficient evidence to disprove these models. If beliefs about property relations and the working of the economy are persistent and difficult to change, this forces us to recalibrate the possibilities for social change. Rather than adapting quickly to new incentives offered

---

[1] Scholars have examined how perceptions of the equity of social mobility in the United States influence support for the redistribution of resources by the state (Fong 2001; Alesina and La Ferrara 2005).

by changes in policy and institutions, we would see some individuals clinging to sub-optimal patterns of behavior that are consistent with prior institutional and cultural environments.

There is certainly evidence to support this view. Some find that the culture of origin of an individual or an individual's ancestors continue to shape economic attitudes even after individuals have moved to new institutional environments (Guiso et al. 2006). Still others observe that even after individuals have moved to another country in Europe, the perceived level of corruption in their parent's country of origin continues to shape attitudes about corruption (Simpser 2016). Most closely related to this chapter is Di Tella et al. (2012), who examine the mutability of attitudes toward property and the extent to which new information can change these attitudes following the privatization of water in Buenos Aires, Argentina. Using a vignette about privatization, they find that reading a critical statement about privatization by the President of Argentina has an impact on attitudes toward privatization about as large as actually receiving a new water line via privatization. In this case, what they call government propaganda about the legitimacy of property rights is about as powerful an influence on attitudes as is the material benefit of privatization itself. They also find that investments by the privatized firm moderate the impacts of governmental statements.

Privatization provides an especially good window for examining societal norms toward property rights because it is frequently a topic of much public discussion, affects broad swaths of the population, and is a high-stakes policy with the potential to create new winners and losers in society. Looking broadly across countries, privatization is very unpopular. A World Bank survey conducted in 28 postcommunist countries in 2006 found that 80 percent of respondents would like to revise the privatization of state enterprises (Denisova at al. 2009). A 2006 survey from Russia finds that just over half of respondents agreed that "the majority of private assets in the country should be nationalized" (Denisova et al. 2010). Survey results from Latin America tell a similar tale. *LatinoBarometer*, a public opinion poll conducted in 17 countries in 2003, found that more than two-thirds of respondents thought that privatization was "not beneficial" for the country and 40 percent disagreed with the statement: "the state should leave productive activities to the private sector" (Lora and Panizza 2003; Panizza and Yanez 2005; Boix 2005). Baker (2003) finds that privatization in Latin America has been far less popular than other types of economic reform, such as trade liberalization. Even where privatization has brought objective benefits the public dislikes it. Di Tella et al. (2012) find that privatization of water services was broadly unpopular in Argentina even though it brought tangible benefits to many. World Bank studies in Latin America find that privatization increased access to telecommunications and electricity, but the beneficiaries of those gains still resented privatization (IADB 2002: 185–186). This "privatization paradox" has been widely noted, but is not well understood (IADB 2002).

Why is privatization so unpopular? Is it because people prefer state ownership or is because they view privatization as illegitimate? Moreover, what can be done about it? Are property rights obtained through legally dubious means forever tainted with original sin or can right-holders make their ill-gotten gains more acceptable by doing good works? Finally, if privatization is so massively unpopular, then why are revisions of privatization so relatively rare? While the economic consequences of privatization have been widely studied, there has been far less research into the questions posed above (but see Kaltenthaler et al. 2006; Denisova et al. 2009; 2012; Di Tella et al. 2012). These questions are important not only for privatization but also for economic and political transformation.

This chapter examines mass attitudes toward revising privatization based largely on a 2006 survey of the mass public from Russia and makes four points. First, I find that despite the highly technical nature of the issue, people are able to evaluate privatization based on their individual interests. Respondents with better human capital are more likely to oppose revising privatization because they prefer private property to state property. Respondents also evaluate privatization based on legitimacy concerns. The severity of violations of the law on privatization influences support for revising privatization in some scenarios in a survey-based experiment of the mass public.

Second, right-holders can make their assets more legitimate post-privatization. Most studies focus on the design of privatization, support for privatization, or the effects of privatization, but there has been very little research into how right-holders can make privatized assets more legitimate after the state has released control (but see Besley 1995; Frye 2006; Di Tella et al. 2012; Markus 2012; 2015). I find that right-holders can increase public support for the status quo privatization by *both* providing public goods for the region and by investing in the firm at high levels. When respondents were told that a privatized firm provided many public goods for the region and invested in their firm at high levels, opposition to privatization declined significantly, in some conditions by as many as 16 percentage points. The original sin of privatization can be expiated in part via good works.

Third, support for revising privatization should not be equated with favoring renationalization. While majorities in all the postcommunist countries want to revise privatization, less than a third of respondents would like assets to remain in state hands. Most respondents prefer that privatized firms remain in private hands. Moreover, this pattern – support for revising privatization while also rejecting state property – holds across the postcommunist region. This distribution of responses suggests that privatized property rights are not secure because a majority of the public supports a specific privatization program. Rather, revisions of privatization are rare in part because it is very difficult for a majority of citizens to coordinate on an alternative to the status quo.

Finally, results from a survey of 28 countries on the legitimacy of privatization suggest that privatization in Russia is viewed as not much more illegitimate than in other countries in the region. Often viewed as the poster child for "reform gone awry," support for revising privatization in Russia is about par for the region. Observers who decry privatization in Russia should recognize that privatization is widely unpopular across the region and in many countries outside the region too.

Privatized Property Rights

Property rights created through privatization are often treated as unproblematic. Having received legal title, right-holders are expected to put those assets to their most productive use. However, the transfer of rights from state to private hands is only a first step in encouraging right-holders to use their assets well. The state, through its monopoly on the use of coercion, retains the ability to redraw property rights in a variety of ways, from expropriation and renationalization to changes in regulation and tax policy. Right-holders who expect the state to alter their rights in the future have weak incentives to use their assets productively today.

The specter of reversing privatization may be heightened where the community opposes existing definitions of property rights. This underlying opposition to privatization may allow political entrepreneurs to bolster their public standing by railing against the current distribution of property rights. Under these circumstances privatization is likely to produce few benefits as right-holders anticipate future limitations on their assets. In contrast, such appeals are likely to fail should the community view property rights as broadly acceptable. This support should allow right-holders to invest with confidence, knowing that their rights are unlikely to be challenged. The extent to which property rights are broadly accepted may have a direct bearing on whether those assets are used productively.

Concerns about the lack of popular support for privatization have special importance in the postcommunist world where the scope and speed of de-etatization were unprecedented. Having inherited massive state sectors and facing pressure from international institutions to privatize, politicians had vast opportunities to abuse privatization. The former Minister of Ownership Transformation in Poland famously observed: "Privatization is when someone who does not know who the real owner is and does not know what it is really worth sells something to someone who does not have any money" (cited in Verdery 1996: 210). Initial privatization outcomes remain a lightning rod in many countries. In Bulgaria the aptly named protest party "Ataka" received 10 percent of the seats in the 2004 parliamentary elections on a platform of reversing privatization, while charges of crony privatization helped to undermine the Kuchma and Yanukovich governments in Ukraine.

Russia presents a prime example of the politically contingent nature of post-privatization property rights. In the 1990s, big business and President Yeltsin sought to balance the exchange of political support for economic benefits while avoiding a populist backlash that would threaten them both.[2] The rapid voucher-based privatization of more than 70 percent of industrial enterprises between 1992 and 1995 provided great benefits for firm managers. In 1995 and 1996, the privatization of 15 very valuable enterprises in the loans for shares program to politically connected businesspeople helped solidify the new economic elite. The speed of the voucher privatization and the opacity of the loans for shares program raised concerns about the legality

[2] See Shleifer and Treisman (2000) on the political economy of Russia's reforms.

of privatization (Black et al. 2000). A 2003 study by ROMIR found that 88 percent of respondents believed that "big capital" in Russia became rich through "dishonest" or "more or less dishonest" means and 77 percent favored a partial or complete revision of privatization (*Vedemosti*, July 18, 2003).

President Putin came to power in 2000 with the backing of some members of big business who expected him to continue the policies of his predecessor, but Putin's unexpected rise in popularity allowed him to build an independent base of support. This popularity gave him leverage over his former backers, and shortly after coming to office, he began to chip away at the power of individual big businessmen – many of whom had grown wealthy from privatization deals of dubious legality.[3] With the transfer of power to President Putin, privatization deals conducted by previous administrations received renewed attention.[4]

The arrest of YUKOS executives Platon Lebedev and Mikhail Khodorkovsky in 2003 on a variety of charges including violations of the Law on Privatization brought this issue sharply into focus. Among other charges the two men were accused of underinvesting in the *Apatit* fertilizer plant whose privatization was conditional upon the owners meeting investment targets. Ironically, both were found guilty on charges related to this privatization, but the judge ruled that the statute of limitations had expired. They were sentenced to eight-year terms based on other charges. The economic and political fallout of this case has been hotly debated. Some argue that the affair had little effect on the economy as investors saw the *YUKOS* affair as a one-off event and returned to the equities market after several months. Others cite a sharp increase in capital flight in 2003 and 2004 against a backdrop of rapid economic growth as evidence of the short-term

---

[3] Wealth redistribution continued after privatization as groups grown powerful from their control over former state assets were especially well placed to shape public policy in their favor. See Barnes (2006.)

[4] In 2003, President Putin insisted that not all privatization deals violated the law: "We often hear that laws were complicated and impossible to comply with. These are the statements of those who did not observe them. This is rubbish. Those who wanted to observe the law did so." More ominously, he added: "if five or seven people did not observe the law it does not mean that everybody did the same." This quote sparked a guessing game about which businessmen would be the next to suffer the fate of Khodorkovsky.

effects of the *YUKOS* affair.[5] There is less debate about the political impact: the prosecutions were very popular. President Putin's approval rating rose from 70 percent in May 2003 to 78 percent in July 2003 after Lebedev's arrest according to the Levada Center.

But concerns about the economic and political consequences of legally dubious privatizations are hardly confined to the postcommunist world. In Bolivia, the nationalization of oil and gas fields by President Evo Morales in 2006 "sent shock waves through the international community," but were "widely supported by Bolivians who see the so-called privatization under former President Gonzalo "Goni" Sanchez as a ripoff" (Stiglitz 2006: 1). President Morales demanded that British Petroleum cede rights over the formerly state-owned gas company (*New York Times* March 28, 2008). In Zimbabwe, President Mugabe's redistribution of farmland held by white commercial farmers to black farmers was politically popular but had disastrous consequences for the economy (Richardson 2004). Malaysia renationalized the country's largest car-marker and national airline (Frye 2014). As usual, Venezuelan President Chavez stood apart from the crowd. His government renationalized not only oil companies but also sugar plantations, foreign-owned concrete-making firms, the largest distributor of dairy products, and the biggest cold storage and distribution company (*New York Times* April 24; A26). More generally, that the market for insurance against nationalization continues to thrive underscores the broad relevance of this threat.

These post-privatization asset redistributions raise important empirical and theoretical questions. Dmitriev (2006) and others argue that select reversals of privatization offer the potential to redress corrupt transfers of property. Stiglitz and Hoff (2005) argue that illegitimate privatizations provide few efficiency gains even where they do not produce great concentrations of wealth. Following this logic, some have argued for re-privatizating select assets on economic grounds (Wolosky 2000; Bunich 2006). One may point to the re-privatization in 2005 of the massive *Kryvoryzhstal* steel works in Ukraine at a market price of US$4.8 billion, which was previously sold to the son-in-law of President

---

[5] In the second quarter of 2003 more capital flowed into Russia than out for only the second time since 1992. In the third quarter, following Lebedev's arrest, capital flight soared to $7.6 billion. In 2004, capital flight exceeded $8 billion in an economy that grew by 7.1 percent.

Kuchma for one-fifth the price, as an economically defensible case of re-privatization.

Others disagree. Borrowing from Coase and the analogy of the Robber Barons in the United States, they suggest that the manner in which property rights are initially distributed is relatively unimportant. This interpretation of the "Coasian" view suggests that once property rights are transferred into private hands economic agents will exchange them until they find a stable arrangement. These observers fear that reversing even a bad privatization may call into question all transfers of property and lead to a never-ending cycle of privatization and re-privatization. With a nod to Trotsky's cry of "permanent revolution," Hellman (2002) and Sonin (2003) refer to this process as "permanent redistribution" and warn of its economic consequences.

Conceptions of Property Rights

The more political treatment of property rights in these theories brings to the fore aspects of privatization that have received less attention. It suggests the importance of gauging the acceptance of existing definitions of property rights in the broader community. Rather than viewing property rights in a static fashion as protected by law, this interpretation suggests that property rights are continually redefined through political competition. Political challenges to existing property rights are likely to be more successful where the initial transfer of rights is seen as illegitimate. Far from being fixed in law, property rights are highly dependent on the political climate. This conception of property rights grants right-holders the capacity to influence popular support for their holdings. Right-holder agency is largely lacking in existing literature that typically depicts right-holders as passively responding to institutional constraints. Here right-holders have the potential to take matters into their own hands and shape public support, and perhaps, ultimately the security of their property rights.

Evaluating Privatization

Why do some support privatization, while others oppose it? This section offers several possibilities.

Material Interests and Human Capital. Respondents may evaluate privatization based on their material interests. Workers with better skills, more education, and an education better suited for a market economy may be more likely to favor private property over state property and to oppose a revision of privatization (Kaltenthaler et al. 2006). Similarly, in a postcommunist context younger respondents typically have skills more suited to a market economy (Brainerd 1998) and may hold similar preferences. This may seem like a straightforward calculation, but privatization is a technically complex policy, and respondents may have difficulty evaluating their fate under different property regimes. Indeed, public opinion researchers often have little faith in respondents' capacity to evaluate complex policies.

Original Sin and the Coasian View of Privatization. Respondents however, also make take non-material factors into account, such as the legitimacy of privatization. The "original sin" argument suggests that the manner in which property is transferred from state to private hands influences evaluations of property rights. Former state-owned assets obtained through serious illegality acquire a birth defect that is long lasting and impervious to treatment. Property rights seen as ill-gotten by the community may provoke uncertainty among rightholders who fear future revisions of their rights due to changes in policy. Absent broad acceptance of the procedures by which assets are privatized, transferring property rights from state to private hands may produce few benefits.

It is straightforward to argue that property transferred through legally dubious means would receive less popular support. However, there is also reason to expect the contrary, especially in the case at hand. Most privatizations in Russia took place in the mid-1990s and memories of the gory details of the initial bargain may have dimmed. The role of private property in a market economy was better understood and more broadly accepted in 2006 than it was during privatization's heyday a decade earlier. And many have noted that formal law in Russia is not held in wide respect (Ledeneva 1998; Stiglitz and Hoff 2005, but see Hendley et al. 2001). In addition, Russia was undergoing an economic boom at the time of the survey in 2006. Therefore, one might expect violations of the Law on Privatization to be forgotten and forgiven at least by some.

Moreover privatizers in Russia, many of whom were not overly concerned about the legal details of privatization, had an intellectual foundation for their stance. Echoing Coase (1960), they suggested that the initial distribution of property rights is relatively unimportant provided that right-holders can exchange their rights in the marketplace. While not condoning illegality, privatizers in Russia sought to transfer rights as quickly as possible so that right-holders would provide a base of political support and eventually assets would reach the most efficient users. The state official in charge of privatization, Anatolii Chubais, reported the following about managers in Russia: "They steal and steal and steal. They are stealing absolutely everything and it is impossible to stop them. But let them steal and take their property. They will then become owners and decent administrators of this property" (Freeland 2000: 70). The "Coasian" view, which undergirds many arguments in favor of rapid privatization, suggests that respondents would downplay violations of the Law on Privatization when judging the legitimacy of property rights.[6] The "original sin" view suggests the opposite. Both theories presented focus on the government, while the next set of arguments explore how right-holders themselves can take steps to increase the legitimacy of property rights by doing "good works." The argument comes in two versions.

Good Use as Good Works. The "good use" view of the "good works" argument suggests that the legitimacy of property rights depends on how the managers have used the resource granted to them by the state. If a manager has modernized and restructured the firm, then others may be willing to view the property rights as legitimate even if the assets were obtained by cutting legal corners. This argument is often made by Russian business elites who justify their wealth by their ability to create jobs, investment, and growth. The good use of the asset generates its own justification for initial privatization outcomes.

Public Goods as Good Works. The public goods version of the "good works" argument suggests that managers who provide public goods may generate greater acceptance for their property rights. Indeed, in recent years, firms in Russia have sponsored opera performances, rock concerts, museum exhibitions, ballet companies, and a variety of religious and social organizations. They have created think tanks that analyze social and economic problems. In addition, they have contributed directly to a range of social projects from scholarship funds to summer camps and hospitals. The movement goes well beyond the oligarchs. The Putin government has made corporate social responsibility an important theme and encouraged firms across the country

---

[6] Hoff and Stiglitz (2004) also treat privatization in Russia as guided by a Coasian view.

to find ways to provide critical services to their communities (Levitov 2006). The largest lobby for big business in Russia, the Russian Union of Industrialists and Entrepreneurs, has adopted corporate social responsibility as a key slogan and developed a variety of plans to encourage businesses to provide public goods. Many of these efforts remain at the level of public relations, but there is little doubt that many businesses are trying to use good works to polish their public image. That firms should support public goods is not a new idea in Russia as during the Soviet period enterprises provided many social services for their workers and the local population.

This good works argument echoes Di Tella et al. (2012), who studied the impact of renationalization of water services in Argentina in 2006. They take advantage of the fact that some, but not all, districts in Buenos Aires had their water services privatized in the 1990s. Using a survey experiment that exposed treatment groups to negative information from the government and to information about investments made by the privatized company, they found that attitudes toward privatiztion were susceptible to negative information from the government, but also that telling respondents about investments made by the privatized company rendered respondents less susceptible to the government's information campaign in favor of renationalization. In addition, they found respondents who had benefitted from the privatization of water prior to renationalization were less vulnerable to information campaigns in support of the government's effort to renationalize water services. More generally, and in line with this work, social norms about privatization are susceptible to change by new information.[7]

The Data

To study support for revising privatization, I commissioned the Levada Center to conduct a survey of 1600 adult residents of Russia in a nationally representative sample in the middle of October 2006.[8] In addition

---

[7] See Della Vigna and Kaplan (2007) and Gerber et al. (2009) for field experiments on how new information shapes beliefs and Zaller (1992) on persuasion and public opinion.

[8] The response rate was 57 percent and 26 percent of respondents were contacted after the interview to check quality. The questions are similar to Frye (2006), which analyzed the perceptions of firm managers rather than citizens. See Data Appendix for details.

Table 6.1 *The Necessity of Privatization*
"For all its faults, the privatization of large industrial
enterprises in Russia in the 1990s was necessary."

	Percent
Strongly agree	5.9
More or less agree	23.8
More or less disagree	26.2
Strongly disagree	29.5
(unread/don't know)	14.6

to a battery of questions asked each month by the Levada Center,
the survey included several questions on privatization. Interviewers
asked respondents to what extent they agreed with the following question: "For all its faults, the privatization of large industrial enterprises
in Russia in the 1990s was necessary."

Table 6.1 reports the results. About 30 percent of respondents
"strongly agree" or" more or less agree" that privatization of large
industrial enterprises in the 1990s was necessary. About a quarter of
respondents "more or less" disagreed and about 30 percent of respondents "strongly disagreed" with the statement.

Interviewers also probed the respondent's perceptions about the frequency of major illegalities in the privatization process. They asked
to what the extent the respondents agreed that: "The privatization
of large enterprises in Russia in the 1990s was often conducted with
major violations of the law."

Three-quarters of respondents "agreed" or "more or less" agreed
that the privatization of industrial enterprises in Russia was conducted with significant violations of the law. Only about 10 percent
of respondents "disagreed" or "more or less disagreed" with the statement, indicating the breadth of the belief that privatization was conducted with little regard for legal niceties.

To focus on theories of support for privatized property, the survey included a question with an experimental design that aims to
capture a familiar situation in Russia. Most firms were privatized
in the early to mid-1990s in an environment of weak legal norms
and observers have spent much of the past decade discussing the
legitimacy of these transfers of property. The experiment manipulates the actions of right-holders by varying whether or not they

Table 6.2 *The Frequency of Major Violations of Privatization*

"The privatization of large industrial enterprises in Russia in the 1990s was often conducted with major violations of the Law on Privatization."

	Percent
Strongly agree	40.3
More or less agree	35.4
More or less disagree	7.1
Strongly disagree	3.2
(unread/don't know)	14.0

have modernized the firm and whether they provided public goods for their region after privatization. It also manipulates the severity of the violations of the Law on Privatization. Again, the differences in responses should only be due to the minor changes in question wording.

An Experiment on Privatization

Let's say that an industrial firm was privatized in the mid-1990s. After privatization, the managers of the firm invested a [little/a great deal] of their own capital in the modernization and restructuring of their firm and they have provided [few/many] social programs for the development of the region.

It turns out that the firm was privatized with [minor/major] violations of the Law on Privatization. Do you believe that this matter should be turned over to the courts?

Yes   More or less   Yes   More or Less No   No

If the respondents answered "yes" or "more less yes" then the interviewers asked:

What steps should the judge take in this matter?

1) Firm should be returned to state ownership
2) Firm should be privatized to new owners
3) The guilty should pay a significant fine
4) The guilty should pay a small fine
5) Since so much time has passed nothing should be done

Table 6.3 *Turning to the Courts: Major Violations*

	Major Violations	
	Mean Response (n)	Difference from Baseline t-test
Baseline	1.75 n = 159	–
High Investment	1.78 n = 184	.03 t = .34
High Public Goods	1.96 n = 164	.21** t = 2.14
High Investment and High Public Goods	2.20 n = 181	.45*** t = 4.7

* p<.10, ** p<.05, and *** p<.01. Mean responses to the question: "Do you believe that this matter should be turned over to the courts?" where 1 = yes, 2 = more or less yes, 3 = more or less no, and 4 = no. n = number of responses. Data from 2006 survey.

I begin by presenting responses to whether those interviewed believed that given the parameters of the violations of the privatization law and the behavior of the right-holder, the case should be turned over to the courts. First, take cases of major violations as depicted in Table 6.3 in which lower average responses mean less secure property rights as more respondents believe that the privatization should be reviewed by the courts.

On the whole, we see that investing at high levels has no effect on privatization attitudes, that providing higher levels of public goods can increase popular support for the legitimacy of a privatization, and that doing both activities at high levels dramatically increases support for privatized property rights. In the baseline category where the right-holder provides little investment and few public goods, 67 percent of respondents thought the courts should review the case, 13 percent said no, and 18 percent were undecided (average of 1.75 on the 1–4 scale).[9]

---

[9] Yes responses include those who said "yes" or "more or less yes" while no includes those who responded "no" or "more or less no."

Table 6.4 *Turning to the Courts: Minor Violations*

	Minor Violations	
	Mean Response (n)	Difference from Baseline t-test
Baseline	1.96 n = 144	–
High Investment	1.99 n = 147	.03 t = .29
High Public Goods	2.05 n = 153	.09 t = .90
High Investment and High Public Goods	2.20 n = 164	.24** t = 2.39

* p<.10, ** p<.05, and *** p<.01. Mean responses to the question: "Do you believe that this matter should be turned over to the courts?" where 1 = yes, 2 = more or less yes, 3 = more or less no, and 4 = no. n = number of responses. Data from 2006 survey.

When the right-holder invests a great deal in the modernization of the firm, attitudes remained unchanged (average 1.78 on the 1–4 scale). However, when respondents were told that the right-holder provided many public goods for the region as depicted in the third row, 59 percent of respondents believed that the courts should review the case, a decline of 8 percentage points (1.96 on the 1–4 scale). These differences are statistically significant as depicted in the column on the right (1.75 versus 1.96, t = 2.14).

Moreover, when right-holders both invested and provided public goods at high levels, only 51 percent of respondents believed that the courts should review the matter (2.20 on the 1–4 scale). This response is significantly different from the baseline condition (2.20 versus 1.79, t = 4.7). These results hold when violations of the Law on Privatization were major.

Table 6.4 reproduces the scenarios except in this case respondents were told that the privatization occurred with only minor violations of the law. As before investing in the firm has no impact on attitudes toward privatization (1.96 versus 1.99); while right-holders who both invested in their firm and provided public goods at high levels can significantly increase support for the privatization status quo (1.79 versus 2.20, t = 2.39). One difference with the preceding scenario is that the increase in support for privatized property when the right-holder had provided public goods for the region falls short of statistical significance (1.96 versus 2.05).

Testing the Original Sin Argument

Comparing levels of support for the status quo privatization in similar scenarios permits an assessment of how the severity of the violations of the Law on Privatization shapes the legitimacy of privatized property. Table 6.5 reports levels of support for the privatization status quo from the two previous scenarios, but places responses when violations of the Law on Privatization were major in bold and responses when violations of the Law on Privatization were minor in normal text. By comparing the two numbers in each cell, we can test the impact of changing the severity of the violations of the law from minor to major in the responses.

Consider the top left cell in Table 6.5 in which managers invested little in their firm and provided few public goods for the region. When violations of the Law on Privatization were minor, 59 percent of respondents said that the privatization should be reviewed and when violations were major this figure was 67 percent (1.96 versus 1.75, t = 2.2). Similar increases in support for revising privatization are found comparing responses in the lower left corners in Table 6.5 in which managers invested in the firm but did not provide public goods (1.99 versus 1.77, t = 2.2). In this condition, when violations of the Law on Privatization were severe, 69 percent of respondents believed that the courts should review the case, but this figure falls to 55 percent when violations of the Law on Privatization were minor. In the two scenarios depicted in column two, however, moving from a severe to a minor violation of the Law on Privatization has no discernible impact on attitudes toward privatization. In sum, in two of the four scenarios testing the original sin argument, we find significant differences in responses when violations of the law were major and minor. This suggests that the manner in which assets are privatized influences the legitimacy of property rights, although these results are mixed.

Table 6.5 *Testing the Original Sin Argument*

	No Investment	Investment
No Public Goods	**1.75 Major**	**1.95 Major**
	1.96 Minor	2.05 Minor
	Difference = .21**	Difference = .09
	t = 2.2	t = 3.9
Public Goods	**1.78 Major**	**2.20 Major**
	1.99 Minor	2.20 Minor
	Difference = .21**	Difference = .00
	t = 2.2	t = 0.0

* $p<.10$, ** $p<.05$, and *** $p<.01$. Mean responses to the question: "Do you believe that this matter should be turned over to the courts?" where 1 = yes, 2 = more or less yes, 3 = more or less no, and 4 = no. Data from 2006 survey.

What Should Be Done?

This section probes responses in more detail by examining what respondents believe should ultimately happen to the privatized firm. Table 6.6 reports the responses to scenarios depicted above when violations of the law on privatization were major, but here we explore what steps the respondents believed that the judge should take in the case. This is important as opposition to privatization is sometimes equated with support for renationalization, but this is not borne out in the data. Here respondents could choose among five responses:

1. the privatized asset should be renationalized
2. the privatized asset should be reprivatized
3. the guilty parties should pay a significant fine
4. the guilty parties should pay a small fine
5. nothing should happen since so much time has passed.

The figures in bold depict the percentage of respondents who support the privatization status quo and include those who believed that the courts should not hear the case and the small number of those who said that "the matter should be reviewed but nothing should be done about it" (3 percent of respondents) and the few respondents who said

that "only a small fine should be levied" (3.6 percent of respondents).
All of these responses indicate support for the privatization status quo.

Table 6.6 reports the responses when violations of the Law on
Privatization were major. In the baseline scenario when respondents
were told that the right-holder had invested little in the firm and
provided few public goods for the region, 25 percent of respondents
favored the privatization status quo; while 33 percent favored renationalization, 22 percent favored reprivatizing the firm to new owners,
and 20 percent favored a large fine. Even in this worst case scenario,
only one-third of respondents favored renationalization and more
than two-thirds of respondents wanted the asset to ultimately remain
in private hands.

Support for the privatization status quo is similar when respondents
were told that the right-holder had invested a great deal in the firm
as depicted in the second row (25 percent in both cases). As in the
baseline condition, only one-quarter of respondents favored allowing
the current right-holders to retain ownership with at most a small fine.

In contrast, providing a high level of public goods increases support
for the privatization status quo by 11 percentage points above the
baseline condition as depicted in the third row (36 percent versus 25
percent). This increase is statistically significant as depicted in the column on the right. Finally, right-holders who had invested a great deal
in the firm and provided a wealth of public goods for the region dramatically increased support for privatized property (41 percent versus
25 percent, t = 3.15). This 16 percentage point increase is substantively
large and statistically significant.

Examining responses when violations of the law were minor yields
a similar picture, but showing somewhat greater support for privatization overall. In the baseline scenario depicted in Table 6.7, in which
right-holders invested little in the firm and provided few public goods
for the region, 33 percent of respondents said that the status quo privatization should prevail and this figure remains unchanged when
respondents were told that the right-holders had invested a great deal
in the firm as depicted in the high investment scenario.

When respondents were told that right-holders had provided many
public goods for the region, 37 percent of respondents supported the
privatization status quo, a difference that is statistically indistinguishable from the baseline condition. However, when right-holders had
both invested in the firm and provided high levels of public goods

Table 6.6 *What Should the Courts Do? Major Violations*

Major Violations		
	Response (%) (n)	Difference from Baseline and t-test
Baseline	34 = renationalization 22 = reprivatization 20 = big fine 04 = small fine 20 = no review/do nothing **25 = no review/small fine** (n = 153)	–
High Investment	33 = renationalization 23 = reprivatization 19 = big fine 06 = small fine 20 = no review/do nothing **25 = no review/small fine** (n = 179)	0.0 t = 0
High Public Goods	34 = renationalization 17 = reprivatization 14 = big fine 04 = small fine 32 = no review/do nothing **36 = no review/small fine** (n = 160)	.11** t = 2.15
High Investment and High Public Goods	24 = renationalization 17 = reprivatization 19 = big fine 03 = small fine 39 = no review/do nothing **41 = no review/small fine** (n = 176)	.16*** t = 3.15

* $p<.10$, ** $p<.05$, and *** $p<.01$. Responses in bold include the percentage of respondents who said that state arbitration courts should not hear the matter and those that said that the judge should do nothing because so much time had passed since the privatization. n = number of respondents. Data from 2006 survey.

Table 6.7 *What Should the Courts Do? Minor Violations*

Minor Violations		
	Responses (%) (n = number of observations)	Difference from Baseline t-test
Baseline	32 = renationalization 20 = reprivatization 15 = big fine 03 = small fine 29 = no review/do nothing **33 = no review/small fine** (n = 138)	–
High Investment	32 = renationalization 11 = reprivatization 24 = big fine 01 = small fine 32 = no review/do nothing **33 = no review/small fine** (n = 144)	0 t = 0
High Public Goods	23 = renationalization 18 = reprivatization 23 = big fine 03 = small fine 34 = do nothing/no review **37 = no review/small fine** (n = 146)	.04 t = .70
High Investment and High Public Goods	31 = renationalization 10 = reprivatization 12 = big fine 04 = small fine 43 = do nothing/no review **47 = no review/small fine** (n = 157)	.14 t = 2.48***

*p<.10, ** p<.05, and *** p<.01. Responses in bold include the percentage of respondents who said that state arbitration courts should not hear the matter and those that said that the judge should do nothing because so much time had passed since the privatization. n = number of respondents. Data from 2006 survey.

for the region, 47 percent of respondents supported the privatization status quo. In this case, providing public goods *and* investing in the firm has a large and statistically significant impact on support for privatization. In sum, it is not easy, but right-holders can take steps to increase support for privatization after they receive their assets and respondents' attitudes toward privatization are susceptible to change via new information.

Who Supports Revising Privatization and Why?

In this section, I probe attitudes toward privatization in two ways. I begin by examining which of the four outcomes different types of respondent prefer. For example, do highly skilled respondents favor renationalization, reprivatization, paying a fine, or preserving the status quo? I then try to divine why respondents hold these views. For example, respondents may favor revising privatization because they prefer state property or because they have concerns about the legitimacy of the process of privatization. These distinctions have implications for policy. If respondents favor revising privatization because they expect their set of skills to be more useful under an economy dominated by state ownership, then retraining programs may mute opposition to privatization. If respondents support revising privatization due to concerns that privatization was conducted in a legally dubious manner, then redistribution of property via a more transparent and just process may be an appropriate response. This latter view also indicates that privatization designers should take into account the perceived fairness of the process as part of any program to transfer state assets to private hands.

Examining the average responses to the question of preferred outcomes for privatization finds that 30 percent of respondents favored renationalization (option 1), 17 percent favored reprivatization (option 2), 18 percent favored having owners pay a large fine (option 3), and 35 percent favored the status quo (option 4). Thus, while a majority of respondents favor revising privatization, only 30 percent of respondents prefer that property ultimately be left in the hands of the state.

In the statistical analysis below, I begin by studying which respondents support which type of privatization outcome. In Table 6.8, I estimate a multinomial logit model, which presents the likelihood that a respondent chooses one of the four different options. I report in columns 1–3 how each factor influences the likelihood of choosing either renationalization

Table 6.8 *Who Supports Revising Privatization and Why?*

	1 Renationalized	2 Reprivatized	3 Large Fine	4 Reprivatize	5 State v. Private	6 Legitimacy
	B1	B2	B3	B1+B2+B3 =B4 (p-value)	B1=B2+B3+B4 (p-value)	B2+B3=B4 (p-value)
High Skill	.68** (.04)	1.14 (.49)	.81 (.29)	(.06) Oppose	(.01) Private	(.84)
Age (log)	1.10** (.03)	1.05 (.45)	1.06 (.33)	(.02) Support	(.23)	(.03) Illegitimate
Primary School	.68 (.20)	.78 (.50)	.67 (.30)	(.11)	(.82)	(.13)
Unfinished High School	.64** (.05)	.100 (.99)	.88 (.64)	(.10) Oppose	.09 Private	(.25)
High School	.68* (.10)	.54** (.04)	.75 (.37)	(.01) Oppose	(.76)	(.01) Legitimate
Some or Finish College	.58** (.05)	.61* (.07)	.79 (.41)	(.00) Oppose	(.46)	(.01) Legitimate
Household Income	.84 (.11)	1.15 (.27)	1.15 (.22)	(.80)	(.00) Private	(.61)

				Oppose		Illegitimate
				Support		Legitimate
City Size	.85*	.80***	.86*	(.02)	(.75)	(.01)
	(.07)	(.01)	(.07)			
Male	1.09	.99	.89	(.92)	(.22)	(.88)
	(.51)	(.97)	(.47)			
Ethnic Russian	1.22	1.58*	1.15	(.10)	(.59)	(.08)
	(.41)	(.07)	(.60)			
Constant	.96	-.19***	.22			
	(.05)	(.01)	(.06)			

ⱷ<.10, ** p<.05, ***p<.01. Multinomial logit. The excluded category for education is vocational students. Robust standard errors with clustering on city. N = 1249; Wald Chi2 =199; Prob> chi = .0000, Pseudo R2 = .04. P-values in parentheses. Data from 2006 survey. Columns 1–3 predict whether respondents prefer firms be renationalized, reprivatized, or pay a fine relative to the privatization status quo. Columns 4–6 explore whether respondents prefer reprivatization of any kind to the status quo, whether they prefer state to private property, and view the process of privatization as legitimate or illegitimate, respectively.

(option 1), reprivatization (option 2), or paying a fine (option 3), relative to keeping the status quo (option 4). The table reports relative risk ratios for each of the variables of interest, including measures of skill, education levels, age, family income, city size, gender, and a dummy variable that equals 1 for ethnic Russians and 0 otherwise.[10]

A relative risk ratio greater than 1 indicates that the variable is associated with an increase in the likelihood of choosing that option relative to option 4. For example, a relative risk ratio of 1.10 in column 1 would suggest that a one-unit change in the variable of interest makes it 10 percent more likely that the respondent would choose option 1 relative to option 4. A relative risk ratio of less than one indicates that this factor makes it less likely to choose that option relative to option 4. As option 4 is keeping the privatization status quo, it is a good reference category. P-values are in parentheses below each relative risk ratio.

In columns 4–6, I explore why respondents hold these views by changing the reference category in the analysis. For example, in column 4, I explore whether respondents favor any form of reprivatization over the privatization status quo. Here I compare whether respondents prefer the privatization status quo option (4) relative to the other outcomes combined (options 1 + 2 +3).[11] If the respondent is significantly more likely to choose option (4), then they oppose revising privatization. Alternatively, if they are more likely to choose any of the other options relative to option 4, they favor revising privatization.

In column 5, I compare whether respondents hold their views about reprivatization because they prefer state property or private property. I assess whether respondents favor leaving assets in state hands (option 1) relative to all other outcomes (options 2 + 3 + 4). If so, the respondent favors state property. Conversely, if respondents are significantly more likely to choose options (2 + 3 + 4) relative to option 1, then the

---

[10] I also control for each version of the question posed to the respondents as they influence responses and use robust standard errors clustered on city. The different versions of the question are significantly related to support for revising privatization, renationalizing state assets, and the legitimacy of privatization in the expected directions. The severity of violations of the law on privatization, the provision of public goods, and the good use of the privatized asset shape attitudes toward revising privatization. The results are available from the author on request.

[11] Thus, rather than comparing each individual coefficient against the status quo option as in columns 1-3 (B1=B4, B2=B4, B3=B4), here I compare the coefficient on support for revising privatization relative to all other outcomes combined (B1+B2+B3=B4).

respondent prefers private property as each of these options ultimately leaves assets in private hands.

Finally, in column 6 I explore how respondents view the legitimacy of the process of privatization. It is difficult to divine how respondents who favor option 1, renationalizing and leaving assets in state hands, view the legitimacy of privatization because they could favor state property due to material interests or due to legitimacy concerns. I can, however, identify the extent of concern for legitimacy among those who ultimately would like to see privatized assets remain in private hands by comparing the probability that a respondent chooses either option 2 or 3 as compared to 4 (option 2 + 3 = 4). Option 2, reprivatizing the assets to new owners and option 3, making owners pay a large fine, both keep privatized assets in private hands, but indicate some concern about the legitimacy of the process. If respondents are significantly more likely to choose option 2 or 3 relative to 4, they view privatization as illegitimate, while the opposite is true if the respondents are more likely to choose option 4 relative to options 2 or 3.

To begin, consider the impact of *HighSkill*, a dummy variable that equals 1 for respondents who work as managers, administrators, technical specialists, or independent entrepreneurs. High-skill respondents are about 32 percent less likely to choose option 1(renationalization) relative to option 4 as indicated by the relative risk ratio of .68 in column 1. This is a large effect. High-skill respondents are no more likely to choose reprivatization or having owners pay a fine than to choose option 4, as indicated by the relative risk ratios on *HighSkill* in columns 2 and 3. The ratios in columns 4 and 5 indicate that *HighSkill* is associated with opposition to changing the status quo privatization and a preference for private over state property. Thus, skill seems to be positively associated with support for the privatization status quo, and for private property, but not with any particular view toward the legitimacy of privatization. These results are consistent with the argument that respondents view privatization through a lens of material interest as high-skill workers are likely to benefit more from privatization than less skilled workers.

Age has a similar relation with attitudes toward reprivatization. Older respondents are more likely to favor renationalization than the status quo, as indicated by the relative risk ratio in column 1, are more likely to support revising privatization, and to view privatization as illegitimate as indicated by the statistically significant results reported in columns 4 and 6. The result in column 6 indicates that among those who prefer private property, older respondents are more likely than younger respondents to view privatization as illegitimate. This result obtains even controlling for skill, education, and income, which suggests the possibility that respondents' attitudes are shaped by the Soviet economic experience.

Education too has predictable associations with views toward reprivatization. The excluded category is those respondents with a vocational education whose skill set is likely to be narrowly defined by their training.[12] Non-vocational education is associated with greater opposition to revising privatization as indicated by the coefficients on the four education variables in column 1. Respondents who had at least some high school, finished high school, or attended college were significantly less likely to favor renationalization relative to the privatization status quo. Moreover, these effect sizes are large, ranging from changes in risk ratios of 36 to 42 percent. It is not just the number of years of education that shapes attitudes toward revising privatization; the content of education also matters and it does so in a predictable fashion

In addition, those with higher education tend to view privatization as more legitimate than do those with vocational education as indicated by the results reported in column 6 for respondents who finished high school or had some college education. This is interesting as we do not see this relationship for those who are less educated as indicated by the relative risk ratios on lower levels of education in column 6.

Measuring household income is admittedly difficult. I use a four-point qualitative scale where 1 indicates that the household "could barely make ends meet and lacked money even for food"; 2 indicates that the household "had enough money for food, but buying clothes is a financial hardship"; 3 indicates that the household "had enough money to buy food and clothes, but that buying consumer durables like a television or refrigerator would be financially difficult"; and 4 indicates that the household "could buy consumer durables, but it was difficult to buy expensive items like an apartment, a summer cottage

---

[12] Vocational education includes those who attended or graduated from "professional-technical institutes" (PTUs), a form of educational institute often run by ministries that trained specialists for narrowly defined tasks within the command economy. Graduates from these PTUs were likely to be especially unprepared for an economy dominated by private property and are not surprisingly strong supporters of revising privatization.

or other items."[13] Respondents in households with higher reported incomes express no clear preference over reprivatization as indicated by the result column 6.

Household income is negatively associated with respondents choosing renationalization over the status quo as indicated by the coefficient in column 1, although this relationship lies just outside standard levels of statistical significance (p = .11). Respondents with higher family incomes are significantly more likely to favor private over state property as indicated by the results in column 5, but are no more likely to choose other options relative to the privatization status quo. These results may be less precisely estimated given the difficulty of measuring household income in Russia.[14]

City size is also associated with attitudes toward revising privatization. City size is a five-category variable where 1 = village; 2 = city less than 100,000; 3 = city less than 500,000; 4 = greater than 500,000; and 5 = Moscow. Respondents in large cities oppose revising privatizing. They also viewed privatization as less legitimate. This is likely due to the great disparities in income in large cities that many attribute to privatization. Unpacking this result finds that residents of Moscow support private property, but residents of other cities greater than 500,000 support state property.

Taken together these results indicate that human capital, such as levels of education, skill, and age, are strong predictors of attitudes toward revising privatization. Moreover, the respondents with human capital most suited for a market economy were likely to oppose revising privatization because they preferred private property. This suggests that despite the technical nature of privatization, respondents evaluate the policy

---

[13] Respondents had the opportunity to select "could buy whatever they wanted including expensive items, like an apartment, a summer cottage, etc." As only 9 respondents out of 1600 reported their income in this category, I include these responses in category 4.

[14] To further explore the relationship of human capital, I interacted the high-skills dummy variable with age. Older respondents with low skills continue to support revising privatization, while older respondents with high skills did not. Respondents who said that they could name a firm that was providing public goods for the region were about five percentage points more likely to support the status quo privatization than were respondents who could not. This result is consistent with the experiment reported above and suggests the value of firms conducting public campaigns to advertise their good works. However, only 19 percent of respondents could name such a firm.

based in part of their personal material interests and are able to calculate the personal costs and benefits of the policy in a reasonable manner.

In addition, legitimacy concerns shape support for revising privatization. College-educated respondents viewed privatization as more legitimate than did respondents with a vocational education. Respondents in larger cities viewed privatization as less legitimate than did their compatriots in smaller towns.

The Results in Comparative Perspective

Within Russia privatization has been wildly unpopular. For some, it was *prikhvatizatsiia* or "grabization" rather than privatization. For others, it was the "Sale of the Century" (Freeland 2000). Anatolii Chubais, the architect of privatization in Russia, is widely regarded as one of Russia's most unpopular officials. Yet, these comments tend to view Russia in a vacuum and do not evaluate privatization in Russia compared to privatizations in other countries. The appropriate question therefore is not: "Was privatization in Russia unpopular?", but rather "Is it more unpopular than privatization in other countries?" And here the answer is "just a little bit more." In 2006, the World Bank and the European Bank for Reconstruction and Development conducted a survey similar to the one analyzed above, but on a much larger scale. One thousand respondents in each of 28 postcommunist countries were asked:

"In your opinion, what should be done with most privatized companies? They should be...
(1) Renationalized and kept in state hands;
(2) Renationalized and then re-privatized again using a more transparent process;
(3) Left in the hands of current owners provided they pay privatized assets' worth;
(4) Left in the hands of current owners with no change."

Table 6.9 summarizes responses to this question.[15] Twenty nine percent of respondents preferred a renationalization that left

[15] Despite the technical nature of the question, non-responses occurred in only 0.6 percent of the cases. Respondents appear to have well-defined views on the issue.

Table 6.9 *The Results in Comparative Perspective*
"In your opinion, what should be done with most privatized companies?
They should be..."

	Renation-alized and kept in state hands %	Renation-alized and then re-privatized again using a more transparent process %	Left in the hands of cur-rent owners provided that they pay privatized assets' worth %	Left in the hands of current owners with no change %
Albania	14.5	18.7	51.7	15.2
Armenia	40.5	22.6	26.8	10.1
Azerbaijan	41.4	26.4	8.6	23.7
Belarus	20.4	7.1	25.8	46.7
Bosnia	25.0	17.9	43.4	13.7
Bulgaria	28.8	15.8	48.3	7.2
Croatia	23.9	29.1	41.0	6.0
Czech Rep.	13.0	11.8	50.6	24.6
Estonia	22.4	10.7	22.6	44.4
FYRoM	35.3	20.7	38.0	6.0
Georgia	30.9	31.9	14.0	23.2
Hungary	24.6	10.2	51.9	13.3
Kazakhstan	47.5	13.4	26.7	12.5
Kyrgyzstan	43.8	11.2	17.7	27.4
Latvia	19.1	14.2	40.4	26.4
Lithuania	17.6	17.3	38.3	26.8
Moldova	34.8	14.6	32.7	17.9
Mongolia	19.9	22.6	21.0	36.5
Montenegro	19.3	20.6	51.3	8.8
Poland	22.4	20.4	37.2	20.0
Romania	19.9	14.4	53.0	12.8
Russia	**36.7**	**13.3**	**31.5**	**18.5**
Serbia	20.0	18.3	50.7	11.0
Slovakia	34.2	8.7	39.9	17.1
Slovenia	12.4	19.6	36.6	31.4
Tajikistan	48.4	13.7	21.9	16.0
Ukraine	43.0	12.5	31.9	12.6
Uzbekistan	51.6	10.6	22.6	15.3
Total	**29.0**	**16.7**	**34.8**	**19.4**

Table **6.9** (*cont.*)

	Renation-alized and kept in state hands %	Renation-alized and then re-privatized again using a more transparent process %	Left in the hands of cur-rent owners provided that they pay privatized assets' worth %	Left in the hands of current owners with no change %
Cumulative	29.0	45.7	80.6	100.0
Observations	8077	4654	9697	5412

Mean responses. Data from European Bank for Reconstruction and Development (2006).

property in state hands. Seventeen percent of respondents supported renationalization followed by privatization to new owners using a more transparent process. Thirty-five percent of respondents favored leaving property in the hands of the current owners provided they pay what the privatized assets are worth. And a little over nineteen percent of respondents favored the status quo of leaving privatized assets in the hands of current owners with no additional payments.

Support for revising privatized property varied considerably across countries. Despite the widespread belief that privatization in Russia was particularly unpopular, responses from Russia are roughly similar to regional averages. Respondents in Russia express slightly higher than average support for renationalizing privatized firms (36.7 versus 29.0). Yet, they are just about as likely to support the status quo privatization (18.5 versus 19.4 percent). In other words, the legitimacy of privatization in Russia is a little bit lower than par for the course. In comparative perspective, the much maligned privatization in Russia is viewed as not much more illegitimate than other privatizations in the region.[16]

---

[16] This question is not aimed at the "Loans for Shares" auctions that have drawn considerable criticism (Black et al. 2000, but see also Treisman (2010).

Why so Few Reversals of Privatization?

Scholars and journalists have paid much attention to high-profile reversals of privatization and rightly so. However, given the great support from the public for revising privatization across every country in the postcommunist region, perhaps the more interesting questions is why reversals of privatization have not been more common. After all, in every country in the sample, a majority of respondents would like to revise privatization in some way.

These results from the World Bank/EBRD survey suggest a partial answer that has broader implications for the study of property rights. It is not so much support for a particular program of privatization making privatized property stable that keeps property rights in place. Indeed, majority support for a particular reprivatization outcome is rare. Rather it is the inability of competing groups within society to coordinate on an alternative that keeps the property rights status quo in place. That is, while a majority of respondents may be unhappy with the status quo privatization, they are unable to agree on how to correct it. To the extent that this argument is valid, creating secure assets post-privatization does not require broad support for a particular privatization program. Secure property rights may emanate in part from diffuse support for a number of alternatives to the status quo that make it difficult to coordinate on a single option.

Caveats

These results are subject to several caveats. First, responses to a public opinion survey are not necessarily indicative of behavior and popular support for moves by the government is rarely translated directly into policy. Yet, the coordination problem facing those in favor of revising privatization may be an important source for the stability of an unpopular privatization program. Second, it is difficult to know the impact of the survey experiments on attitudes over time. Does the new information gained from the survey experiments have a lasting or fleeting impact on attitudes? It is noteworthy that small changes in wording in a survey experiment can produce significant changes in attitudes and a much more intense campaign of these messages could produce more substantive changes. But it could be that a much noisier environment with contrasting claims about the severity of violations or the extent of public goods provision would dilute these results. Di Tella et al. (2012), for example, find smaller substantive effects in their survey experiment on water privatization in Buenos Aires – a design that takes advantage of a more realistic environment by discriminating between those that did and did not benefit from privatization.

Conclusion

Many studies examine the impact of privatization on economic outcomes, but these works rarely examine the legitimacy of privatization among the public. This is a critical issue for developing and transition countries where privatization is rarely transparent. In addition, of the few studies that examine popular support for and against privatization, few examine why respondents hold their view, and fewer still explore the possibility that legitimacy concerns could shape support for policy.

Moreover, there is a considerable debate about the extent to which fundamental economic attitudes can be changed via new information (Denzau and North 1994). Indeed, the substantive importance and technical nature of privatization lead one to expect that it would be rather difficult to change attitudes toward privatized property simply by giving respondents new information. The immutability of norms is far from just an academic question. If attitudes toward fundamental economic issues such as privatized property are largely immune to change, then the prospects for social or economic transformation may be muted (Di Tella et al. 2012).

This chapter found that in the case of Russia the original sin of a legally dubious privatization helped to undermine support for privatized property, but with some effort, right-holders could increase public support for privatization. When respondents were told that right-holders had both invested in the firm and provided public goods for the region at high levels, support for the privatization status quo was about 14–16 percentage points higher than the baseline condition. Investing at high levels on its own had no impact on attitudes; whereas providing public goods at high levels significantly increased support for privatized property when violations of the Law on Privatization were major. In addition, human capital, as measured by education, skill, and age are all associated with attitudes toward reversing privatization as were concerns about the process of privatization. It is not easy to change public attitudes toward privatized property, but it can be done.

Further research is necessary to learn how well these insights on privatization travel outside of Russia and the postcommunist region. The scope and speed of industrial privatization in the postcommunist region is far larger than in other settings, which makes generalizations difficult, but given the frequency of corrupt privatizations and weak property rights in developing countries, the empirical results have theoretical importance beyond the case at hand. One hypothesis worth exploring is whether the unpopularity of privatization may be traced to the manner in which privatization was conducted. Further research could also examine whether these results extend to other reforms, such as trade liberalization.

More generally, the results have implications for business–state relations. Existing literature has paid considerable attention to the role of the state in shaping the legitimacy of property rights. The results here indicate that the state and business elites share the capacity to influence the legitimacy of property rights. Rather than viewing right-holders as passively responding to institutional constraints, we should recognize that they can shape the legitimacy of their property rights. Even without a change in the legal status of their property, right-holders can increase its legitimacy. This result introduces agency into a literature in which it has been largely absent (but see Besley 1995; Frye 2006; Di Tella et al. 2012; and Markus 2012; 2015).

More speculatively, the results may provide insights into the disappointing results of privatization in some settings. To the extent that the legitimacy of privatization is reflected in the security of property rights, the birth defect of an illegitimate privatization may dull incentives to use assets productively. A legally dubious privatization may lead right-holders to perceive their ill-gotten assets as illegitimate and, therefore, vulnerable to political attack. Even where privatizations are not reversed, the illegitimacy of rights may ultimately impair economic performance. This, too, is a topic for more research.

The results have some implications for policy. First, as human capital poorly suited for a market is an important source of support for revising privatization, training programs that better prepare citizens for the market may be appropriate. That older, better-skilled respondents did not support revising privatization (while older, less-skilled respondents did) provides some evidence that this may already be taking place.

Second, in contrast to the implications of the Coasian view of privatization, the findings suggest that the design and implementation of privatization programs are important determinants of the subsequent legitimacy of property rights. To the extent possible, privatizers should favor designs that are broadly acceptable to the community. This may involve greater transparency, simplicity, and public discussion of privatization policies than has often been the case to date.

Third, the results suggest a possible, but long, path out of the illegitimacy trap that bedevils privatization in many countries. Governments may encourage the private provision of some public goods and the good use of assets, in part so right-holders can increase the legitimacy of their property rights. There are limits to this policy as the state is a more efficient provider of public goods than are private firms. But the private provision of public goods may be less socially costly than renationalization or reprivatization.

7 | *Conclusion*

You'd think I could change anything in this country. Like hell I can. No matter what changes I propose and carry out, everything stays the same. Russia is like a tub full of dough, you put your hand down in it, down to the bottom, and think you're master of the situation. When you first pull out your hand, a little hole remains, but then, before your very eyes, the dough expands into a spongy, puffy mass. That's what Russia is like.

Nikita Khrushchev to Fidel Castro in 1963 (Taubman 2004: 598)

Creating strong property rights after the fall of a command economy was never going to be easy and this is especially true in Russia. For 25 years rulers of Russia have reached down deep into the tub of dough, pulled out their hands, and been frustrated by the results. Yet Khrushchev's colorful quote is only half right. For all the frustrations, Russia has changed, for better and for worse, in many ways, and before our very eyes.

To try to understand these changes I have used a variety of survey experiments, a natural experiment, statistical analyses, and administrative data to explore these attempts to shape property rights in Russia. Rather than making blanket claims about the state of property in Russia or trying to develop a unified theory of property rights, I focused on several key potential shapers of property rights, including the bargaining power of rulers and right-holders, social norms, such as attitudes toward privatization; informal institutions, such as reputation, and formal institutions, such as courts and elections.

That bargaining power and political connections shape property rights is well accepted, but bargaining power is multifaceted and scholars debate which dimensions are most important. I unpack the bargaining power of right-holders by exploring how firm size, mobility, and various forms of political connections shape perceptions of property rights and find that managers of state-owned, smaller, and less mobile firms view themselves as especially likely to be the target of a hostile takeover, as do managers who previously worked in the state bureaucracy or do not know the governor personally. In addition, political connections can mitigate these vulnerabilities as managers of state-owned, smaller, and less mobile firms who know the governor personally view their property rights as significantly more secure than those who do not.

Exogenous shocks to the bargaining power of the ruler also shape perceptions of property rights. Following the surprisingly poor performance of the ruling United Russia party in parliamentary elections, managers of immobile, small, and state-owned firms viewed their property rights as less vulnerable to a hostile takeover. Because the bargaining power of the ruler is both shaped by and shapes property rights, it is important for causal identification to find an exogenous source of change in bargaining power in order to determine the direction of causation.

Looking beyond bargaining power, I find that social norms about the legitimacy of privatized property rights are not fixed, but depend on the context and are subject to change. It is not easy to change these norms, but it is possible under some conditions. By providing public goods and by investing in their firms, the right-holders of privatized assets can increase the legitimacy of their property rights in the eyes of the public. More generally, the results indicate that while large majorities in all postcommunist countries revile privatization, they also prefer that privatized assets remain in private rather than in state hands.

Property rights in Russia depend not only on bargaining power and social norms but also on a rich mixture of informal and formal institutions. As have others I find that informal institutions, such as reputation, are an important influence on the security of property rights in Russia. Reputation is a powerful predictor of property rights in trade and political connections are perceived to be a great benefit, particularly during a dispute. Many works have pointed to the relevance of informal institutions, such as reputation and political connections for property rights in Russia, but this work also identifies the relative impact of these institutions while controlling for a range of other factors. This is important because informal institutions and political connections are likely correlated with many other factors that may produce more secure property rights. Larger, better performing firms with more experienced managers are likely to have better personal connections with public officials, and better reputations, and they are also likely to receive better treatment from judges and firms. Without controlling for these factors, it is difficult to identify the independent impact of reputation and personal connections on the security of property rights.

Moreover, many studies struggle to identify the magnitude of the impact of informal or private institutions on property rights. How important are political connections or a good reputation? Is a good relationship with a state official more important for receiving favorable treatment in a dispute than the size or sector of the firm? I find that a good reputation has a stronger impact on the propensity to trade than a 15 percent reduction in property rights and, that during a court case respondents perceive that political connections increase the chances of winning a dispute by about 10 percentage points. By controlling for other factors that might influence the security of property rights, I begin to identify the relative magnitude of the importance of these factors in comparison to other influences on the security of property rights.

Formal institutions too are important in protecting some types of property right in Russia. Businesspeople in Russia use state courts of arbitration for all their many flaws and perceive them to be somewhat effective in everyday disputes. Respondents perceive that political connections matter when going to court, but they also perceive that facts of the case are important too. In addition, the state courts of arbitration that decide most commercial cases are perceived to be far more effective than the courts of general jurisdiction that handle most criminal cases. This may be a low bar given how badly the courts of general jurisdiction are perceived to work.

Yet, these same state courts of arbitration offer far less protection against corporate raids by powerful state agents, who are often in league with economic rivals of the firm being raided. Indeed, it is powerful agents within the legal system itself – the Procuracy, the Investigative Committee, Ministry of Internal Affairs and the Federal Security Services – that are frequently behind these attacks on property rights.

Thus, everyday threats to firms such as non-payment and non-performance of contractual obligations, and existential threats to firms such as *reiderstvo* have different dynamics, sources, and outcomes. Rather than trying to make broad statements about the condition of property rights in Russia, it is more useful to embrace the heterogeneity of economic conflict, to recognize how differences in stakeholders, strategies, and institutions shape different types of economic conflict over property, and to orient our research accordingly.

Broader Points

The results also have implications for three broad bodies of work. For scholars of economic development the findings point to the importance of the politically contingent nature of property rights. Rather than viewing property rights as exogenously given or driven primarily by efficiency considerations, the results here suggest the heavy hand of politics on the nature of property rights. Politics can shape social norms about property rights as politicians use populist appeals to rally those who perceive privatization as illegitimate. Firms with political connections are perceived to get significantly better treatment in courts and to be less likely to be the target of a hostile takeover even after controlling for a range of other factors. Political connections are central to the security of property rights, but not all types of political power are easily translated into greater protection.

In addition, while traditional treatments, such as Eggertson (1990: 59–60) and Pejovich (1998: 60–61) assume that property rights can usefully be seen as public goods equally available to all citizens, the analysis here suggests the value of viewing property rights as a private good or club good that is available to some, but not to others (Haber et al. 2003: 10–20; Lawson-Remer 2012). Even within a single institutional framework of contemporary Russia, the security of property rights varies greatly among right-holders – a type of heterogeneity that is often overlooked in analyses that use national-level indicators of the security of property rights. This point is not new. Much of the literature on revenue-maximizing rulers and state capture by interest groups implicitly relies on the assumption that property rights may be selectively enforced, but we know far less about the conditions under which rulers choose to assign and enforce property rights selectively or universally (Stigler 1971; North 1981). More generally, there is much to learn about how the interaction of rulers and right-holders influence whether property rights become a public good or private good.

Moreover, this study contributes to empirical studies of property rights by focusing more explicitly on political factors. Firm surveys have become a staple of research in development economics, but tend to focus on manager-specific features, such as skills and training; firm-specific factors, such as level of centralization or type of governance; or on market-specific factors, such as levels of competition or exposure to exports. While not neglecting these factors, this work puts political factors, such as relations with state officials, political preferences, or prior experience in the government, front and center. This is important as in many countries businesspeople are important political actors in their own right and their political activities shape economic outcomes.

For scholars of comparative politics, this work reinforces the importance of studying the formal institutions of autocracy. For many years, scholars argued that elections under autocracy were merely window-dressing, but in the last decade scholars have made considerable headway to overturn this view. They have shown that holding elections influences the tenure of autocratic rulers, the prospects for leadership turnover, and the content of economic policy (Magaloni 2006; Chiozza and Goemans 2011; Blaydes 2011; Pop-Eleches and Robertson 2015). However, this body of work has paid little attention to how elections under autocracy shapes property rights. By showing that elections in an autocratic setting can have real consequences for perceptions of property rights, this work hopes to deepen our understanding of the impact of formal institutions under autocracy.

This work also points to the benefits of looking beyond elections, parties and legislatures to also explore how formal legal institutions can be used to shape policy and regime durability (Lust-Okar 2006a 2006b; Magaloni 2006; Gandhi 2008). The tendency to charge political opponents with economic crimes, rather than political crimes, leaves defendants in the hands of the prosecutor-friendly criminal courts rather than international courts, such as the European Courts of Human Rights. The subservience of the state courts, especially the courts of general jurisdiction, is a useful tool to keep political opposition in check.

A focus on courts is also helpful because this study found significant variation in state support for empowering courts over time. During the economic boom of 2000–2008, President Putin significantly increased spending on the courts and courthouses even as he increased accountability for judges. As the boom continued, President Medvedev took a number of measures to humanize the legal system for entrepreneurs from 2008–2012. However, President Putin returned to power in 2012 and, after putting down a series of anti-government protests, reversed many of the efforts of his predecessor to strengthen property rights. In addition, he undermined the power of the state courts of arbitration by merging the Supreme Court of Arbitration with State Courts of General Jurisdiction. These variations in court performance and state strategies over time map well on to the interests of the ruler's constituencies and the bargaining power of the ruler.

These results also suggest a larger point about property rights under hybrid or autocratic rule that should be of interest to scholars of comparative politics: the tendency to create dual legal systems that provide secure property rights to some but not others. Ideally, this form of legal dualism allows rulers to use the legal system to reward key constituencies on whose political support they depend, while also encouraging economic activity in areas that do not directly threaten important constituencies of the ruler.

Take two extreme examples. If all economic disputes were resolved according to the political needs of the autocrat, economic activity would shrivel – even among constituencies who do not pose a threat to the ruler. Rather than investing their assets and risk losing them to a politically more powerful business rival, economic agents would hide their assets, send them abroad, or consume them. While this strategy would benefit the political supporters of the autocrat, it would also rob the ruler of much-needed tax revenue from economic activity generated in politically non-sensitive cases. Moreover, the costs to the autocrat of deciding whose side to take in every case would likely far exceed the political benefits of doing so.

Consider another extreme. If all economic disputes were resolved according to legal principles that treated all subjects equally without regard to their political connections and affiliations, businesspeople could invest with confidence in the knowledge that their rights would be protected from the state. This would generate significant tax revenue for the ruler, but the autocrat would lose the ability to use the state to benefit key political constituencies.

In an ideal situation for the ruler and his coalition in a hybrid or autocratic regime, this dualism would allow the ruler to use the legal system to deliver specific benefits to key constituents on whose political support he depends, while also giving him the opportunity to collect taxes on investment from businesspeople in non-politically sensitive cases. Rulers in hybrid regimes therefore may seek to provide some mix of legal institutions that allows a degree of bias in the legal system to protect core constituencies while also minimizing the losses of revenue that is inevitably generated by protecting politically important if economically less efficient supporters.

This tendency to divide legal systems and protect rights in some areas but not others is hardly unique to contemporary Russia. In Egypt, Moustafa (2007) finds that President Mubarak built separate legal institutions for foreign investors in an effort to attract capital. In Mexico, Magaloni (2008) shows how rulers used the *ampare* courts to allow citizens to monitor misbehavior by local officials, but not to challenge more fundamental political rights. In Pinochet's Chile, Hilbink (2008) finds that while courts under the purview of the Supreme Court were subservient to the regime, the Constitutional Tribunal was not. Ginsburg (2008: 69) notes that "administrative law in China is used to constrain low officials, but not high officials."

The dualism of legality in various forms also has deep roots in Russian and Soviet history and scholars have consistently pushed back against the view that legal norms have always been irrelevant. Burbank notes (2012: 339): "To sum up, this study of legal legacies shows that in the imperial period Russian subjects were active litigants in lower level courts. Peasants were familiar with legal procedures and used them in their own interests. However, as at present, spectacular trials in cities with political significance or social interest were what attracted elite society's attention, and the ordinary life of the law remained invisible to elites, including foreigners." In the Soviet period, Hazard (1962) and Feifer (1964) found that administrative law functioned reasonably well even in the face of the strictures of communist ideology, but provided few human or political rights. Hendley (2011: 23) finds that this dualism of legality has not disappeared in contemporary Russia. Based on her research with focus groups, she notes: "Notwithstanding the societal lack of trust in the capacity of law and those entrusted with its enforcement to stand up to bribery and connections, some are still willing to work through formal channels... Particularly surprising was the respondents' use of law to challenge the state and other powerful interests." More generally, she notes (2012b: 523) that: "the instrumentalism that politicized cases evidence exists in uneasy harmony with the vast majority of mundane cases that courts resolve in accord with the written law. My research, which is based on focus groups and interviews with ordinary Russians, finds that Russians are sufficiently savvy to appreciate the unspoken differences between these various categories of cases."

The size of these two legal spheres between the privileged and the rest likely depends on the bargaining power of the ruler with respect to the most politically important right-holders. Where the autocrat is sufficiently autonomous from these right-holders due to personal popularity or alternative sources of revenue, he may be able to expand control over property rights. However, exogenous shocks that weaken the bargaining position of the ruler relative to these right-holders may yield property rights less favorable to the ruler. These latter points are necessarily speculative, but worthy of more research.

Finally, for observers of Russia, this discussion of legal dualism suggests a reframing of debates over property rights. Legal dualism – in which property rights in run-of-the-mill disputes are much better protected than in politically sensitive disputes – need not be a halfway house on the path to a rule-of-law state or some other final endpoint. Nor need it be the result of a weak state incapable of providing the public good of justice (Holmes 1996). Nor, in this specific case, need it be the result of uniquely Russian cultural traditions (Newcity 1997). Rulers in hybrid or autocratic regimes such as Russia may prefer this legal dualism to either the complete dependence of property rights on political authority or the complete independence of property rights from political authority. This dualism allows them to reward politically important supporters, while also retaining some incentives for right-holders to use their assets productively. How rulers make this trade-off between the political benefits of rationing property rights and the economic benefits of making them available to all likely depends on the relative bargaining power of rulers and right-holders as well as prevailing institutions and social norms.

This view suggests that improvements in property rights in Russia and other weakly institutionalized countries, are tightly linked to changes in bargaining power between rulers and right-holders. This is not much help in predicting the shape of property rights as shifts in bargaining power are not always easy to foresee. But this view does help us better understand where to look for changes in the nature of property rights in the future and it reminds of the fundamental importance of politics in shaping property rights.

More generally, it suggests that scholars and policymakers should pay greater attention to how autocrats seek to create dual legal systems that provide secure property rights to some but not to others. Exploring how autocrats use personal relations to protect property rights for the privileged while compelling others to rely on formal institutions should be high on the research agenda. Why is the gap between the security of property rights for the privileged and for other right-holders greater in some settings than others? Under what conditions can right-holders without political connections increase the security of their property? Can institutions that bolster property rights for ordinary right-holders undermine the personal ties that protect the property of the privileged? Under what conditions do the privileged support and oppose stronger property rights for ordinary right-holders? Clearly there is much more to learn about property rights under autocratic rule.

Data Appendix

Introduction

I conducted surveys of firm managers in 2000, 2005, 2008, and 2011. Before reporting the details and descriptive statistics from each survey, I note several commonalities across the four surveys. Full data, original questions, and replication data are available at the Harvard Dataverse and on my personal webpage, www.TimothyFrye.com

In each survey, interviewers spoke with respondents face to face in the place of work of the respondents. Chief executive officers, chief financial officers, and chief legal officers were included as potential respondents and interviewers spoke with only one person per firm. The surveys included firms from 22 to 24 different economic sectors as categorized by the State Statistical Agency and ranged from industrial giants in metals and energy to retail trading firms. The samples excluded firms in agriculture, communal services, and health and social services. Firms were chosen using stratified random sampling. Researchers stratified the sample by firm size and sector to mirror the population of firms in each region and firms were selected at random from within each of the strata. Each firm within each stratum had an equal probability of being included in the sample. In all surveys, the survey company called back at least 20 percent of respondents to ensure consistency with reported data. In each of the four surveys, firms were based in Moscow, Voronezh, Nizhnii Novgorod, Ekaterinburg, Smolensk, Ufa, Tula, and Novgorod. In 2005 and 2011, I added to the sample three and seven regions, respectively. All interviews were done in the capital city of each region. For each survey, I provide details on the field work, descriptive statistics of managers, firms, and variables used in the analyses.

206

Firm Survey 2000: Used Briefly in Chapter 4

On my behalf, the Levada Center (then known as VCIOM) conducted a survey of businesspeople from October 10 to November 23, 2000. The response rate among managers contacted was 56 percent. The lowest response rate was in Smolensk at 44 percent and in four regions the response rate was over 70 percent.

Table DA1 *Descriptive Statistics: Firm Survey 2000*

	Mean (st.dev)	Min/Max	Observations
Size, # of employees	840	3/53327	495
Size, Log # of employees	5.19	1.10/10.88	495
Age director	46	23/82	495
Education levels	2.9 (.58)	1/4	495
Privatized	.64 (.49)	0/1	495
Any state ownership	.10 (.31)	0/1	495
Competition as problem	3.38 (1.34)	1/5	494
Energy sector	.02 (.15)	0/1	495
Heavy industry	.31 (.47)	0/1	495
Light industry	.21 (.40)	0/1	495
Construction	.17 (.37)	0/1	495
Communications	.04 (.18)	0/1	495
Transportation	.06 (.21)	0/1	495
Retail/wholesale trade	.15 (.35)	0/1	495
Financial sector	.03 (.19)	0/1	495
Foreign investment	.08 (.27)	0/1	459
Foreign ownership	.09 (.28)	0/1	426
Rating of arbitration courts	3.19 (.93)	1/5	354
Rating of general courts	2.87 (.79)	1/5	305

Firm Survey 2005: Data from Chapters 4 and 5

I commissioned a survey of 666 managers in 11 of Russia's (then) 89 regions to address these and other questions. Interviewers from the Levada Center spoke face to face with managers in January and February 2005. Regions included the original eight, plus Khabarovsk, Omsk, and Rostov. The overall response rate was 53 percent for firms contacted by the interviewer. Fully one-third of all refusals came from the capital city. Absent Moscow the response rate increases to 62 percent. At least one region from each of Russia's 7 "super-regions" was included in the sample.

Table DA2 *Descriptive Statistics: Firm Survey 2005*

	Mean (st.dev)	Min/Max	Observations
Size., # of employees	726	4/70000	666
Size, Log # of employees	4.99 (1.53)	1.38/11.15	666
Age of the director	47 (10.2)	21/72	666
Male	.79 (.41)	0/1	666
Education levels	2.9 (.58)	1/4	666
Privatized	.58 (.49)	0/1	666
Competition as problem	3.38 (1.34)	1/5	657
Energy sector	.02 (.16)	0/1	666
Heavy industry	.28 (.45)	0/1	666
Light industry	.21 (.40)	0/1	666
Construction	.18 (.38)	0/1	666
Transportation	.07 (.36)	0/1	666
Communications	.04 (.19)	0/1	666
Retail/wholesale trade	.15 (.36)	0/1	666
Financial sector	.05 (.26)	0/1	666
Foreign investment	.06 (.25)	0/1	666
Rating of arbitration courts	3.21 (.83)	1/5	565
Rating of general courts	2.87 (.79)	1/5	501
Foreign ownership	.05 (.22)	0/1	569
Give credit	.49 (.50)	0/1	645
Weak reputation	.27 (.45)	0/1	590
Medium reputation	.19 (.40)	0/1	590
Strong reputation	.53 (.50)	0/1	590
Courts (recoded as in text)	2.22 (.67)	0/3	565

Firm Survey 2008: Data from Chapters 2, 3, and 4

The 2008 survey included only the original 8 regions. Interviewers from the Levada Center interviewed 503 firm managers between June 19 and August 14, 2008. The survey was completed just before the financial crash of 2008 and 2009. The response rate among firms with whom the Levada Center was able to make contact was 55 percent. Among all firms included in the initial sample of firms the response rate was 44 percent. Almost half of the refusals – 353 of 624 – were from Moscow, which is typical of these types of survey.

Table DA3 *Descriptive Statistics: Firm Survey 2008*

	Mean (st.dev)	Min/Max	Observations
# of employees	436 (1401)	3/22000	503
Log # of employees	4.9 (1.6)	.1/9.99	503
Age director	47 (10.56)	22/72	503
Male	.70 (.46)	0/1	503
Education levels	2.9 (.53)	1/6	503
Fully state-owned firm	.06 (.22)	0/1	503
Privatized	.62 (.49)	0/1	503
No competition	.06 (.22)	0/1	503
Export	.30 (.46)	0/1	503
Energy	.03 (.16)	0/1	503
Heavy industry	.28 (.45)	0/1	503
Light industry	.20 (.25)	0/1	503
Construction	.16 (.37)	0/1	503
Transport	.06 (.22)	0/1	503
Communication	.03 (.16)	0/1	503
Trade	.18 (.39)	0/1	503
Financial sector	.05 (.22)	0/1	503
Hostile takeover threat	2.35 (.60)	1/3	432
United Russia voter	.56 (.50)	0/1	503
Government experience	.20 (.40)	0/1	487
Foreign investment	.09 (29)	0/1	481
Profit in 2008	1.28 (.52)	1/3	485
Foreign ownership	.04 (.21)	0/1	503
Hostile takeover threat	2.35 (.60)	1/3	432
Rating of arbitration courts	3.41 (.78)	1/5	415
Rating of general courts	3.23 (.81)	1/5	371

Firm Survey 2011: Data from Chapters 1, 2, 3, and 4

With colleagues from the International Center for the Study of Institutions and Development in Moscow, I employed VCIOM, a Moscow-based polling company, to survey 922 firms drawn from 24 sectors in 15 regional capitals in Russia from November 15 to December 22, 2011. Of 1240 firm managers contacted, 318 refused to take part in the survey for a response rate of 74 percent. Interviews were conducted face to face in the employers' place of work. The 15 regional capitals included at least one regional capital drawn from each of Russia's 7 federal districts. Regional capitals included: Voronezh, Ekaterinburg, Kemerovo, Kursk, Moscow, Nizhnii Novgorod, Novgorod, Omsk, Rostov, Smolensk, Tula, Ulyanovsk, Ufa, Irkutsk, and Khabarovsk.

Table DA4 *Descriptive Statistics: Firm Survey 2011*

	Mean (st.dev)	Min/Max	Observations
Size, # of employees	253 (600)	1/6500	893
Size, Log # of employees	4.05 (1.84)	.01/8.78	893
Age director	44 (9.79)	20/73	900
Male	.67 (.47)	0/1	922
Higher education	.89 (.31)	0/1	873
Fully state owned firm	.04 (.18)	0/1	922
Competition as problem	3.5 (1.39)	1/5	902
Energy sector	.03 (.11)	0/1	922
Heavy industry	.16 (.35)	0/1	922
Light industry	.20 (.40)	0/1	922
Construction	.11 (.31)	0/1	922
Transport	.05 (.22)	0/1	922
Trade	.26 (.44)	0/1	922
Communication	.04 (.20)	0/1	922
Real estate	.07 (.26)	0/1	922
Financial sector	.07 (.26)	0/1	922
United Russia member	.04 (.19)	0/1	922
UR sympathizer	.26 (.43)	0/1	922
Immobile	.20 (.40)	0/1	922
Know governor	.30 (.46)	0/1	856
Government experience	.14 (.35)	0/1	793
Some state ownership	.09 (.28)	0/1	922
Rating of arbitration court	3.42 (.89)	1/5	694

Table DA4 (*cont.*)

	Mean (st.dev)	Min/Max	Observations
Rating of general court	3.28 (.91)	1/5	722
Hostile takeover index	2.54 (.56)	1/3	846
Federal government renationalization index	2.49 (.60)	1/3	838
Regional government takeover index	2.43 (.64)	1/3	842

Mass Survey 2006: Data from Chapter 6

I also conducted a survey of the Russian public in November 2006. I added 15 questions to the monthly omnibus survey run by the Levada Center known as the Courier. A multi-stage, stratified sample of interviewing locations was employed in the study and is described blow. The survey is designed to be nationally representative and respondents are drawn from 128 primary sampling units across 45 subnational units of Russia.

FIRST STAGE: The sample was distributed among 7 federal regions (North-Western, Central, Southern, Povolzhskii, Uralskii, Siberian, and Far Eastern), and inside each region – among 5 strata of settlements proportionally to number of population of adults. All cities with a popoulation of over 1 million were included in the sample as self-representative objects. Other urban settlements (rural districts in rural areas) were selected based on probability proportional to the size of a settlement. In each settlement 10–15 interviews were conducted. The number of interviews, falling onto one strata, is divided equally among selected settlements. In total there are 128 PSUs (88 urban settlements and 40 rural districts).

SECOND STAGE: In each selected PSU one or more SSUs/sampling points (polling-districts in urban settlements, villages in rural districts) were randomly selected from the list of all SSUs of the given PSU based on the method of constant step. The necessary number of sampling points was found from the calculation – about ten respondents per one sampling point.

THIRD STAGE: Selection of households in the territory of sampling points was done by random route method.

FOURTH STAGE: Only one respondent was selected within a household using the sex-by-age and educational quotas.

The sampling is based on data from the 2002 National Census.

FIELDWORK interviews were conducted face to face in the respondent's home.

Table DA5 *Fieldwork Report: Mass Survey 2006*

The total number of visited addresses	3880
Non-dwelling buildings	62
The door of multi-apartment building is locked	105
No one home	837
The total number of contacts	2876
Bad health/unable to answer	49
Refusals	1190
Interrupted interviews	19
Completed interviews	1618
Rejected during control	18
Included into the data file	1600
QUALITY CONTROL	
The work of the interviewers was controlled by the regional offices' supervisors.	
The following ways of control were used:	
Callbacks	121 cases
Telephone control	306 cases
Total	427 cases

Thus, about 26 percent of the interviews were controlled.

Table DA6 *Description of Variables: Mass Survey 2006*

Age	Age of respondent (log value)
High skill level	Dummy variable 1 = Manager, independent entrepreneur, specialist without managerial function, security force worker, white collar worker; 0 = worker, student, pensioner, invalid, house-wife, unemployed.
Education levels	Dummy variable Highest degree attained: Primary education – 9 years of coursework or less (primary school) Unfinished high school (less than high school_ High school graduate – 11 years of coursework (high school) Unfinished or finished professional technical institute (vocational) Some college – either technikhum or VUZ (vocational education) (some college)
Household income	Categorical variable: 1 = We barely make ends meet. We lack money even for food. 2 = We have money for food, but buying clothes is a financial hardship. 3 = We have money for food and clothes, but buying consumer durables, like a television or refrigerator, is a financial hardship. 4 = We can buy consumer durables, but it is difficult for us to buy expensive items like an apartment, a summer cottage or other items. 5 = We can permit ourselves to buy even expensive items, like an apartment, a summer cottage or other items.
Urbanization	Categorical variables 1 = Moscow 2 = City with more than 500,000 inhabitants 3 = City of 100,000–500,000 inhabitants 4 = Town of less than 100,000 5 = Rural village (Selo)
Unemployed	Dummy variable
Female	Dummy variable
Ethnic Russian	Dummy variable

Table DA7 *Descriptive Statistics: Mass Survey 2006*

	Mean (st.dev)	Min/Max	Observations
High skill	.33 (.47)	0/1	1600
Age	44.75	18/87	1600
Primary	.17 (.38)	0/1	1600
Less than high school	.19 (.39)	0/1	1600
High school	.29 (.45)	0/1	1600
Some college	.20 (.40)	0/1	1600
Vocational school	.14 (.29)	0/1	1600
Household income	2.65 (.86)	1/4	1597
Urbanization	3.44 (1.3)	1/5	1600
Male	.45 (.49)	0/1	1600

References

Abel, Richard L. 2010. "Law and Society: Project and Practice." *Annual Review of Law and Society* 6, 1–23.

Acemoglu, Daron and Simon Johnson. 2005. "Unbundling Institutions." *Journal of Political Economy* 113:5, 949–995.

Acemoglu, Daron and James Robinson. 2006. *Economic Origins of Dictatorship and Democracy*. New York: Cambridge University Press.

Acemoglu, Daron and James Robinson. 2012. *Why Nations Fail: The Origins of Power, Prosperity and Poverty*. New York: Crown Publishing.

Acemoglu, Daron, Simon Johnson, and James Robinson. 2001. "The Colonial Origins of Comparative Development: An Empirical Investigation." *American Economic Review* 91 (December), 1369–1401.

Acemoglu, Daron, Tarek Hassan, and James Robinson. 2011. "Social Structure and Development in Russia." *Quarterly Journal of Economics* 126:2, 895–946.

Adachi, Yuko. 2010. *Building Big Business in Russia*. New York: Routledge Press.

Albertus, Michael and Victor A. Menaldo. 2012. "If You're Against Them You're With Us: The Effect of Expropriation on Autocratic Survival." *Comparative Political Studies* 45:8, 973–103.

Alesina, Alberto and Eliana La Ferrara. 2005. "Preferences for Redistribution in the Land of Opportunities." *Journal of Public Economics* 89, 897–931.

Alina-Pisano. 2008. *Post-Soviet Potemkin Village: Politics and Property Rights in the Black Earth*. New York: Cambridge University Press.

Ang, Yuen Yuen and Nan Jia. 2014. "Political Connections and the Use of Courts among Private Firms in China." *Journal of Politics* 76:2, 318–332.

Antonov, Sergei. 2011. "Law and the Culture of Debt in Moscow 1850–1870." Unpublished Ph.D. Dissertation, Columbia University Department of History.

Baird, Vanessa A. and Debra Javeline. 2007. "The Persuasive Power of Russian Courts." *Political Research Quarterly* 60:3, 429–442.

Baker, Andy. 2003. "Why is Trade Reform So Popular in Latin America? A Consumption-Based Theory of Trade Policy Beliefs." *World Politics* 55:3, 423–55.

Balmforth, Tom. 2013. "Putin's Legal Vertical: Kremlin Seeks to Consolidate Court System." www.rferl.org/a/russia-judicial-reform-arbitration-court/25131950.html

Banerjee. Abhijit and Esther Duflo. 2010. "Giving Credit Where It Was Due." *The Journal of Economic Perspectives* 24:3, 61–79.

Banfield, Edward C. 1958. *The Moral Basis of a Backward Society.* New York: Free Press

Barnes, Andrew. 2006. *Owning Russia: The Struggle Over Factories, Farms, and Power.* Ithaca, NY: Cornell University Press.

Barzel, Yoram. 1989. *The Economic Analysis of Property Rights.* New York: Cambridge University Press.

Bates, Robert. H. 1981. *Markets and States in Tropical Africa*: Berkeley, CA: University of California Press.

    1989. *Beyond the Miracle of the Market.* New York: Cambridge University Press.

    2001. *Prosperity and Violence: The Political Economy of Development.* New York: Norton.

Bates, Robert H. and Donald Lien Da-Hsiang. 1985. "A Note on Taxation, Development, and Representative Government." *Politics and Society* 14:1, 53–70.

Becker, Gary. 1996. "Preferences and Values." In Gary Becker (ed.) *Accounting for Taste.* Cambridge, MA: Harvard University Press, 3–23.

Belanovsky Sergei and Mikhail Dmitriev. 2011. *"Political Crisis in Russia and How it May Develop."* Moscow: Center for Strategic Research.

Belanovsky Sergei, Mikhail Dmitriev, Svetlana Miskhina, and Tatyana Omelchuk. 2011. *"Socio- Economic Change and Political Transformation in Russia."* Moscow: Center for Strategic Research.

Berglof, Erik, Andrey Kounov, Julia Shvets, and Ksenia Yudaeva. 2003. *The New Political Economy of Russia.* Cambridge, MA: MIT Press.

Berliner, Joseph. 1957. *Factory and Manager in the USSR.* Cambridge, MA: Harvard University Press.

Bernhard, Willam and David Leblang. 2006. *Democratic Processes and Financial Markets: Pricing Politics.* New York: Cambridge University Press.

Bernstein, Lisa. 1992. "Opting Out of the Legal System: Extralegal Contractual Relations in the Diamond Industry." *Journal of Legal Studies* 21:1, 115–157.

Besley, Timothy. 1995. "Property Rights and Investment Incentives: Theory and Evidence from Ghana." *The Journal of Political Economy* 103:5, 903–937.

Besley, Timothy and Maitreesh Ghatak. 2009. "Property Rights and Economic Development." In D. Rodrick and M.R. Rosenzweig (eds.),

Handbook of Development Economics. Handbooks in Economics, 5. North Holland: Elsevier, 4525–4595.

Besley, Timothy and Masa Kudamatsu. 2009. "Making Autocracy Work." In Elhanan Helpman (ed.) *Institutions and Economic Performance.* Cambridge, MA: Harvard University Press, 452–510.

Black, Bernard, Reinier Kraakman, and Anna Tarassova. 2000. "Russian Privatization and Corporate Governance: What Went Wrong." *Stanford Law Review* 52: 1731–1806.

Blair, Robert, Christopher Blattman, and Alexandra Hartman, 2014. "How to Promote Order and Property Rights Under Weak Rule of Law: An Experiment in Changing Dispute Resolution Behavior Through Community Education." *American Political Science Review* 108:1, 100–120.

Blattman, Christopher and Edward Miguel. 2010. "Civil War." *Journal of Economic Literature* 48:1, 3–57.

Blaydes, Lisa. 2011. *Elections and Distributive Politics in Mubarak's Egypt.* New York: Cambridge University Press.

Boix, Carles. 2003. *Democracy and Redistribution.* New York: Cambridge University Press.

  2005. "Privatization and Public Discontent in Latin America." Paper prepared for Inter-American Development Bank, Sustainable Development Department. 1–31.

Boix, Carles and Milan W. Svolik. 2013. "The Foundations of Limited Authoritarian Government: Institutions, Commitment, and Power-Sharing in Dictatorships." *The Journal of Politics* 75:2, 300–316.

Boone, Catherine. 2014. *Property and Political Order in Africa: Land Rights and the Structure of Politics.* New York: Cambridge University Press.

Boycko, Maxim, Andrei Shleifer, and Robert Vishny. 1995. *Privatizing Russia.* Cambridge, MA: MIT Press.

Brainerd, Elizabeth. 1998. "Winners and Losers in Russia's Economic Transition." *American Economic Review* 88:5, 1094–1116.

Browder, William. 2015. *Red Notice.* New York: Simon and Schuster.

Bunich, Andrei. 2006. *Osen' Oligarkhov.* Moscow: Yauza Publishing.

Burbank, Jane. 2004. *Russian Peasants Go To Court: Legal Culture in the Countryside, 1905–1917.* Bloomington, IN: Indiana University Press.

  2012 "Rights of the Ruled: Legal Activism in Imperial Russia." *Wisconsin International Law Journal* 29:2, 319–342.

Burger, Ethan. 2004. "Corruption in Russian Arbitrazh Courts: Will There Be Significant Progress in the Near Term?" *The International Lawyer* 38:1, 15–25.

Burger, Ethan and Evgenia Sorokina 2003. "Putin's 'Dictatorship of Law': Its Potential Implications for the Business and Legal Communities." *BNA East Europe Reporter* 13:12, 19–23.

Bush, Jason. 2008. "Russia's Raiders." June 4. www.bloomberg.com/bw/stories/2008-06-04/russias-raiders

Butorina, Ekaterina. 2014. "Sudi popadayut v cherniye spiski." *Vremya Novosteie online* 102, June 10.

Campbell, Angus, Philip E. Converse, Warren E. Miller, and Donald E. Stokes. 1960. *The American Voter*. New York: John Wiley & Sons, Inc.

Campos, Jose Edgardo and Hilton Root. 1994. *The Key to the Asian Miracle: Making Shared Growth Credible*. Washington DC: Brookings Institution.

Carbonell, Brenden, Dimtry Foux, Vera Krimnis, Ed Ma, and Lisa Safyan. 2009. "Hostile Takeovers Russian Style." Knowledge@Wharton. http://knowledge.wharton.upenn.edu/article/hostile-takeovers-russian-style/

Caro, Robert. 2002. *Master of the Senate: The Years of Lyndon Johnson*. New York: Alfred A. Knopf.

Carothers, Thomas. 2006. "The Problem of Knowledge." In Thomas Carothers (ed.) *Promoting the Rule of Law Abroad: In Search of Knowledge*. Washington, DC: Carnegie Endowment for International Peace, 15–30.

Charny, David. 1990. "Nonlegal Sanctions in Commercial Relationships." *Harvard Law Review* 104, 373–467.

Chemin, Matthieu. 2012. "Does Court Speed Shape Economic Activity? Evidence from a Court Reform in India." *Journal of Law, Economics and Organization* 28:3, 460–485.

Chernykh, Lucy. 2011. "Profit or Politics? Understanding Renationalizations in Russia." *Journal of Corporate Finance* 17, 1237–1253.

Chiozza, Giacomo and H.E. Goemans. 2011. *Leaders and International Conflict*. New York: Cambridge University Press.

Coase, Ronald. 1960. "The Problem of Social Cost." *Journal of Law and Economics* 3:1, 1–44.

Deirmeier, Daniel, Joel Ericson, Timothy Frye, and Steven Lewis. 1997. "Credible Commitment and Property Rights: The Role of Strategic Interaction between Political and Economic Actors." In David Weimer (ed.) *The Political Economy of Property Rights*. New York: Cambridge University Press, 20–42.

Della Vigna, Stefano and Ethan Kaplan 2007. "The Fox News Effect: Media Bias and Voting," *Quarterly Journal of Economics* 122 (August), 1187–1234.

Demidova, Elena. 2007. "Hostile Takeovers and Defenses Against Them in Russia." *Problems of Economic Transition* 50:5, 44–60.

Demsetz, Harold. 1967. "Toward a Theory of Property Rights." *American Economic Review Papers and Proceedings* 57:2, 347–359.

Denisova, Irina, Markus Eller, Timothy Frye, and Ekaterina Zhuravskaya. 2009. "Who Wants to Revise Privatization? The Complementarity of Market Skills and Institutions." *American Political Science Review* 103:2, 284–304.

Denisova, Irina, Markus Eller, and Ekaterina Zhuravskaya. 2010. "What Do Russians Think about Transition?" *Economics of Transition* 18:2, 249–280.

Denisova, Irina, Markus Eller, Timothy Frye, and Ekaterina Zhuravskaya. 2012. "Everybody Hates Privatization, but Why? Survey Evidence from 28 Post-communist Countries." *Journal of Comparative Economics* 40, 44–61.

Denzau, Arthur T. and North, Douglass C. 1994. "Shared Mental Models: Ideologies and Institutions." *Kyklos* 47:1, 3–31.

Derlugian, Georgi. 2000. "A Tale of Two Cities." *New Left Review* May–June, 47–71.

DeSoto, Hernando. 1989. *The Other Path: The Invisible Revolution in the Third World*. London: I. B. Tauris.

DFID, Department for International Development UK Aid. 2014. *Secure Property Rights and Development: Economic Growth and Household Welfare, Property Rights Evidence Paper*. April, 1–94. www.gov.uk/government/uploads/system/uploads/attachment_data/file/304551/Property-rights-evidence-paper.pdf

Dickson, Bruce. 2003. *Red Capitalists in China: Private Entrepreneurs, the Party and the Prospects for Political Change*. New York: Cambridge University Press.

Di Tella, R, S. Galiani, and E. Shargrodsky. 2007. "The Formation of Beliefs: Evidence from the Allocation of Land Titles to Squatters." *Quarterly Journal of Economics* 122:1, 209–241.

Di Tella, Rafael, Sebastian Galiani, and Ernesto Schargrodsky. 2012. Reality Versus Propaganda in the Formation of Beliefs About Privatization." *Journal of Public Economics* 96:5, 553–567.

Djankov, Simeon, Rafael La Porta, Florencio Lopez-De-Silanes, and Andrei Shleifer. 2003. "Courts." *Quarterly Journal of Economics* (May), 453–517.

Dmitriev, Mikhail. 2006. "V zashchitu natsionalizatsii." *Kommersant'* January 30.

Dmitrieva, Irina. 2013. "Arbitrazhniie Sudi: Advokat Gosudarstva ili Biznesa?" *Vedomosti*, November 21. www.vedomosti.ru/newspaper/ articles/2013/11/21/gosudarstvo-protiv-biznesa-v-arbitrazhe#/cut

Duch, Raymond R. 1993. "Tolerating Support for Economic Reform: Popular Support for Transition to a Free Market in the Former Soviet Union." *American Political Science Review* 87:3, 590–608.

Dunning, Thad. 2012. *Natural Experiments in the Social Sciences: A Design-Based Approach*. New York: Cambridge University Press.

Duvanova, Dinissa. 2012. *Building Business in Postcommunist Russia, Eurasia and Eastern Europe*. New York: Cambridge University Press.

Dzis'-Voinarskii, Nikolai. 2012. "Naskol'ko na Samom Dele Zhestoki Rossisskie Sudi?" Slon.Ru August 17. http://slon.ru/economics/ naskolko_na_samom_dele_zhestoki_rossiiskie_sudy-820268.xhtml

Earle, John and Scott Gehlbach. 2015. "The Productivity Consequences of Political Turnover: Firm-Level Evidence from Ukraine's Orange Revolution." *American Journal of Political Science* 59:3, 708–723.

Easter, Gerald. 2012. *Capital, Coercion, and Postcommunist States*. New York: Cambridge University Press.

Eggertson, Thrainn. 1990. *Economic Behavior and Institutions*. Cambridge: Cambridge University Press.

Ellickson, Robert C. 1991. *Order Without Law: How Neighbors Settle Disputes*. Cambridge, MA: Harvard University Press.

Enikolopov, Ruben, Vasily Korovkina, Maria Petrova, Konstantin Sonin, and Alexei Zakharov. 2013. "Field Experiment Estimate of Electoral Fraud in Russian Parliamentary Elections." *Proceedings of the National Academy of Science* 110:2, 448–452. www.pnas.org/content/110/2/ 448.full.pdf

European Bank for Reconstruction and Development. 2006. *Life in Transition Survey*. London: European Bank for Reconstruction and Development.

Evans, Gregory and Stephen Whitefield. 1995. "The Politics and Economics of Democratic Commitment: Support for Democracy in Transitional Societies." *British Journal of Political Science* 25, 485–514.

Faccio, Mara, Ronald W. Masulis, and John J. McConnel. 2006. "Political Connections and Corporate Bailouts." *Journal of Finance*, 61:6, 2597–2635.

Feifer, George. 1964. *Justice in Moscow*. New York: Simon and Schuster.

Fenske, James. 2011. "Land Tenure and Investment Incentives: Evidence From West Africa." *Journal of Development Economics* 95:2, 137–156.

Field, Erica. 2007. "Entitled to Work: Urban Property Rights and Labor Supply in Peru." *The Quarterly Journal of Economics* 122:4, 1561–1602.

Finifter, Ada and Ellen Mickiewicz. 1992. "Redefining the Political System of the USSR- Mass Support for Political Change." *American Political Science Review* 86:4, 857–874.

Fiorina, Morris P. 1981. *Retrospective Voting in American National Elections.* New Haven, CT: Yale University Press.

Firestone, Thomas. 2008. "Criminal Corporate Raiding in Russia." *International Lawyer* 42:4, 1207–1229.

2009. "Armed Injustice: Abuse of Law and Complex Crime in Post-Soviet Russia." *Denver Journal of International Law and Policy* 38:4, 555–580.

Fisman, Raymond, 2001. "The Value of Political Connections." *The American Economic Review* 91:4, 1095–1102.

Fisman, Raymond and Yongxiang Wang. 2015. "The Mortality Costs of Political Connections." NBER Working Paper 21266, 1–52. www.nber.org/papers/w21266

Fong, Christina. 2001. "Social Preferences, Self-interest and the Demand for Redistribution." *Journal of Public Economics* 82:2, 225–246.

Freeland, Christia. 2000. *Sale of the Century. Russia's Wild Ride From Communism to Capitalism.* New York: Verso Books.

Frey, Bruno. 1997. "A Constitution for Knaves Crowds Out Civic Virtues." *Economic Journal* 107, 1043–53.

Frieden, Jeffry, 1991. "Invested Interests: The Politics of National Economic Policies in a World of Global Finance." *International Organization* 45:4, 425–451.

Frye, Timothy. 2000. *Brokers and Bureaucrats: Building Market Institutions in Russia.* Ann Arbor, MI: University of Michigan Press.

2002. "Private Protection in Russia and Poland." *American Journal of Political Science* 46 (June), 572–584.

2004. "Credible Commitment and Property Rights: Evidence from Russia." *American Political Science Review* 98:3, 453–466

2006. "Original Sin, Good Works, and Property Rights in Russia." *World Politics* 58:4, 479–504.

2010. *Building States and Markets after Communism: The Perils of Polarized Democracy.* New York: Cambridge University Press.

2014. "Limits of Legacies: Property Rights in Russian Energy." In Mark R. Beissinger and Stephen Kotkin (eds.) *Historical Legacies of Communism in Russia and Eastern Europe.* New York: Cambridge University Press. 90–110.

2015. "Property Rights and Development." In Robert A. Scott and Stephen M. Kosslyn (eds.) *Emerging Trends in the Social and Behavioral Sciences* New York: John Wiley. http://onlinelibrary.wiley.com/doi/10.1002/9781118900772.etrds0266/pdf DOI: 10.1002/9781118900772.etrds 0266.

Frye, Timothy and Ekaterina Borisova. 2015. *Elections and Trust in Government: A Natural Experiment from Russia*. Moscow: Ms. Higher School of Economics.

Frye, Timothy and Andrei Shleifer 1997. "The Invisible Hand and the Grabbing Hand." *American Economic Review Papers and Proceedings* 87 (May), 554–559.

Frye, Timothy and Andrei Yakovlev. 2016. "Elections and Property Rights: A Natural Experiment from Russia." *Comparative Political Studies* 49:4, 499–528.

Frye, Timothy and Ekaterina Zhuravskaya. 2000. "Rackets, Regulation and the Rule of Law." *Journal of Law, Economics, and Organization* 16:2, 478–502.

Frye, Timothy, Ora John Reuter, and David Szakonyi. 2014. "Political Machines at Work: Voter Mobilization and Electoral Subversion in the Workplace." *World Politics* 66:2, 195–228.

Frye, Timothy, Scott Gehlbach, Kyle Marquardt, and Ora John Reuter. 2016. "Is Putin's Popularity Real?" *Post-Soviet Affairs* 33:1. www.tandfonline.com/doi/abs/10.1080/1060586X.2016.1144334

Gaddy, Clifford and Barry W. Ickes. 2002. *Russia's Virtual Economy*. Washington, DC: Brookings Institution.

Gaines, Brian J., James H. Kuklinski and Paul J. Quirk. 2007. "The Logic of the Survey Experiment Reexamined." *Political Analysis* 15, 1–20.

Galanter, Marc. 1975. "Why the Haves Come Out Ahead: Speculations on the Limits of Legal Change." *Law and Society Review* 91:1, 95–160.

Gandhi, Jennifer. 2008. *Political Institutions Under Dictatorship*. New York: Cambridge University Press.

Gambetta, Diego. 1994. *The Sicilian Mafia: The Business of Private Protection*. Cambridge, MA: Harvard University Press.

Gans-Morse, Jordan. 2012. "Threats to Property Rights in Russia: From Private Coercion to Sate Aggression." *Post-Soviet Affairs* 28:3, 263–295.

2017. *Property Rights in Post-Soviet Russia: Violence, Corruption and the Demand for Law*. New York: Cambridge University Press.

Garcia-Ponce, Omar and Benjamin de Pasquale. 2014. "How Political Repression Shapes Attitudes Toward the State." Unpublished MS. New York.

Gasiorowski, Mark. 1995. "Economic Crisis and Political Regime Change: An Event-History Analysis." *American Political Science Review* 89:4, 882–897.

Geertz, Clifford. 1978. "The Bazaar Economy: Information and Search in a Peasant Economy." *American Economic Review* 68, 28–32.

Gehlbach, Scott and Philip Keefer. 2012. "Private Investment and the Institutionalization of Collective Action in Autocracies: Ruling Parties and Legislatures." *Journal of Politics* 74:2, 621–635.

Gehlbach, Scott and Alberto Simpser. 2014. "Electoral Manipulation as Bureaucratic Control." *American Journal of Political Science* 59:1, 212–224.

Gerber, Alan S. and Donald P. Green. 2012. *Field Experiments: Design, Analysis and Interpretation*. New York: Norton Press.

Gerber, Theodore and Oleg Kharkhodin. 1994. "Russian Directors' Business Ethics: A Study of Industrial Enterprises in St. Petersburg." *Europe-Asia Studies* 47:7, 1075–1108.

Gerber, Alan S., Dean Karlan, and Daniel Bergan. 2009. "Does the Media Matter? A Field Experiment Measuring the Effect of Newspapers on Voting Behavior and Political Opinions." *American Economic Journal: Applied Economics* 1:2, 35–52.

Gerber, Alan, Gregory A. Huber, and Ebonya Washington. 2010. "Party Affiliation, Partisanship and Political Beliefs." *American Political Science Review* 104:4, 72–74.

Gerschenkron, Alexander. 1960. *Economic Backwardness in Historical Perspective*. Cambridge, MA: Belknap Press of Harvard University.

Gibson, James. 1996. "Political and Economic Markets: Changes in the Connections Between Attitudes Toward Political Democracy and a Market Economy Within the Mass Culture of Russia and Ukraine." *Journal of Politics* 58:4, 954–984.

Gilbert, Daniel. 2007. *Stumbling on Happiness*. New York: Random House.

Ginsburg. Tom. 2003. *Judicial Review in New Democracies: Constitutional Courts in Asian Cases*. Cambridge: Cambridge University Press.

2008. "Administrative Law and the Judicial Control of Agents in Authoritarian Regimes." In Tom Ginsburg and Tamir Moustafa (eds.) *Rule by Law: The Politics of Courts in Authoritarian Regimes*. New York: Cambridge University Press, 58–72.

Ginsburg, Tom and Alberto Simpser. 2014. *Constitutions in Authoritarian Regimes*. New York: Cambridge University Press.

Glaeser, Edward, Simon Johnson, and Andrei Shleifer. 2001. "Coase Versus The Coasians." *The Quarterly Journal of Economics* 116:3, 853–899.

Goldstein, Markus and Christopher Udry. 2008. "The Profits of Power: Land Rights and Agricultural Investment in Ghana." *Journal of Political Economy* 116:6, 981–1022.

Gordon, Sanford C. and Gregory A. Huber. 2002. "Citizen Oversight and the Electoral Incentives of Criminal Prosecutors." *American Journal Political Science* 46:2, 334–351.

Goriaev, Alexei and Konstantin Sonin. 2005. "Is Political Risk Company-Specific? The Market Side of the YUKOS Affair." Unpublished MS. Moscow.

Granovetter, Mark. 1985. "Economic Action and Social Structure: The Role of Embeddedness." *American Journal of Sociology* 91:3, 481–510.

Green, Donald P. and Alan S. Gerber. 2002. "Reclaiming the Experimental Tradition in Political Science." In Ira Katznelson and Helen V. Milner (eds.) *Political Science: The State of the Discipline.* New York: Norton, 785–832.

Greene, Kenneth. 2007. *Why Dominant Parties Lose: Mexico's Democratization in Comparative Perspective.* New York: Cambridge University Press.

Greene, Samuel. 2014. *Moscow in Movement: Power and Opposition in Putin's Russia.* Stanford, CA: Stanford University Press.

Greif, Avner. 1994. "Cultural Beliefs and the Organization of Society: A Historical and Theoretical Reflection on Collectivist and Individualist Societies." *Journal of Political Economy* 103 (October), 912–950.

  2006. *Institutions and the Path to the Modern Economy: Lessons From Medieval Trade.* New York: Cambridge University Press.

Grigoriev, Leonid, Alfred Zhalinsky, Elena Novikova, and Andrei Fedotov. 2011. "Problemy Sverkhkriminalizatsii i dekriminalizatsii ekonomicheskoi deiatelnosti: Ugolovnaya Politika V Sfere Ekonomiki." Tsentr Pravovykh i Ekonomicheskikh Isledovanii. Vysshaya Shkola Ekonomiki, June 1–8. Also available as "Problems of the Hyper-Criminalization and Decriminalization of Economic Activity." In *Legal Policy: In Economics.* Moscow: Liberal Mission, 22–36.

Grosjean, Pauline and Claudia Senik. 2011. "Democracy, Market Liberalization and Political Preferences." *The Review of Economics and Statistics* 93:1, 365–381.

Grossman, Guy. 2011. "Lab in the Field Experiments." *Newsletter of the American Political Science Association Experimental Section.* 2:2. https://sites.sas.upenn.edu/sites/default/files/ggros/files/apsa_newletter_fall2011.pdf

Guiso, Luigi, Paola Sapienza, and Luigi Zingales. 2004. "The Role of Social Capital in Financial Development." *The American Economic Review* 94:3, 526–56.

2006. "Does Culture Affect Economic Outcomes?" *Journal of Economic Perspectives* 20:2, 23–48.

Guriev, Sergei and Andrei Rachinsky. 2005. "The Role of Oligarchs in Russian Capitalism." *Journal of Economic Perspectives* 19:1, 131–150

Guriev, Sergei, Anton Kolotilin, and Konstantin Sonin. 2011. "Determinants of Nationalization in the Oil Sector: A Theory and Evidence From Panel Data." *Journal of Law, Economics, and Organization* 27:2, 301–323.

Gustaffson, Par. 2013. "The Emergence of the Rule of Law in Russia." *Global Crime* 14:1, 82–109.

Gustafson, Thane. 2012. *Wheel of Fortune. The Battle for Oil and Power in Russia*. Cambridge, MA: Harvard University Press.

Haber, Stephen, Armando Razo, and Noel Maurer. 2003. *The Politics of Property Rights: Political Instability, Credible Commitments, and Economic Growth in Mexico, 1876–1929*. New York: Cambridge University Press.

Haddock, David and Lynne Kiesling. 2002. "The Black Death and Property Rights." *Journal of Legal Studies* 31 (Spring), S545–S587.

Haley, John. 1978. "The Myth of the Reluctant Litigant." *Journal of Japanese Studies* 4, 359–390.

Han, Jianlei and Guangli Zhang. 2015. "Politically Connected Boards, Value or Cost: Evidence from A Natural Experiment in China." Unpublished MS. University of Queensland, 1–25.

Hanson, Philip. 2014. "*Reiderstvo*: Asset Grabbing in Russia." *Chatham House* 2014:3, 1–12.

Hazard, Johnathan. 1962. *The Soviet System of Government*. Chicago, IL: University of Chicago Press.

Hellman, Joel. 1993. "Breaking the Bank. Bureaucrats and the Creation of Markets in a Transition Economy." Unpublished Ph.D. Dissertation, Columbia University.

　　1998. "Winners Take All: The Pitfalls of Partial Reforms." *World Politics* 50:2, 203–234.

　　2002. "Russia's Transition to a Market Economy: A Permanent Redistribution?" In Andrew C. Kuchins (ed.) *Russia After the Fall*. Washington, DC: Carnegie, 93–109.

Hellman, Joel S., Geraint Jones, and Daniel Kaufmann. 2003. "Seize the State, Seize the Day: An Empirical Analysis of State Capture and Corruption in Transition Economies." *Journal of Comparative Economics* 31:4, 751–773.

Helmke, Gretchen. 2005. *Courts Under Constraints: Judges, General, and Presidents in Argentina*. New York: Cambridge University Press.

Hendley, Kathryn. 1998. "Struggling to Survive: A Case Study of Adjustment of a Russian Enterprise." *Europe-Asia Studies* 50:1, 91–119.

2002. "Suing the State in Russia." *Post-Soviet Affairs* 18:2, 122–147.

2004. "Business Litigation in the Transition: A Portrait of Debt Collection in Russia." *Law and Society Review* 38:2, 305–348.

2007a. "Handling Economic Disputes in Russia: The Impact of the 2002 Arbitrazh Procedure Code." In Kathryn Hendle (ed.) *Remaking the Role of Law: Commercial Law in Russia and the CIS.* Huntington, NY: Juris Publishing, 171–189.

2007b. "Are Russian Judges Still Soviet?" *Post-Soviet Affairs* 23:3, 240–276.

2009. "'Telephone Law' and the 'Rule of Law': The Russian Case." *Hague Journal of International Law* 1, 241–262.

2011. "Varieties of Legal Dualism: Making Sense of the Role of Law in Contemporary Russia." *Wisconsin International Journal of Law* 29:2, 233–263.

2012a. "Assessing the Role of the Justice of the Peace Courts in the Russian Judicial System." NCEER Working Paper.

2012b. "The Puzzling Non-Consequences of Societal Distrust of Courts: Explaining the Use of Russian Courts." *Cornell International Law Journal* 45, 517–567.

Hendley, Kathryn and Peter Murrell. 2003. "Which Mechanisms Support the Fulfillment of Sales Agreements? Asking Decision-Makers in Firms." *Economic Letters* 78:1, January, 49–54.

2015. "Revisiting the Emergence of the Rule of Law in Russia." *Global Crime* 16:1, 19–33.

Hendley, Kathryn, Peter Murrell, and Randi Ryterman. 1999. "Law Works in Russia: The Role of Legal Institutions in the Transactions of Russian Enterprises." SSRN 151132, March 13, 1–55.

2000. "Law, Relationships, and Private Enforcement: Transactional Strategies or Russian Enterprises." *Europe-Asia Studies* 52:4, 627–656.

2001. "Law Works in Russia: The Role of Law in Interenterprise Transactions." In Peter Murrell (ed.) *Assessing the Value of the Rule of Law in Transition Economies.* Ann Arbor, MI: University of Michigan Press, 56–93.

Higino, Carlos and Ivo Gico. 2010. "When Crime Pays: Measuring Judicial Efficacy Against Corruption in Brazil." SSRN working paper 1591223. April 12, 1–42.

Hilbink, Elisabeth. 2007. *Judges Beyond Politics in Democracy and Dictatorship: Lessons from Chile.* New York: Cambridge University Press.

2008. "Agents of Anti-Politics: Courts in Pinochet's Chile." In Tom Ginsburg and Tamir Moustafa (eds.) *Rule by Law: The Politics of*

Courts in Authoritarian Regimes. New York: Cambridge University Press, 102–131.

Hille, Kathrin. 2013. "Putin Tightens Grip on Legal System." *Financial Times*. November 27, 4:29 pm. www.ft.com/intl/cms/s/0/a4209a42-5777-11e3-b615-00144feabdc0.html#axzz3obh3Jb4L

Hoff, Karla and Joseph Stiglitz. 2004. "After the Big Bang: Obstacles to the Emergence of the Rule of Law in Postcommunist Societies." *American Economic Review* 94:3, 753–763.

Hoffman, David. 2003. *The Oligarchs: Wealth and Power in the New Russia*. New York: Public Affairs.

Holmes, Stephen. 1995. "Conceptions of Democracy in the Draft Constitutions of Postcommunist Countries." In Beverly Crawford (ed.) *Markets, States, and Democracy: The Political Economy of Postcommunist Transition*. Boulder, CO: Westview Press, 71–80.

  1996. "Cultural Legacies or State Collapse?" In Michael Mandelbaum (ed.) *Perspectives on Postcommunism*. New York: Council on Foreign Relations, 22–76.

  2003. "Lineages of the Rule of Law." In Jose Maria Maravall and Adam Przeworski (eds.) *Democracy and the Rule of Law*. New York: Cambridge University Press, 19–61.

Holmstrom, Bengt and Steven N. Kaplan. 2001. "Corporate Governance and Merger Activity in the US: Making Sense of the 1980s and 1990s." NBER Working Paper 8220, 1–47.

Hou, Yue. 2016. "Participatory Autocracy: Private Entrepreneurs, Legislatures, and Property Protection in China." Paper presented at Annual Meeting of the American Political Science Association, Philadelphia, PA, 1–42.

Huang, Yasheng, 2008. *Capitalism with Chinese Characteristics*. New York: Cambridge University Press.

Humphreys, Macartan, Raul Sanchez de la Sierra, and Peter Van der Windt. 2013. "Fishing, Commitment, and Communication: A Proposal for Comprehensive Nonbinding Research Registration." *Political Analysis* 21:1, 1–20.

IADB, Inter-American Development Bank. 2002. "The Privatization Paradox." *Latin American Economic Policies* 18, 1–8.

Ingram, Matthew C., Octavio Rodriguez, and David Shirk. 2011. "Assessing Mexico's Judicial Reform: Views of Judges, Prosecutors, and Public Defenders." Special Report. Joan B. Kroc School of Peace Studies, University of San Diego. 1–38. https://justiceinmexico.files.wordpress.com/2010/07/tbi-assessing-judicial-reform1.pdf

Ivanov, Anton. 2014. "O proekte zakona Rossiiskoi Federatsii o popravke k Konstitutsii Rossisskoi Federatsii" No. 352924-6 "O Verkhovnom Sude Rosssiskoi Federatsii i Prokurature Rossisskoi Federatsii."

Jackson, John and Elizabeth Gerber. 1993. "Endogenous Preferences and the Study of Institutions." *American Political Science Review* 87:3, 639–656.

Jappelli, Tulio, Marco Pagano, and Magda Bianco. 2005. "Courts and Banks: Effects of Judicial Enforcement on Credit Markets." *The Journal of Money, Credit, and Banking* 37:2, 223–244.

Jha, Saumitra. 2015. "Financial Asset Holdings and Political Attitudes: Evidence From Revolutionary England." *Quarterly Journal of Economics* 130:3, 1485–1545.

Johnson, Simon, Daniel Kaufmann, and Andrei Shleifer. 1997. "The Unofficial Economy in Transition." *Brookings Papers on Economic Activity* 2, 159–239.

Johnson, Simon, John McMillan, and Christopher Woodruff. 2002a. "Property Rights and Finance." *American Economic Review* 92 (December), 1335–1356.

2002b. "Courts and Relational Contracting." *Journal of Law, Economics, and Organization* 18:1, 221–277.

Jordan, Pamela. 2009. "Strong-Arm Rule or Rule of Law? Prospects for Legal Reform in Russia?" *Jurist*, http://jurist.law.pitt.edu

Kaltenthaler, Karl C., Stephen J. Ceccoli, and Andrew Michtal. 2006. "Explaining Individual-level Support for Privatization in European Post-Soviet Economies." *European Journal of Political Research* 45, 1–29.

Kapeliushnikov, Rostislav, Andrei Kuznetsov, Natalie Demina, and Olga Kuznetsova. 2013. "Threats to Security of Property Rights in a Transition Economy: An Empirical Perspective." *Journal of Comparative Economics* 41:1, 245–264.

Kasara, Kimuli. 2007. "Tax Me If You Can: Ethnic Geography, Democracy, and the Taxation of Agriculture." *American Political Science Review* 101:1, 159–171.

Kaufmann, Daniel, Aart Kray, and Pablo Zoido-Laboton. 1999. "Governance Matters." Policy Research Working Paper #2196. Washington, DC: World Bank.

Kaufmann, Daniel, Art Kraay, and Massimo Mastruzzi. 2007. "Growth and Governance: A Defense." *Journal of Politics* 69:2, 555–562.

King, Gary, Michael Tomz, and Jason Wittenberg. 2000. "Making the Most of Statistical Analyses: Improving Interpretation and Presentation." *American Journal of Political Science* 44:2, 341–355.

Khurana, Rakesh, Raymond Fisman, Julia Galef, and Yongxiang Wang. 2012. "Estimating the Values of Connections to Vice President Cheney." *B.E. Journal of Economic Analysis & Policy* 13:3, Article 5, 1–18.

Klebnikov, Paul. 2000. *Godfather of the Kremlin: Boris Berezovsky and the Looting of the Kremlin.* New York: Harcourt.

Klimentova, Lyudmila. 2013. "Vysshii Arbitrazh Raskritikoval Proekt Sozdaniia Yedinogo Verkhovnogo Suda." *Vedemosti,* November 12.

Knack, Steven C. and Philip Keefer. 1995. "Institutions and Economic Performance: Cross-Country Tests Using Alternative Measures." *Economics and Politics* 7:3, 207–227.

Kobak, Dmitri, Sergey Shpilkin, and Maxim Pshenichnikov. 2012. "*Statistical Anomalies in 2011–2012 Russian Elections revealed by 2D correlation analysis.*" London. 1–12. http://arxiv.org/pdf/1205.0741v2.pdf

Kramer, Andrew E. 2013. "Russia's Stimulus Plan: Open Gulag Gates." *New York Times.* August 9. www.nytimes.com/2013/08/09/business/global/russias-stimulus-plan-open-the-gulag-gates.html

Kramer, Gerald. 1983. "The Ecological Fallacy Revisited: Aggregate-versus Individual-level Findings on Economics and Elections, and Sociotropic Voting." *American Political Science Review* 77:1, 92–111.

Kreps, David. 1990. "Corporate Culture." In James E. Alt and Kenneth Shepsle (eds.) *Perspectives on Positive Political Economy.* New York: Cambridge University Press, 90–143.

Kuran, Timur. 2005. *Islam and Mammon: The Economic Predicaments of Islamism.* Princeton, NJ: Princeton University Press.

Kurtz, Marcus and Andrew Schrenk. 2007. "Growth and Governance: Models, Measures, and Mechanisms." *Journal of Politics* 69:2, 538–554.

Lambert-Mogiliansky, Ariane, Konstantin Sonin, and Ekaterina Zhuravskaya. 2007. "Are Russian Commercial Courts Biased: Evidence From a Bankruptcy Law Transplant." *Journal of Comparative Economics* 35:2, 254–277.

Landes, David. 2000. "Culture Makes Almost All the Difference." In L. E. Harrison and S. P. Huntington (eds.) *Culture Matters: How Values Shape Human Progress.* New York: Basic Books, 2–13.

Landry, Pierre. 2008. *Decentralized Authoritarianism in China: The Communist Party's Control of Local Elites in the Post-Mao Era.* New York: Cambridge University Press.

Lawson-Remer, Terra. 2012. "Property Insecurity." *Brooklyn Law Journal* 38:1, 145–188.

Lazzarini, Sergio, Gary Miller, and Todd Zenger. 2004. "Order With Some Law: Complementarity Versus Substution of Public and Private

Arrangements." *Journal of Law, Economics and Organization* 20:2, 261–298.

Leblang, David. 1996. "Property Rights, Democracy, and Economic Growth." *Political Research Quarterly* 49:1, 5–26.

Ledeneva, Alena. 1998. *Russia's Economy of Favours.* Cambridge: Cambridge University Press.

2006. *How Russia Really Works: The Informal Practices that Shaped Post-Soviet Politics and Business.* Ithaca, NY and London: Cornell University Press.

2013. *Can Russia Modernise? Sistema, Power Networks and Governance.* Cambridge: Cambridge University Press.

Levi, Margaret. 1988. *Of Rule and Revenue.* Berkeley, CA: University of California Press.

1998. "A State of Trust." In Valerie Braithwaite and Margaret Levi (eds.) *Trust and Governance.* New York: Russell Sage, 77–101.

Levitov, Maria. 2006. "State Pressure Motivates Most Corporate Giving." *Moscow Times,* February 14.

Levitt, Steven D. and Sudhir Alladi Venkatesh. 2000. "An Economic Analysis of a Drug-Selling Gang's Finances." *Quarterly Journal of Economics* 115:3, 755–789.

Libecap, Gary. 1992. *Contracting for Property Rights.* New York: Cambridge University Press.

Lindblom, Charles. 1977. *Politics and Markets: The World Politco-Economic Systems.* New York: Basic Books.

Lora, Eduardo and Ugo Panizza. 2003. "The Future of Structural Reforms." *The Journal of Democracy* 14:2, 123–127.

Lu, Yi, Ivan Png, and Zhigang Tao. 2013. "Do Institutions Matter in China: Evidence from Manufacturing Enterprises." *Journal of Comparative Economics* 41:1, 74–90.

Lust-Okar, Ellen. 2006a. *Structuring Conflict in the Arab World: Incumbents, Opponents, and Institutions.* New York: Cambridge University Press.

2006b. "Elections under Authoritarianism: Preliminary Lessons from Jordan." *Democratization* 13:3, 456–471.

Macauley, Stewart. 1963. "Noncontractual Relations in Business: A Preliminary Study." *American Sociological Review* 28:1, 55–67.

Magaloni, Beatriz. 2006. *Voting for Autocracy: Hegemonic Party Survival and its Demise in Mexico.* New York: Cambridge University Press.

2008. "Enforcing the Autocratic Political Order and the Role of Courts: The Case of Mexico." In Tom Ginsburg and Tamir Moustafa (eds.) *Rule by Law: The Politics of Courts in Authoritarian Regimes.* New York: Cambridge University Press, 18–26.

Malesky, Edward and Kristin Samphantharak. 2008. "Predictable Corruption and Firm Investment: Evidence from a Natural Experiment and Survey of Cambodian Entrepreneurs." *Quarterly Journal of Political Science* 3:3, 227–267.

Markus, Stan. 2012. "Secure Property Rights as a Bottom-Up Process: Firms, Stakeholders and Predators in Weak States." *World Politics* 64:2, 242–277.

2015. *Property, Protection, and Predation: Piranha Capitalism in Russia and Ukraine*. New York: Cambridge University Press.

Mattingly, Daniel. 2016. "Elite Capture: How Decentralization and Informal Institutions Weaken Political Accountability in China." *World Politics* 68:3, 383–412.

McGregor Burns, James. 2010. *Leadership*. New York: Harper.

McMillan, John and Christopher Woodruff. 1999. "Dispute Prevention Without Courts in Vietnam." *Journal of Law, Economics, and Organization* (October), 18:1, 637–658.

2000. "Private Order under Dysfunctional Public Order." *Michigan Law Review* 98 (August), 101–138.

McCubbins, Mathew D. and Thomas Schwartz. 1984. "Congressional Oversight Overlooked: Police Patrols versus Fire Alarms." *American Journal of Political Science* 28:1, 165–179

McDermott, Gerald. 2002. *Embedded Politics: Industrial Networks and Institutional Change in Post-Communism*. Ann Arbor: MI. University of Michigan Press.

Medushevsky, Andrei. 2006. *Russian Constitutionalism: Historical and Contemporary Development*. London. Routledge.

Mereu, Frances 2004. "Judges Who Lost Their Jobs Speak Out." *Moscow Times*, October 6.

Meyer, Henry. 2011 "Kremlin Panel Backs Pardon for Economic Crimes, Khodorkovsky." *Bloomberg News*, July 11.

Migdal, Joel. 1988. *Strong Societies and Weak States: Power and Accommodation*. Princeton, NJ: Princeton University Press.

Milgrom, Paul, Douglass C. North, and Barry Weingast. 1990. "The Role of Institutions in the Revival of Trade: The Law Merchant. Private Judges, and the Champagne Fairs." *Economics and Politics* 2:1, 1–23.

Miller, Arthur, Vicki Hesli, and William Reissinger. 1994. "Reassessing Mass Support for Political and Economic Change in the Former USSR." *American Political Science Review* 88:3, 339–411.

Mokyr, Joel, 2009. *The Enlightened Economy: An Economic History of Britain 1700–1859*. New Haven, CT and London: Yale University Press.

Morton, Rebecca B. and Kenneth C. Williams. 2010. *Experimental Political Science and the Study of Causality*. New York: Cambridge University Press.

Moustafa, Tamir. 2007. *The Struggle for Constitutional Power: Law, Politics, and Economics Development in Egypt.* New York: Cambridge University Press.

2008. "Law and Resistance in Authoritarian States: The Judicialization of Politics in Egypt." In Tom Ginsburg and Tamir Moustafa (eds.) *Rule By Law: The Politics of Courts in Authoritarian Regimes.* New York: Cambridge University Press.

Mulders, Joera. 2011. "Legal Reforms: Medvedev's Achievements." Russia Watchers, April 25. http://russiawatchers.ru/daily/legal-reforms/.

Murdoch, James C. and Todd Sandler. 2004. "Civil Wars and Economic Growth: Spatial Dispersion." *American Journal of Political Science* 48:1, 138–151.

Myers, Stephen Lee. 2006. "Phone Seizure Seen as Example of Russian Corruption." *New York Times*, June 14.

Nazrullaeva, Evgeniiya, Yakovlev, Andrei, and Alexei Baranov. 2013. *Criminal Persecution of Russian Business in Russia's Regions: Private Interests versus the 'Stick System'.* Moscow: Higher School of Economics, 1–34.

Newcity, Michael. 1997. "Russian Legal Tradition and the Rule of Law." In Jeffrey D. Sachs and Katharina Pistor (eds.) *The Rule of Law and Economic Reform in Russia.* Boulder, CO: Westview Press, 41–54.

North, Douglass. 1981. *Structure and Change in Economic History.* New York: W.W. Norton.

1990. *Institutions, Institutional Change and Economic Performance.* New York: Cambridge University Press.

1993. "Institutions and Credible Commitment." *Journal of Institutional and Theoretical Economics* 149:1, 11–23.

North, Douglass C. and Robert Paul Thomas. 1973. *The Rise of the Western World: A New Economic History.* New York: Cambridge University Press.

North, Douglass C. and Barry R. Weingast. 1989. "Constitutions and Commitment: The Evolution of Institutions Governing Public Choice in Seventeenth Century England." *Journal of Economic History* 59:4, 803–32.

North, Douglass, Wallis, John J., and Weingast, Barry. 2009. *Violence and Social Orders: A Conceptual Framework for Interpreting Recorded Human History.* New York: Cambridge University Press.

Novikov, Vladimir. 2014. "Who Will Lead Renewed Russia's Supreme Court?" RAPSI News, April 9. www.rapsinews.com/judicial_analyst/20140409/271113785.html

Novikova, Elena V. 2011. *Doklad na nauchnom seminare E. Yasina. 'Biznes v zale Sudya: Den'gi, Vlast' i Pravo.* Moscow: Higher School of Economics.

O'Brien, Kevin and Lianjing Li. 2004. "Suing the Local State: Administrative Litigation in Rural China." *The China Journal* 51 (January), 75–96.

Olken, Benjamin. 2007. "Measuring Corruption: Evidence from a Field Experiment in Indonesia." *Journal of Political Economy* 115:2, 200–249.

Olson, Mancur. 1993. "Democracy, Dictatorship and Development." *American Political Science Review* 87:3, 567–576.

Ostrom, Elinor. 1990. *Governing the Commons: The Evolution of Institutions for Collective Action*. New York: Cambridge University Press.

Paneyakh, Ella. 2014. "Faking Performance Together: Systems of Performance Evaluation in Russian Enforcement Agencies and Production of Bias and Privilege." *Post-Soviet Affairs* 30: 2–3, 115–136.

Panin, Alexander and Elena d'Amora. 2013. "Putin Takes Input on Tax Investigation Bill." *Moscow Times*. November 18. www.themoscowtimes.com/news/article/putin-takes-inputs-on-tax-investigation-bill/489738.html

Panizza, Ugo and Moniza Yanez. 2005. "Why are Latin Americans So Unhappy About Reforms?" *Journal of Applied Economics* 8:1, 1–29.

Partlett, William. 2013. "Putin's Artful Jurisprudence." *National Interest* (January/February), 35–45.

   2014. "Vladimir Putin's New Court System." *The Fletcher Forum*. www.fletcherforum.org/home/2016/9/7/vladimir-putins-new-court- system, 1–3.

Pejovich, Svetozar. 1998. *Economic Analysis of Institutions and Property Rights*. Boston, MA: Kluwer Academic Publishers.

Pepinsky, Thomas. 2014. "The Institutional Turn in Comparative Authoritarianism." *British Journal of Political Science* 44:3, 631–653.

Perenboom, Randall. 2003. *China's Long March Toward the Rule of Law*. New York: Cambridge University Press.

Petrov, Nikolai. 2011. "An Exciting End to a Dull Election." Carnegie Center, Moscow. http://carnegie.ru/2011/12/06/exciting-end-to-dull-election/auh1

Pincus, Stephen C.A. and James A. Robinson. 2014. "What Really Happened at the Glorious Revolution." In Sebastian Galliani and Itai Sened (eds.) *Institutions, Property Rights, and Economic Growth: The Legacy of Douglass North*. New York: Cambridge University Press, 192–222.

Pipes, Richard. 1974. *Russia Under the Old Regime*. New York: Penguin Press.

Polanyi, Karl. 1957. *The Great Transformation: The Political and Economic Origins of Our Time*. Boston, MA: Beacon Press.

Polischuk, Leonid and Gyorgi Sunyaev. 2013. "Ruling Elites' Rotation and Asset Ownership: Implications for Property Rights. Working Papers by NRU Higher School of Economics Series WP BRP Economics/EC #43.

Pomerantsev, Peter. 2014. *Nothing is True and Everything is Possible.* New York: Public Affairs Books.

Pomeranz, Will. 2014. "Russia's Fading Judiciary." *National Interest.* http://nationalinterest.org/commentary/russias-fading-judiciary-9313

Pop-Eleches, Grigore and Graeme Robertson. 2015. "Elections, Information and Political Change in the Post-Cold War Era." *Comparative Politics* 47:4, 459–495.

Popova, Maria 2006. "Watchdogs or Attack Dogs: The Role of the Russian Courts and Central Election Commission in the Resolution of Electoral Disputes." *Europe-Asia Studies* 58:3, 391–414.

Posner, Eric. 2008. "Does Political Bias in the Judiciary Matter? Implications of Judicial Bias Studies for Legal and Constitutional Reform." *University of Chicago Law Review* 75, 853–884.

Putnam, Robert D. 1993. *Making Democracy Work: Civic Traditions in Modern Italy.* Princeton, NJ: Princeton University Press.

Pyle, William. 2005. "Contractual Disputes and the Channels for Inter-firm Communication." *Journal of Law, Economics, and Organization* 21:2, 547–575.

   2011. "Organized Business, Political Competition and Property Rights: Evidence from the Russia Federation." *Journal of Law, Economics, and Organization* 27:1, 2–31.

Qian, Yingyi, 2003. "How Reform Worked In China." In Dani Rodrik (ed.) *In Search of Prosperity: Analytic Narratives on Economic Growth.* Princeton, NJ: Princeton University Press, 297–333.

Raiser, Martin, Rousso, Franklin Steves, and Utko Teksos. 2007. "Trust in Transition: Cross-Country and Firm Evidence." *Journal of Law, Economics, and Organization* 24:2, 407–433.

Ramseyer, Mark. 1994. "The Puzzling (In)dependence of Courts." *Journal of Legal Studies* 24 (June), 721–747.

   1996. *Odd Markets in Japanese History: Law and Economic Growth.* New York: Cambridge University Press.

Rauch James and Peter Evans. 2000. "Bureaucratic Structure and Economic Performance." *Journal of Public Economics* 75 (January), 49–71.

Reuter, Ora John and Thomas Remington. 2009. Dominant Party Regimes and the Commitment Problem: The Case of United Russia." *Comparative Political Studies* 42:4, 501–526.

Richardson, Craig. J. 2004. *The Collapse of Zimbabwe in the Wake of the 2000–2003 Land Reforms.* Lewiston, NY: Edwin Mellen.

Richerson, Peter J. and Robert Boyd. 2005. *Not By Genes Alone: How Culture Transformed Human Evolution.* Chicago, IL: University of Chicago Press.

Riker, William and Itai Sened. 1991. "A Political Theory of the Origin of Property Rights: Airport Slots." *American Journal of Political Science* 35 (October), 951–969.

Riker, William and David Weimer. 1993. "The Economic and Political Liberalization of Socialism: The Fundamental Problem of Property Rights." *Social Philosophy and Policy* 10:2, 79–102.

Riley, Alan. 2011. "Russia's Courts of Last Resort." *New York Times*, August 5. www.almendron.com/tribuna/russias-courts-of-last-resort/.

Rochlitz, Michael. 2014. "Corporate Raiding and the Role of the State in Russia." *Post-Soviet Affairs* 2014: 2–3, 89–114.

Roese, Neal J. and Kathleen D. Vohs. 2012. "Hindsight Bias." *Perspectives on Psychological Science* 7:5, 411–420.

Roland, Gerard. 2000. *Transition and Economics: Politics, Markets, and Firms*. Cambridge, MA: MIT Press.

   2004. "Understanding Institutional Change: Fast Moving and Slow Moving Institutions." *Studies in Comparative International Development* 38:4, 109–131

   2012. "The Long-Run Weight of Communism or the Weight of Long Run History." In Gerard Roland (ed.) *Economies in Transition*. London: Palgrave Macmillan, 153–171.

Romano, Roberta 1992. "A Guide to Takeovers: Theory, Evidence and Regulation." Faculty Scholarship Series. Paper 1954. http://digitalcommons.law.yale.edu/fss_papers/195

Ross, Cameron. 2004. *Russian Politics Under Putin*. Manchester: Manchester University Press.

Rubinstein, Ariel. 1982. "Perfect Equilibrium in a Bargaining Model." *Econometrica* 50:1, 97–109.

Ruvinsky, Vladimir. 2011. "Russian Entrepreneurs Lead Fight Against Corruption." *The Daily Telegraph*, April 27.

Safford, Daniel. 2011. "Russian Entrepreneur Jailed for 'Not Selling'." *BBC News*. May 25.

Sakwa, Richard. 2009. *The Quality of Freedom: Khodorkovsky, Putin and the YUKOS Affair*. Oxford: Oxford University Press.

   2011. "Raiding in Russia." *Russian Analytical Digest* 105:5, 9–13.

Satarov, G.A. 2003. "Prorzhavevshee pravosudie." *Otechestvennye zapiski* 2:11, 87–98. www.strana-oz.ru/

Satarov, G.A., V.L. Rimskii, and Yu N. Blagoveshchenskii. 2010. *Sotsiologicheskoe Issledovanie Rossiiskoi Sudebnoi Vlasti*. Moscow: Norma Publishing.

Schultz, Andre, Vladimir Kozlov, and Alexander Libman. 2014. "Judicial Alignment and Criminal Justice: Evidence from Russian Courts." *Post-Soviet Affairs* 30:2–3, 137–170.

Scott, James. 1972. *Comparative Political Corruption*. New York: Prentice Hall.

Sedaitis, Judith. 1994. "Start-ups or Spinoffs under Market Transition." Ph.D. Dissertation. Columbia University, Department of Sociology.

Shapiro, Martin. 1981. *Courts: A Comparative and Political Analysis*. Chicago, IL: University of Chicago Press.

  1988. *Who Guards the Guardians: Judicial Control of Administration*. Athens, GA: University of Georgia Press.

Sharlet, Robert. 1977. "Stalinism and Legal Culture." In Robert C. Tucker (ed.) *Stalinism: Essays in Historical Interpretation*. New York: W.W. Norton, 155–56.

Shleifer, Andrei and Daniel Treisman. 2000. *Without a Map: Political Tactics of Economic Reform in Russia*. Cambridge, MA: MIT Press.

Shiller, Robert I., Maxim Boycko, and Vladimir Korobov, 1991. "Popular Attitudes Toward Free Markets: The Soviet and United States Experience Compared." *American Economic Review* 81:3, 385–400.

Shvartsman, Oleg. 2007. "For Us, the Party is Represented by the Power Bloc Headed by Igor Ivanovich Sechin." *Kommersant*, December 3, English language version. www.kommersant.com/p831089/r_530/Oleg_Shvartsman_discloses_his_companys_relations_with_power_ministries/

Shvets, Julia. 2005. *Selection of Judges and Policy Enforcement: Theory and Evidence from Russian Commercial Courts*. London: London School of Economics, 1–32.

  2013. "Judicial Institutions and Firms' External Finance: Evidence from Russia." *Journal of Law Economics and Organization* 29, 735–764.

Shvetsova, Lilia and Andrew Wood. 2011. "Russia: The Beginning of the End of Putin's Epoch." Carnegie Moscow Center, December 8, http://carnegie.ru/2011/12/08/russia-beginning-of-end-of-putin-s-epoch/auh0

Skidanova, Liliya Alekseevna. 2010. "Reiderstvo Kak Sotsialno-Ekonomicheskii Fenomenon," Ph.D. Dissertation, Economic Sociology and Demography. Moscow State University, *Avtoreferat*, 1–23.

Simachev, Yurii. 2003. *Arbitrazh kak instrument uregulirovaniia sporov v korporativnoi sfere*. Moscow: Institute for Complex Strategic Research.

Simis, Konstantin. 1982. *USSR: The Corrupt Society*. New York: Simon and Shuster.

Simpser, Alberto. 2013. *Why Governments and Parties Manipulate Elections*. New York: Cambridge University Press.

  2016. "The Culture of Corruption across Generations: An Empirical Study of Bribery Attitudes and Behavior." https://papers.ssrn.com/sol3/papers.cfm?abstract_id=2241295.

Solomon, Peter Jr. 2002. "Putin's Judicial Reform: Making Judges Accountable as well as Independent." *East European Constitutional Review* 11:1–2, 101–107.

2003. "The New Justices of the Peace in the Russian Federation: A Cornerstone of Judicial Reform." *Demokratizatsiya* 11:3, 363–380.

2004. "Judicial Power in Russia: Through the Prism of Administrative Justice." *Law and Society Review* 38:3, 549–582.

2008. "Assessing the Courts in Russia: Parameters of Progress under Putin." *International Journal of Court Administration*, October. www.iaca.ws/files/LWB-PeterSolomon.pdf

2010. "Authoritarian Legality and Informal Practices: Judges, Lawyers and the State in Russia and China." *Communist and Post-Communist Studies* 43:4, 351–362.

Sonin, Konstantin, 2003. "Why the Rich May Favor Poor Protection of Property Rights." *Journal of Comparative Economics* 31:4, 715–731.

Spence, Matthew. 2006. "The Complexity of Success in Russia." In Thomas Carothers (ed.) *Promoting the Rule of Law Abroad: In Search of Knowledge*. Washington, DC: Carnegie Endowment for International Peace, 217–250.

Stark, David. 1996. "Recombinant Property in East European Capitalism." *American Journal of Sociology* 101:4, 993–1027.

Stasavage, David. 2003. *Public Debt and the Birth of the Democratic State: France and Great Britain, 1688–1789*. New York: Cambridge University Press.

Stigler, George. 1971. "The Theory of Economic Regulation." *Bell Journal of Economics and Management Science* 2, 3–21.

Stiglitz, Joseph. 1999. "Whither Reform." *Paper presented at the Annual Bank Conference on Development Economics*. Washington, DC: World Bank. April 28–30.

2006. "Who Owns Bolivia?" www.project-syndicate.org, accessed July 16, 2006.

Stligitz, Joseph and Karla Hoff. 2005. "The Creation of the Rule and Law and the Legitimacy of Property Rights: The Political and Economic Consequences of a Corrupt Privatization." NBER Working Papers #11772. Cambridge, MA.

Stoner-Weiss, Kathryn. 2006. *Resisting the State: Reform and Retrenchment in Post-Soviet Russia*. New York: Cambridge University Press.

Svolik, Milan W. 2012. *The Politics of Authoritarian Rule*. New York: Cambridge University Press.

Szakonyi, David. 2016. "Elected Public Office and Private Benefit: Firm-Level Returns from Businesspeople Becoming Politicians in Russia." Unpublished MS. New York, 1–45. https://papers.ssrn.com/sol3/papers.cfm?abstract_id=2844901

Taubman, William. 2004. *Khrushchev: The Man and His Era*. New York: Norton Press.

Taylor, Brian. 2011. *State-Building in Putin's Russia Policing and Coercion After Communism*. New York: Cambridge University Press.

Thompson, William. 2005. "Putting YUKOS in Perspective." *Post-Soviet Affairs* 21:2, 159–181.

Tilly, Charles. 1992. *Coercion, Capital and European States*. Oxford: Blackwell.

   2005. *Trust and Rule*. New York: Cambridge University Press.

Tirole, Jean. 2006. *Theory of Corporate Finance*. Princeton, NJ: Princeton University Press.

Tischenko, Kirill. 2009. "Effective Defense Methods Against Hostile Takeovers and Raiders in Russia." MA Thesis. Finance, Helsinki School of Finance. 1–90.

Titaev, Kirill. 2012. "U nas uzhe est' spravedlivaia sudebnaia sistema – arbitrazhnaia." *Vedemosti*, May 12. www.vedemosti.ru. Accessed May 13, 2012.

Titaev, Kirill, Anna Dmitrieva, and Irina Chetvirikova. 2014. "Gosudarstvo i Bizness v Arbitraznhom Protsesse." *Voprosy Ekonomiki* 6, 40–62.

Treisman. Daniel. 2007. "Putin's Silovarchs." *Orbis* 51:1, 141–153.

   2010. "Loans for Shares Revisited." *Post-Soviet Affairs* 26:3, 207–227.

Trenin, Dmitri, Maria Lipman, Alexey Malashenko, Sergei Aleksashenko, Natalia Bubnova, and Nikolay Petrov. 2011. "Duma Elections: Expert Analysis." Carnegie Moscow Center, December 13, http://carnegie.ru/publications/?fa=46205

Trochev, Alexei. 2012. "Suing Russia at Home." *Problems of Post-Communism* 59:5, 18–34.

Tsai, Kellee. 2002. *Back-Alley Banking: Private Entrepreneurs in China*. Ithaca, NY: Cornell University Press.

Udensiva-Brenner, Masha. 2011. "Putin's Russia and the Elections." *At The Harriman Institute*. December 12 http://harriman.columbia.edu/files/harriman/Putin%27s%20Russia%20and%20the%20Elections.pdf

Umbeck, John. 1981. "Might Makes Rights: A Theory of the Formation and Initial Distribution of Property Rights." *Economic Inquiry* 19, 38–54.

Varese, Federico. 2002. *The Russian Mafia: Private Protection in a New Market Economy*. Oxford: Oxford University Press.

Vasilyeva, Nataliya. 2011. "Russian Independent Election Watchdog Found Guilty." *Associated Press*, December 2. www.boston.com/news/world/europe/articles/2011/12/02/russian_independent_election_watchdog_found_guilty/

Verdery, Kathryn. 1996. *What Was Socialism and What Comes Next?* Princeton, NJ: Princeton University Press.

Volkov, Denis. 2011. "Elections in Russia: Polling and Perspectives." *At The Harriman* September 15, 1–2.

Volkov, Vadim. 2002. *Violent Entrepreneurs: The Use of Force in the Making of Russian Capitalism.* Ithaca, NY: Cornell University Press.

2004. "Selective Use of State Capacity in Russia's Economy: Property Disputes and Enterprise Takeover." *Review of Central and East European Law* 4, 427–48.

Volkov, Vadim, A.V. Dmitrieva, E. Paneyakh. M. Pozdnyakov, and K. Titaev. 2011. "Активность правоохранительных органов РФ по выявлению преступлений в сфере экономической деятельности, 2000–2011 гг." "The Activity of the Security Services of the RF on the Reporting of Economics Crimes, 2000–2011." *St. Petersburg: Institut Problem Pravoprimeniniia Evropeiskii Universitet.*

Wang, Yuhua. 2015. *Tying the Autocrat's Hands: The Rise of the Rule of Law in China.* Cambridge: Cambridge University Press.

Weingast, Barry. 1997. "The Political Foundations of the Rule of Law." *American Political Science Review* 91:2, 245–264.

West, Mark. 2005. *Law in Everyday Japan: Sex, Sumo, Suicide, and Statutes.* Chicago, IL: University of Chicago Press.

White, Gregory. 2009. "Once Jailed Executive Pushes Law Changes." *Wall Street Journal*, December 30.

Willerton, John P. 1992. *Patronage and Politics in the USSR.* Cambridge: Cambridge University Press.

Williamson, Oliver. 1985. *The Economic Institutions of Capitalism.* New York: Free Press.

Wolosky, Lee. 2000. "Putin's Plutocrat Problem." *Foreign Affairs.* March/April, 18–31.

World Bank. 2012. "Doing Business in the World." Washington, DC www.doingbusiness.org/.

Yaffa, Joshua. 2015. "The Double Sting: A Power Struggle Between Russia's Rival Security Agencies." *New Yorker*, July 27. www.newyorker.com/magazine/2015/07/27/the-double-sting

Yakovlev, Andrei. 2006. "The Evolution of Business-State Interaction in Russia: From State Capture to Business Capture." *Europe-Asia Studies* 58:7, 1033–1056.

Yakovlev, Andrei, Anton Kazun, and Anton Sobolev. 2014. "Means of Production Versus Means of Coercion: Can Russian Business Limit the Violence of a Predatory State?" *Post-Soviet Affairs* 2–3, 171–194.

Yarkov, Vladimir. 2013. "Creating a Unified Supreme Court in Russia: Expectations and Consequences." Urals State Law Academy, Ekaterinburg, Russia, MS. 1–11.

Yorke, Thomas. 2014. "State-Led Coercive Takeovers in Putin's Russia: Explaining the Underlying Motives." London School of Economics and Political Science, April, 1–332.

Zaller, John. 1992. *The Nature and Origins of Mass Opinion.* Cambridge: Cambridge University Press.

Index

Acemoglu, Daron, 57
adminstrative law, 18, 20, 116, 203
appeals, 107, 116–117
Argentina, 14, 164, 165, 173, 194
asset immobility, 40, 41, 56–57, 65
  hostile corporate takeover, 41, 77
  political connections, 60
asset mobility, 56–57
  hostile corporate takeover, 56–57,
    65, 76
autocracies, 18, 202
  elections, 99, 202
  formal institutions, 19–21, 201–202

BAC
  see Business Against Corruption
bad reputation, 12, 139, 154
  trade, 147–148, 151, 154
bankruptcy, 44–45, 61, 117
bargaining power, 4–5, 19, 82,
  197–198
  property rights, 6–7, 84–86, 204
  rulers, 84–86, 98–99, 204
Belanovsky, Sergei, 88
blat
  see connections
Bolivia, 169
Boycko, Maxim, 29
Browder, William, 47
Business Against Corruption (BAC), 53
business associations, 52–53, 65
  hostile corporate takeover, 72
  trade, 148–150, 162
business organizations, 10, 11
  hostile corporate takeover, 72
Business Solidarity, 48, 52, 53
businesses, 1, 7, 52–53, 55–56, 102,
  113, 200
  courts, 17, 18, 31, 102

businesspeople, 6, 12, 19, 40, 41, 42,
  49, 52, 90–91
  courts, 17, 18, 102, 103–104, 121,
    135
  dispute resolution, 55, 103–104,
    117–118, 121, 136
  negotiations, 121, 135
  returned losses, 118–119, 120
  state arbitration courts, 102, 107,
    121–122, 140

case studies, 32
causal identification, 2, 6, 42, 198
Chile, 203
China, 28, 203
civic associations, 11, 138
civic institutions, 11
Coase, Ronald, 25, 26
coercion, 2, 29, 42, 43
  corporate raiding, 42, 44
commitments, 8
connections, 3, 10
corporate raiding, 33, 40, 41, 42,
  43–46, 49, 55–56, 82, 99, 199
  coercion, 42, 44
  economic crimes, 55
  firm surveys, 62, 63–64
  political connections, 60–61
  state officials, 42, 49
  state ownership, 41
corruption, 9, 164
court cases, 9, 10, 31–32, 135
courts, 9, 11, 17–18, 30, 31–32,
  101–103, 113, 201
  businesspeople, 17, 18, 102,
    103–104, 121, 135
  credit, 160–161
  dispute resolution, 117–118, 119
  firm size, 129–131

property rights protection, 27
reputation, 12, 140, 152–154, 162
returned losses, 119, 120
trade, 152–154, 159
credit, 140, 157–158, 159
courts, 160–161
reputation, 159
culture, 13–14, 163–164

Deirmeier, Daniel, 8
Demina, Natalie, 56, 63
Denzau, Arthur T., 163
developed economies, 2
Di Tella, Rafael, 14, 164, 165, 173,
194–95
dispute resolution, 117–118, 136–137,
199
businesspeople, 55, 103–104,
117–118, 121, 136
courts, 117–118, 119
firm size, 128–129
negotiations, 117–118, 119,
124–125, 127
political connections, 123, 124–127,
136
regional government, 129
security forces, 118, 119, 131, 132,
134, 135
state arbitration courts, 17, 18, 31,
113, 121–122, 125–127, 136–137,
199
supplier firms, 134–135
disputes, 9, 17, 55, 102, 117
economic, 9, 17, 102, 202
regional government, 118, 120, 121,
122
Dmitriev, Mikhail, 88
Dmitrieva, Irina, 115
dubious privatization, 169, 171, 194,
195

economic agents, 27, 42, 43, 170
economic crimes, 46–47, 49–50,
54–55, 201
economic development, 1, 3, 12,
13–14, 27–28, 43, 200
economic disputes, 9, 17, 102, 202
economic performance, 14, 25, 123, 195
economic repression, 47, 54

Egypt, 20, 203
elections, 3, 6–7, 61, 86–90
autocracies, 99, 202
United Russia party, 6, 86, 87,
88–89, 98
electoral fraud, 89
electoral shock, 83–84, 86, 94, 97–98
immobile firms, 83, 93–94, 95, 98
large firms, 83, 94, 98
partisan connections, 98
personal connections, 83, 94
political connections, 94–95
small firms, 95, 97
state ownership, 83, 94, 97, 98
endogeneity, 21, 22, 64, 65, 67
England, 8, 13
entrepreneurs, 18, 50, 51, 53–54
Ericson, Joel, 8
expropriation, 9, 10, 11, 57
external validity, 23, 135
extortion, 46

Federal Security Agency (FSB), 46, 67,
131
Fedotov, Andrei, 54
field experiments, 23
Firestone, Thomas, 44
firm size, 40, 57–58, 129–131
dispute resolution, 128–129
hostile corporate takeover, 65, 73,
75
negotiations, 128–129
political connections, 128–129
firm surveys, 33–34, 35, 36–37,
42, 62, 63–64, 140,
200–201
Fisman, Raymond, 85–86
foreign investors, 20, 30, 64, 72–73
Egypt, 20
Mexico, 8
formal institutions, 1, 2, 3, 7, 11, 12,
19, 30, 142–144, 162, 199
autocracies, 19–21, 201–202
property rights protection, 138, 139
trade, 141, 142
Frye, Timothy, 9, 11, 34, 52, 60, 117,
122, 144, 169
FSB
see Federal Security Agency

Galiani, Sebastian, 173
Gans-Morse, Jordan, 17, 41, 55, 102
Gehlbach, Scott, 94
general jurisdiction courts, 18, 50–52, 105, 106–107, 199
good reputation, 11, 12, 139, 154, 162
trade, 145–146, 147–148, 151, 154, 199
good works, 166, 172–173
Grigorev, Leonid, 54

Haber, Stephen 3-4, 8, 11, 200
Hendley, Kathryn, 17, 43, 50, 102–03, 113–18, 144, 203
Hobbes, Thomas, 9
hostile corporate takeover, 5, 18, 40, 42, 43, 53, 55–56, 71–72, 74, 77
asset immobility, 41, 77
asset mobility, 56–57, 65, 76
business associations, 72
business organizations, 72
firm size, 65, 73, 75
immobile firms, 68, 70, 71, 74, 75
institutional connections, 59, 67, 70–71, 77
large firms, 57–58, 61, 65, 82
mobile firms, 82
partisan connections, 60, 67–68, 74
personal connections, 59–60, 67, 69, 70, 82
political connections, 58–60, 66–68, 69–71, 76–77
secure property rights, 64–65
small firms, 65, 66, 71
state ownership, 59, 67, 68–69, 71, 73, 75
United Russia party members, 60, 67–68, 69, 72, 73
human capital, 165, 170–171, 189, 194, 195
Hungary, 29

Iakovleva, Iana, 48, 52
illegitimate privatization, 169, 174, 187, 195, 200
immigrants, 13
immobile assets
  see asset immobility
immobile firms, 56, 65
electoral shock, 83, 93–94, 95, 98

hostile corporate takeover, 68, 70, 71, 74, 75
India, 113
informal institutions, 1, 2, 3, 10–12, 30, 142–144, 162, 198–199
property rights protection, 138–139
trade, 141, 142
insecure property rights, 1, 6
institutional connections, 6, 41, 94
hostile corporate takeover, 59, 67, 70–71, 77
institutional reform, 3
internal validity, 23
Investigative Committee, 39, 46, 50, 67, 131
investment decisions, 9
Islam, 12
Ivanov, Anton, 107, 110, 111, 112

Johnson, Simon, 144
judges, 9

Kapeliushnikov, Rosrislav, 56, 63
Khodorkovsky, Mikhail, 17
Koran, 12
Kuznetsov, Andrei, 56, 63
Kuznetsova, Olga, 56, 63

laboratory experiments, 23
Landes, David, 13
large firms, 40, 57–58
electoral shock, 83, 94, 98
hostile corporate takeover, 57–58, 61, 65, 82
Latin America, 164, 165
Law on Bankruptcy (1998), 44, 61
Lebedev, Viacheslav, 106, 112
Ledeneva, Alena, 10, 59–60, 117, 138
legal code, 46, 47
legal dualism, 18, 102, 136–137, 202, 203–204
legal formalism, 113
legal institutions, 20, 31, 108, 121, 162, 202–203
legal subterfuge, 2
legal system, 47, 51, 102, 103–104, 105–107, 108–112
legitimate privatization, 164, 166, 169, 174–175, 176–177, 178, 183, 187, 194, 195

Levada Center, 34, 73, 173–174
Levi, Margaret, 84
Lewis, Steven, 8
Locke, John, 9

Magaloni, Beatriz, 203
Magnitsky Act, US, 47
Magnitsky, Sergei, 16, 47
Malov, Dmtrii, 48
market institutions, 3
Markus, Stan, 5, 11, 41, 165
mass public, 3
McMillan, John, 144
Medvedev, Dmitrii, 46, 47, 49, 54, 88, 111
Mexico, 8, 20, 203
Middle East, 12
Minneapolis business, 24, 25
minority shareholders, 45
mobile assets, 60
mobile firms, 4–5, 57, 82
Moscow business, 24
multivariate regression, 22
Mumbai business, 24
Murrell, Peter, 114–115, 144

natural experiment, 2
Navalny, Alexei, 108
negotiations
    businesspeople, 121, 135
    dispute resolution, 117–118, 119, 124–125, 127
    firm size, 128–129
    returned losses, 119
North, Douglass C., 84, 163
Novikova, Elena, 54

observational analyses, 21, 24
opposition parties, 86–87, 89
original sin, 166, 171, 178, 194
ownership, 28–29

partisan connections, 6, 8, 41, 77
    electoral shock, 98
    hostile corporate takeover, 60, 67–68, 74
personal connections, 5, 6, 40, 41, 77
    electoral shock, 83, 94
    hostile corporate takeover, 59–60, 67, 69, 70, 82

political connections, 6, 9, 10, 40–41, 58–60, 122–123, 197, 198–199
    corporate raiding, 60–61
    dispute resolution, 123, 124–127, 136, 199
    disputes, 104–105
    electoral shock, 94–95
    firm size, 128–129
    hostile corporate takeover, 66–68, 69–71, 76–77
    property rights, 5, 19
    property rights protection, 104–105
political power, 2, 5, 6, 9, 41, 200
political rights, 26
Popova, Maria, 116–117
postcommunist countries, 14, 15, 190–192, 198
    privatization, 164, 166, 167, 190, 195
power, 82
powerful elites, 8
pre-trial detention, 46, 47, 48, 49
private businesses, 9, 18
private firms, 68, 82, 141, 196
private institutions, 2, 141, 143
private property, 2, 14–16, 28
private property rights, 14, 15–16, 84
private protection rackets, 43
privatization, 2, 16, 29, 164–166, 167–168, 169–171, 174
    dubious, 169, 171, 194, 195
    illegitimate, 169, 174, 187, 195, 200
    legitimate, 164, 166, 169, 174–175, 176–177, 178, 183, 187, 194, 195
    revising, 165–166, 183–190, 193, 195
    Russia, 16, 164, 166, 167–168, 190, 192
    status quo, 165, 178, 179–183, 193, 194
privatized property rights, 166–167, 193, 194
property right power, 39–40
property rights, 1–3, 7–8, 16–18, 21, 24–27, 28–29, 30, 32, 36, 137, 170
    bargaining power, 4–5, 6–7, 84–86
    coercion, 29
    firm survey, 36–37
    legitimacy, 195

political connections, 5, 19
political power, 5
right-holders, 7, 27, 30, 170, 195,
    198, 200
rulers, 7, 137, 200, 204
social norms, 12, 13–14
property rights institutions, 9
property rights protection, 18, 27, 53
    formal institutions, 138, 139
property transfer, 2
property-based connections, 6, 59, 67
public goods, 166, 172–173, 196, 198,
    200
public institutions, 2, 8, 11, 34, 101
Putin, Vladimir, 17, 34, 47, 83, 88, 98,
    169
    entrepreneurs, 50, 54
    legal system, 109–110, 111
    privatization, 168

regional government
    dispute resolution, 129
    disputes with, 118, 120, 121, 122
regression analysis, 42, 140
reiderstvo
    see corporate raiding; hostile
        corporate takeover
renationalization, 61, 85, 166, 173,
    179, 190
reprivatization, 169
reputation, 10, 11, 12, 139–140, 154,
    198–199
    courts, 12, 152–154, 157
    credit, 159
    trade, 143–144, 145, 147, 150,
        151–153, 156–157, 158, 162
    see also bad reputation; good
        reputation
returned losses, 118–119
    businesspeople, 118–119, 120
    courts, 119, 120
    negotiations, 119
    security forces, 119, 120
revising privatization, 165–166,
    183–190, 193, 195
revisionists, 17, 18
right-holders, 4, 7, 24–25, 29, 30
    bargaining power, 82
    formal institutions, 7
    hostile corporate takeover, 5

privatization, 165
property rights, 7, 27, 30, 170, 195,
    198, 200
property rights protection, 18, 27
Robinson, James, 57
Rochlitz, Michael, 62
Romania, 29
RUIE, Russian Union of Industrialists
    and Entrepreneurs, 148, 149–150
rule of law, 28, 162
rulers, 4, 6
    bargaining power, 82, 84–86, 98–99
    formal institutions, 7
    property rights, 7, 137, 200, 204
Russia, 3, 9, 14–16, 29, 197
    privatization, 16, 164, 166,
        167–168, 190, 192
Ryterman, Randi, 114–115, 144

Schargrodsky, Ernesto, 173
secure property rights, 1, 4, 6, 7, 18,
    27, 29, 64–65
    economic development, 27
Secure Property Rights Index, 73, 91
security forces, 49
    dispute resolution, 118, 119, 131,
        132, 134, 135
    returned losses, 119, 120
Shleifer, Andrei, 29
Shvets, Julia, 115
siloviki
    see security forces
small firms, 40, 58, 61
    electoral shock, 95, 97
    hostile corporate takeover, 65, 66,
        71
SMARTS Group, 45, 46
social institutions, 143
social networks, 10, 11, 12
social norms, 1, 2, 12–15, 163–164,
    198, 200
    economic development, 13–14
    property rights, 12, 13–14
social organizations, 52
Sofex Co., 48
stable government, 1
state agents, 29, 47, 199
state arbitration courts, 9–10, 18,
    50–52, 105–106, 107, 108–109,
    110, 114–116

appeals, 108
businesspeople, 102, 107, 121–122, 140
dispute resolution, 17, 18, 31, 113, 121–122, 125–127, 136–137, 199
Supreme Arbitration Court, 106, 108–109, 111–112
state institutions, 2, 19–21, 101, 136, 141, 143
state officials, 7, 9, 11, 18, 51
corporate raiding, 42, 49
disputes with, 9
economic crimes, 50
violence, 62
state ownership, 6, 28, 41
electoral shock, 83, 94, 97, 98
hostile corporate takeover, 59, 67, 68–69, 71, 73, 75
status quo privatization, 165, 178, 179–183, 193, 194
supplier firms, 131, 132, 134–135, 140, 151
Supreme Arbitration Court, 106, 108–109, 111–112
Supreme Court, 111–112
survey experiments, 2, 21–24, 135–136
surveys, 33–35, 73
survivor bias, 33

theft, 2
Titaev, Kirill, 50–52, 102, 107, 115
Togliattiazot, 38–39
trade, 139, 140, 141–142, 150, 151
bad reputation, 147–148, 151, 154
business associations, 148–150, 162

courts, 152–154, 159
formal institutions, 141, 142
good reputation, 145–146, 147–148, 151, 154, 199
informal institutions, 141, 142
reputation, 143–144, 145, 147, 150, 151–153, 156–157, 158, 162
trading networks, 10, 142
transaction costs, 26
transition, 18, 28, 59, 139
Treisman, Daniel, 43
trust-based social networks, 11, 12

United Russia party, 83–84, 90, 99
elections, 6, 86, 87, 88–89, 98
United Russia party members, 64, 94–95, 98
hostile corporate takeover, 60, 67–68, 69, 72, 73

validity, 23
Venezuela, 169
violence, 41, 43, 62, 77
Vishny, Robert, 29
vote fraud, 89
voucher privatization, 29, 167

weak property rights, 1, 27, 41
Woodruff, Christopher, 144

Yeltsin, Boris, 108, 167
YUKOS affair, 54, 86, 168–169

Zhalinsky, Alfred, 54
Zimbabwe, 169